Contents

Here are some treats for sipping and snacking.

Enjoy a bounty of breads, even when you're counting carbs.

Eat more fish and receive heart-healthy benefits.

Focus on soy proteins and high-protein beans and grains.

Bring more to the table with our best beef, pork, and lamb selections.

Just "wing it" with these easy chicken and turkey recipes.

Go beyond basic chopped lettuce and tomato with salads featuring fruits, vegetables, and lean meats.

Get out of the brown bag rut with these delectable sandwiches.

Round out meals with simple low-carb veggies and high-fiber grains.

Simmer a pot of vegetable soup or spicy chili for a simple supper.

Satisfy your sweet tooth without sugar.

Dear Friends,

The research continues to show that controlling blood glucose levels can prevent or slow the development of diabetes complications, reduce the incidence of heart disease, and result in a better quality of life for people with diabetes. There's no reason not to start today and take charge of your diabetes. As a person who has lived with type 1 diabetes for over 34 years, I know that managing diabetes can be a daunting task. But with our five-step plan and collection of over 300 recipes, we give you the tools to manage your diabetes in a way that works for you.

The **ALL-NEW Complete Step-By-Step Diabetic Cookbook** provides information on assembling your health care team, setting goals, using resources, counting carbs, stocking your kitchen, and eating away from home. One of the biggest complaints I hear from folks who are following a diabetic diet is that they're tired of eating the same things day after day. So we've filled this collection with too-good-to-be-true main dishes, breakfasts, soups, sandwiches, snacks, and desserts that your whole family will enjoy.

At last!

A new cookbook and a new plan for people with diabetes who love great food.

Here are just a few of the benefits you'll get from the **ALL-NEW Complete Step-By-Step Diabetic Cookbook**:

- over 300 kitchen-tested, dietitian-approved recipes
- complete nutrient breakdown for every recipe including carbohydrate, fiber, calories, fat, protein, and sodium
- recipe tips and shortcuts
- grocery shopping list for stocking up your kitchen
- strategies for eating on the run
- family-pleasing holiday menus
- sugar substitute guide

When it gets down to it, the basic question everyone asks when they find out they have diabetes is "What can I eat?" You'll be pleased with the answers in the **ALL-NEW Complete Step-By-Step Diabetic Cookbook**.

In health,

Anne Cain

Anne Cain, R.D., Editor

ALL-NEW COMPLETE Step-by-Step

DIABETIC
COOKBOOK

ISBN: 0-8487-3112-3

Printed in China
First printing 2006

Be sure to check with your health care provider before making any changes
in your diet.

Oxmoor House, Inc.
Editor in Chief: Nancy Fitzpatrick Wyatt
Executive Editor: Katherine M. Eakin
Copy Chief: Allison Long Lowery

ALL-NEW Complete Step-By-Step Diabetic Cookbook
Editor: Anne C. Cain, M.S., M.P.H., R.D.
Copy Editor: Terri Laschober
Editorial Assistant: Brigette Gaucher
Director, Test Kitchens: Elizabeth Tyler Austin
Assistant Director, Test Kitchens: Julie Christopher
Test Kitchens Staff: Kristi Carter, Nicole Lee Faber,
      Kathleen Royal Phillips, Elise Weis, Kelley Self Wilton
Director of Photography: Jim Bathie
Senior Photo Stylist: Kay E. Clarke
Publishing Systems Administrator: Rick Tucker
Director of Production: Laura Lockhart
Production Manager: Greg Amason
Production Assistant: Faye Porter Bonner

Contributors:
Designer: Carol O. Loria
Indexer: Mary Ann Laurens
Editorial Interns: Rachel Quinlivan, R.D.;
      Mary Catherine Shamblin

Cover: *Chocolate-Macadamia Nut
Pie, page 345*

To order additional copies
of this book or others,
call 1-800-765-6400.
For more books to enrich
your life, visit
oxmoorhouse.com

five steps to diabetes control

Five Steps to Success

The *All-New Complete Step-by-Step Diabetic Cookbook* can help you control diabetes without it controlling you. These five basic steps will have you on the way to diabetes control as you eat well, live well, and enjoy a new level of health and well-being.

1. Take Charge. A diagnosis of diabetes can be overwhelming, but here are ten basic things you need to do when you're newly diagnosed (page 7).

2. Eat Smart. Use the 2005 Dietary Guidelines for Americans as a framework for healthy eating when you have diabetes (page 11).

3. Count Carbs. Not all carbs are bad. It's a matter of picking the right kind of carbs in the right amounts so that you can control blood sugar levels (page 15).

4. Create a "Diabetes-Friendly" Kitchen. Learn how to stock your kitchen to simplify healthy cooking (page 17).

5. Dine for Pleasure. Eating out is not off-limits when you have diabetes. It's all about making choices. We've got restaurant strategies (page 27) as well as a holiday menu planning guide (page 37).

1 Take Charge

You've just learned that you have diabetes. For some, the news comes as a big surprise—even a shock. For others, the diagnosis only confirms what you've suspected for some time but were afraid to admit.

You have a million questions and very few answers. Where can you start? What should you do first? The following checklist offers a tried-and-true plan to help you "get your balance."

What to Do When You're Newly Diagnosed

Before you begin the search for answers, take a deep breath and relax! Diabetes management is a process that will take time and effort, but it's important to understand that you are not alone. There are many people and resources to help you as you learn to control your blood glucose.

Assemble Your Health Care Team

Each member of your health care team plays an important role in your care. Your doctor will design your treatment plan, which may include:
- meal planning
- exercise
- medication
- self blood glucose testing

Your doctor may encourage you to visit with other health care professionals, including the following:
- diabetes nurse educator
- registered dietitian
- pharmacist
- podiatrist
- exercise specialist
- ophthalmologist

Set Reasonable, Measurable Goals

Learning to live well with diabetes is a balancing act: You must be able to acknowledge that diabetes is a serious condition without becoming overwhelmed by its day-to-day demands. Again, remember that others stand ready to help you.

Analyze the tasks that lie ahead as you learn to manage your diabetes. And if you need to make several important lifestyle changes, don't try to change everything at once. Ask members of your team which changes will have the biggest positive impact on your health, and start there.

Plan Your Diet Carefully

Treatment for everyone with diabetes involves meal planning. While making proper food choices, you will learn to eat the foods you enjoy, control portion sizes, control carbohydrate intake, and time meals to avoid high and low blood glucose levels. Some strategies for meal planning and weight loss may include:

- keeping a food diary
- measuring portion sizes
- reading food labels
- modifying recipes
- using low-fat cooking methods
- drinking two quarts of water each day
- checking and recording your weight weekly

There is no single, correct meal plan for everyone. Your dietitian will help you construct the meal plan that's best for you. The recipes in the *All-New Complete Step-by-Step Diabetic Cookbook* can be used in almost all diabetic meal plans. Use the nutrient analysis at the end of each recipe for the specific amounts of carbohydrate, protein, fat, and calories in one serving to determine how the recipe can best fit into your meal plan.

Exercise Regularly

To control your blood glucose, exercise a minimum of three or four times a week for 30 to 45 minutes. Exercise improves heart, blood vessel, and muscle function. Let your doctor know if you are beginning a new exercise program. Set reasonable exercise goals. Begin slowly and keep a record of your exercise activity. Some examples of heart-healthy exercises include:

- walking
- running
- biking
- swimming
- hiking
- cross-country skiing
- group exercise classes such as step, spinning, and Jazzercise

The more physically active you are, the better, and activities such as housework, gardening, dancing, golf, and bowling all contribute to better blood sugar control.

Test Blood Glucose

Your doctor may ask you to do self blood glucose testing. Testing shows how well food, exercise, and medication are working to help achieve your blood glucose goals. Good times to test blood glucose include:
- before meals
- before bedtime
- before and after exercise

Your doctor or nurse educator will teach you how to test and will determine when and how often to test. Always bring your blood glucose testing record when you visit your doctor.

Use Medication Wisely

Your doctor may prescribe pills or insulin to lower your blood glucose. When taking medication, you need to know:
- the name of the medication you are taking
- the amount to take and when to take it
- side effects to report
- what to do if you skip a dose
- what to do if you're unable to take pills (because of nausea or vomiting due to the flu or other sickness, for instance)

You should take diabetes pills or insulin at the same time every day. Also, remember that diabetes medication cannot take the place of regular exercise and a healthy diet.

The way your diabetes medication works may be affected by some over-the-counter medicines. Ask your doctor or pharmacist which over-the-counter medications you can take safely.

Share Concerns with Family and Friends

Many people find the support of family, friends, and co-workers invaluable in achieving control and enhancing their feeling of well-being. Individuals who are knowledgeable and encouraging can help you stay focused. But if they are misinformed, loved ones can become the "diabetes police." You may see them as people who are always handing out citations for violations of the rules. It's important to teach your loved ones how to give effective support. Check with diabetes organizations and agencies in your area to see if there are any diabetes support groups. These groups can provide tremendous support and information for people with diabetes and their parents, spouses, and friends.

(continued on next page)

Tap Resources

Members of your health care team are your first resource. The local hospital, pharmacy, and library may provide information about special programs and classes. Consult your insurance company to clarify benefits.

National organizations such as the American Diabetes Association, the Juvenile Diabetes Research Foundation, and the National Diabetes Information Clearinghouse can be good sources of information. (See the box at right for phone numbers and Web site addresses.)

The manufacturers of supplies and equipment can provide product information. Several magazines and Web sites publish the latest information and provide an opportunity to exchange ideas with other people with diabetes from around the world.

Value Your Strengths

When you identify areas where you need improvement, you'll want to take action: Ask your health care team for help.

But it's also important to take some time every day to congratulate yourself on achieving balance in management. Focus on your accomplishments, not on your less-than-successful moments. You may even want to keep an ongoing journal where you can record your big and little victories—a reminder of how much you are learning from day to day.

American Diabetes Association
800-232-3472
www.diabetes.org

American Association of Diabetes Educators
800-Team-UP4
www.AADEnet.org

Juvenile Diabetes Research Foundation
800-JDF-CURE
www.jdfcure.org

National Diabetes Information Clearinghouse
301-654-3327
www.niddk.nih.gov/health/diabetes/ndic.htm

Diabetes Education and Research Center
215-829-3426
www.diabeteseducationandresearchcenter.org

The American Dietetic Association
800-877-1600
www.eatright.org

2 Eat Smart

The Dietary Guidelines for Americans are a set of recommendations to promote health and prevent disease. While these guidelines are not specifically directed to people with diabetes, they do provide a framework for healthy eating and activity that you can modify more specifically to apply to your particular diabetes care plan. We've listed the guidelines below and included a statement with each one (designated by an ▶ and **bold type**) about how it might specifically impact diabetes.

2005 Dietary Guidelines

Weight Management

Guideline: Balance calories from foods and beverages with calories expended. Follow the USDA Food Guide for appropriate calorie requirements based on age and physical activity level.

▶**Weight control is particularly important for those with diabetes. A loss of even a little weight has been shown to help improve blood glucose control or, for those with insulin-dependent type 2 diabetes, reduce the amount of insulin you need.**

Adequate Nutrients

Guideline: Consume a variety of nutrient-dense foods and beverages. Follow a balanced eating pattern such as the USDA Food Guide or DASH Eating Plan (Dietary Approaches to Stop Hypertension). For more information on the USDA Food Guide or the DASH Eating plan, go to these websites:

www.nal.usda.gov/fnic
www.dashforhealth.com

▶Foods contain a wide variety of nutrients and other compounds that are essential for good health and disease prevention. No one food provides all of what you need, and sometimes it's the combination of foods that promotes health. **When you have a chronic condition such as diabetes, it becomes even more important to do all you can to prevent other diseases such as heart disease and cancer.**

Food Groups to Encourage

Guideline: Consume enough fruits and vegetables while staying within energy needs. Have 2 cups of fruit and 2.5 cups of vegetables per day for a reference 2,000-calorie intake. Make adjustments for various calorie levels. At least half of total grains consumed should be whole grains (at least 3 ounces or more of whole grains per day). Consume 3 cups per day of fat-free or low-fat milk or equivalent.

▶When you have diabetes, the recommendation to eat more fruits and vegetables, whole grains, and low-fat milk or other dairy products is good advice. However, you need to talk to your dietitian about the specific number of servings that you should have from each group. Weight loss goals, diabetes medications, and activity levels all impact the calorie level and number of servings that are right for you.

Fat

Guideline: Keep total fat between 20-35 percent of calories, with most fats coming from sources of polyunsaturated and monounsaturated fats.

▶Those with diabetes are at an increased risk for heart disease. Eating a diet that is low in saturated fat and emphasizes heart-healthy monounsaturated fats will help keep your cholesterol levels in check and help prevent heart disease.

By using the "good fats" in just-enough amounts, you can satisfy your taste buds, keep your heart healthy, and improve diabetes control.

	sources of monounsaturated fats	sources of polyunsaturated fats
GOOD FATS	avocados nuts olive oil peanut oil peanut butter	nuts sunflower seeds corn oil safflower oil sunflower oil
BAD FATS	sources of saturated fats	
	animal fats (beef, chicken, lamb, pork) butter lard	coconut oil palm kernel oil whole milk whole milk cheeses

Salt

Guideline: Consume less than 2,300 milligrams of salt per day and include potassium-rich foods such as fruits and vegetables.

▶ **People with diabetes are at higher risk for heart disease, stroke, and high blood pressure. Controlling the amount of sodium you consume can help decrease your blood pressure and keep your heart healthy.**

Sugar

Guideline: Choose and prepare foods with little added sugars or caloric sweeteners.

▶ **Sugar (sucrose) and sugar-containing foods can cause a rapid increase in blood sugar and make diabetes difficult to control. While sugar is not pro-hibited on most diabetic eating plans, it's usually recommended that you eat sugar only in moder-ate amounts and replace it with more complex forms of carbohy-drate such as whole grains. (See "Count Carbs" on page 15 for more information about sugar, carbohydrates, and diabetes.)**

Physical Activity

Guideline: Engage in at least 30 minutes of moderate physical activity on most days of the week. To manage weight, engage in about 60 minutes (60-90 minutes to lose weight) of moderate to vigorous activity on most days of the week while not exceeding calorie requirements.

▶ **Being physically active can help control blood sugars and help you lose weight. Physical activity decreases blood sugars because the glu-cose moves into the muscles to replace the fuel you used to exercise.**

HALT THE SALT

Here are some ways to shake the salt habit.

• Cut back on salt intake gradually, giving your taste buds time to adjust.

• Don't add salt to your food during cooking. Instead, use herbs and spices for extra zest.

• Avoid high-sodium flavor enhancers like garlic salt, celery salt, onion salt, or MSG.

• Read the labels on packaged and processed foods because high-sodium foods don't always taste salty. Avoid products with more than 15 percent daily value for sodium. (The % Daily Values give you a general idea of how one serving contributes nutritionally to a 2,000-calorie diet. Look on the right-hand column of the Nutrition Facts label for the % Daily Value numbers.)

• Limit your intake of cheese and processed meats.

• Limit intake of condiments such as soy sauce, ketchup, mustard, salad dressings, pickles, and olives.

• Choose low-salt crackers, chips, and snacks.

• Choose no-salt-added or low-sodium versions of canned soups and vegetables.

Alcohol

Guideline: Be sensible, drink in moderation, defined as one drink per day for women and two per day for men. Alcohol should not be consumed by some individuals (pregnant women, children, people who cannot limit their drinks, people who are taking medications that may interact). Alcohol should be avoided by individuals engaging in activities that require attention, skill, or coordination such as driving.

►**Consuming alcohol can be dangerous for diabetics, particularly if consumed on an empty stomach because it can cause low blood sugar. Never drink on an empty stomach. People with diabetes also need to limit alcohol that is mixed with high-carbohydrate fruit juices or sodas.**

HOW MUCH IS ONE SERVING?

12 ounces regular beer

5 ounces wine

1.5 ounces 80-proof distilled spirits

Food Safety

Guideline: Clean hands, surfaces, and produce. Meat or poultry should not be washed or rinsed. Avoid raw unpasteurized milk or any products made from unpasteurized milk, raw or partially cooked eggs or foods containing raw or undercooked eggs, meat, poultry, unpasteurized juices, and raw sprouts.

►**People with diabetes often have compromised immune systems and have difficulty fighting infections, so it becomes even more important to follow food safety practices and prevent exposing yourself or your family to any type of food-borne illness.**

Common Food Safety Mistakes

Make your kitchen a safer place by avoiding the following practices:

- thawing food on the countertop
- leaving leftovers out of the refrigerator
- using an unclean cutting board
- marinating at room temperature
- waiting too long after buying groceries to put them in the refrigerator or freezer
- using one spoon for stirring and tasting
- using the same knife (without cleaning) for trimming raw meat and chopping vegetables
- undercooking high-risk foods such as eggs, meat, poultry, and fish

3 Count Carbs

Carbohydrate is your body's preferred source of fuel. The brain depends exclusively on carbohydrate for its energy when that fuel is available. If there is no carbohydrate available (either from the foods that are eaten or in storage in the liver or muscles), the body will convert protein and/or fat to glucose (the form of carbohydrate the body uses for energy).

But if you eat more carbohydrate than your body needs for fuel, a small amount of it is stored in the liver or the muscles to be used later for energy. The rest of it gets changed and is stored in the body as fat.

Understanding Carbohydrate

Ideal Carbohydrate Level

There's no specific recommended amount of carbohydrate. The amount of carbohydrate you need depends on many factors, including the following:

- current weight and height
- physical activity level
- gender
- health status
- diabetes medications

Most diabetic eating plans don't completely restrict carbohydrate— they allows a specific amount of the right kinds of carbohydrate.

Preferred Carbohydrate

Most diabetic eating plans don't completely restrict carbohydrate—they allow a specific amount of the right kinds of carbohydrate. The ideal carbohydrates in terms of weight loss and disease prevention have the following characteristics:

- high in fiber
- absorbed slowly
- do not cause rapid increases in blood glucose

The carbohydrates in fruits and vegetables are good for you because when you eat them, you get a whole package of disease-fighting vitamins and minerals. Fruits and vegetables, as well as whole grains and cereals, also contain carbohydrate in the form of fiber. Since fiber isn't digested by the body, these foods are absorbed slowly and don't cause a rapid rise in blood glucose. When the blood glucose rises slowly, the carbohydrate isn't stored as fat as easily. (For recipes to help you increase your intake of high-fiber fruits and vegetables, turn to Salads, page 205, and Side Dishes, page 259.)

Carbohydrates can be classified two ways: simple and complex. Simple carbohydrates are sugars like glucose, sucrose, lactose, and fructose that are found in fruit and refined sugar.

Complex carbohydrates (or starches) are chains of simple sugars bonded together and are found in starches like beans, vegetables, and whole grains. Once they're digested by the body, complex carbohydrates (starches) are broken down into simple sugars. Complex carbohydrates are considered healthier because they contain fiber and are digested slower, providing a steady energy source.

Sucrose is another name for table sugar and is only one of several types of sugar referred to as "simple carbohydrates."

See the chart below for a general list of food groups that can impact blood glucose and those that usually don't. Some of the foods in the right-hand column, however, can increase blood sugar if they're eaten in large quantities.

Food groups that can increase blood sugar	Food groups that usually don't increase blood sugar
Breads, cereals, pasta, rice	Meat
Starchy vegetables	Fats, oils, salad dressing*, butter, margarine
Beans, peas, lentils	Seeds, nuts, peanut butter*
Fruit	Cream cheese, sour cream
Juice	Sugar-free hard candy and gum*
Regular soda, carbonated beverages	Sugar substitutes
Candy	Coffee, tea, sugar-free soft drinks
Chocolate	Herbs and spices
Milk, yogurt	

*Check the label for carbohydrate content because some products do contain a significant amount of carbohydrate.

4 Create a "Diabetes-Friendly" Kitchen

When you have the equipment and supplies you need on hand, healthy cooking becomes a way of life instead of a challenge. You don't need a lot of fancy gadgets and gourmet foods—just start with the basics.

Top 10 Healthy Cooking Tools

Quick and easy healthy cooking is no problem when you have the right tools. Here are the 10 items our food editors say they can't do without.

1 Set of sharp knives:
Chopping fresh fruits and vegetables is quick and easy when you use sharp knives.

2 Microwave oven:
Use for melting, steaming vegetables, toasting nuts, and defrosting, as well as a host of other "quick-fix" steps that will reduce your prep time.

3 Measuring spoons:
Select a set of spoons that graduate from 1/8 teaspoon to 1 tablespoon so you don't have to guess at amounts.

4 Dry and liquid measuring cups:
Use the appropriate measuring cup, either dry or liquid, so your amounts will be accurate.

5 Nonstick skillets, saucepans, and baking pans:
You don't have to use much fat, if any, when you cook or bake in nonstick pans. And cleanup is a breeze!

6 Food Scales:
Use a scale to make sure pieces of meat, poultry, and fish are the specified weight or to measure the correct amount of cheese.

7 Kitchen scissors:
Scissors are handy for mincing herbs, chopping tomatoes in the can, trimming fat from meats and poultry—plus many more uses.

8 Instant-read thermometer:
A key safety factor is cooking food to the proper temperature, so use an instant-read thermometer to check eggs, meats, and poultry.

9 Steam basket or vegetable steamer:
Steaming veggies is an easy, healthy way to cook vegetables because it preserves nutrients as well as flavor.

10 Broiler pan/broiler pan rack:
When you broil, much of the fat drips away into the pan, so broiling is a quick, low-fat cooking method.

Stocking Up

Use this handy list to keep your kitchen stocked with the basic ingredients you need for quick low-fat, low-sugar cooking.

Check the pantry for these staples:
- ☐ Baking powder
- ☐ Baking soda
- ☐ Bouillon granules: chicken, beef, and vegetable
- ☐ Broth, canned: reduced-sodium chicken and beef, vegetable
- ☐ Cornstarch
- ☐ Flour: all-purpose, self-rising, whole wheat
- ☐ Milk: nonfat dry milk powder, fat-free evaporated
- ☐ Oats: quick cooking
- ☐ Oils: olive, sesame, and vegetable
- ☐ Sugar substitutes and sugar
- ☐ Unflavored gelatin and sugar-free gelatin mixes

Keep these fruits and vegetables on hand:
- ☐ Canned beans
- ☐ Canned tomato products: paste, sauce, whole, diced, and seasoned tomatoes
- ☐ Canned vegetables
- ☐ Canned fruits packed in juice
- ☐ Dried fruits

You can always make a meal when you have these grains and pastas:
- ☐ Bulgur
- ☐ Couscous
- ☐ Dry pastas
- ☐ Rice and rice blends
- ☐ Dry cereals without added sugar

Add flavor with these condiments and seasonings:
- ☐ Bottled minced garlic
- ☐ Dried herbs and spices
- ☐ Mayonnaise, low-fat
- ☐ Mustards
- ☐ Salad dressings and vinaigrettes: fat-free and reduced-fat
- ☐ Seasoning sauces: hot sauce, ketchup, low-sodium soy sauce, Worcestershire sauce
- ☐ Vinegars

Fill the fridge with these items:
- ☐ Cheeses, reduced-fat
- ☐ Eggs and egg substitute
- ☐ Milk: fat-free milk and low-fat buttermilk
- ☐ Margarine, reduced-calorie margarine, and light butter
- ☐ Rolls and pizza dough
- ☐ Sour cream, low-fat
- ☐ Yogurt, low-fat

Stock up and store these foods in the freezer:
- ☐ Cooked chicken: diced or strips
- ☐ Ground round, pork chops, other meats
- ☐ Frozen fruits
- ☐ Frozen vegetables
- ☐ Juice concentrates

Low-Fat Substitutions

Here are a few simple reduced-fat substitutions for high-fat ingredients.

	Ingredient	Substitution
FATS & OILS	Butter	Light butter, reduced-calorie margarine *(except for baking)*
	Margarine	Light butter, reduced-calorie margarine *(except for baking)*
	Mayonnaise	Fat-free, light, or low-fat mayonnaise
	Oil	Polyunsaturated or monounsaturated oil in a reduced amount (canola, olive)
	Salad Dressing	Fat-free or reduced-fat salad dressing or vinaigrette
	Shortening	Polyunsaturated or monounsaturated oil in a reduced amount
MEAT & POULTRY	Bacon	Reduced-fat bacon; turkey bacon; lean ham; Canadian bacon
	Ground Beef	Ground round, extra-lean ground beef, or ground turkey
	Sausage	50%-less-fat pork sausage; turkey sausage
	Luncheon Meat	Sliced turkey, chicken, lean roast beef, or lean ham
	Tuna Packed in Oil	Tuna packed in water
	Egg, whole	2 egg whites or ¼ cup egg substitute
DAIRY	Sour Cream	Fat-free or reduced-fat sour cream; fat-free or low-fat plain yogurt
	Cheese, Cheddar, Swiss, Monterey Jack, Mozzarella	Reduced-fat cheeses (or use less of the regular cheese)
	Cottage Cheese	Fat-free or 1% low-fat cottage cheese
	Cream Cheese	Fat-free or light cream cheese
	Ricotta Cheese	Part-skim or fat-free ricotta
	Whole Milk	Fat-free or skim milk; 1% low-fat milk
	Evaporated Milk	Fat-free evaporated milk
	Half-and-Half	Fat-free half-and-half or fat-free evaporated milk
	Whipped Cream	Fat-free or reduced-calorie frozen whipped topping
	Ice Cream	Fat-free or low-fat ice cream or frozen yogurt; sherbet; sorbet
OTHER	Soups, canned	Low-fat, reduced-sodium soups
	Fudge Sauce	Fat-free chocolate syrup
	Nuts	A reduced amount of nuts (one-third to one-half less)
	Unsweetened Chocolate, 1 ounce	3 tablespoons unsweetened cocoa and 1 tablespoon butter

Label Reading

Here are some things to consider when you use food labels to select items for your diabetic eating plan.

Serving size: Values are for one serving of the food. A portion may be more or less than what you expect, so pay attention to the amount given.

Total Carbohydrate: Total Carbohydrate is just that—the total amount of carbohydrate in one serving. **This value doesn't indicate what specific type of carbohydrate the food contains, simply a total amount.**

Dietary Fiber: Fiber is a type of carbohydrate, so even though it's listed separately, the value is included in the amount of Total Carbohydrate. In some carbohydrate-counting plans, you are instructed to subtract the grams of Dietary Fiber from the Total Carbohydrate to get the "net carbohydrate" that is actually absorbed.

Sugars: The value for sugars is also part of the amount of Total Carbohydrate. This value refers to both natural sugars and added sugars. You cannot tell from this value what types of sugar are in the food, only the amount of sugars. It may be one type of sugar, or it may be a mix of sugars, but you need to look on the ingredients list panel to determine the types of sugar. **The value for sugars gives part of the picture, but the main number to look at is the Total Carbohydrate.**

Nutrition Facts	
► Serving Size 2 Cookies (24g)	
Servings Per Container about 6	

Amount Per Serving	
Calories 110	Calories from Fat 60

	% Daily Value*
Total Fat 6g	10%
Saturated Fat 4g	19%
Polyunsaturated Fat 0g	
Monounsaturated Fat 1g	
Cholesterol 0mg	0%
Sodium 80mg	3%
►**Total Carbohydrate** 16g	5%
► Dietary Fiber 1g	4%
► Sugars 0g	
► Sugar Alcohol 6g	
Protein 1g	

Vitamin A 0% • Vitamin C 0% • Calcium 0% • Iron 4%

*Percent Daily Values are based on a 2,000 calorie diet. Your daily values may be higher or lower depending on your calorie needs:

	Calories:	2,000	2,500
Total Fat	Less than	65g	80g
Sat Fat	Less than	20g	25g
Cholesterol	Less than	300mg	300mg
Sodium	Less than	2,400mg	2,400mg
Total Carbohydrate		300g	375g
Dietary Fiber		25g	30g

g = grams   mg = milligrams

Sugar Alcohol: Some foods contain sweeteners in the form of sugar alcohols such as sorbitol, manitol, and xylitol. You won't see the specific name of the sugar alcohol listed on the Nutrition Facts panel; they're listed generally as Sugar Alcohol.

Some product package labels display "Net Carb," which is usually the Total Carbohydrate minus the Sugar Alcohol. **"Net Carb," however, is not an approved FDA label term, so it does not have an approved definition.**

How Much Is a Serving?

For many people, controlling portions is the biggest challenge in controlling diabetes. Whether you are counting carbohydrate or watching portion sizes in order to lose weight, the guide below will help you see in your mind's eye the appropriate serving size for each of a variety of foods.

1 ounce cooked meat, poultry, or fish	=	Matchbook
3 ounces cooked meat, poultry, or fish	=	Deck of playing cards, cassette tape, or the palm of a woman's hand
1 slice cheese	=	3.5-inch computer disk
1 ounce cheese	=	4 dice or a tube of lipstick
2 tablespoons peanut butter	=	Golf ball
1 standard bagel	=	Hockey puck or 6-ounce can of tuna
1 cup potatoes, rice, or pasta	=	Size of a fist or a tennis ball
1 medium potato	=	Computer mouse or 1 small bar of soap
½ cup cooked vegetables	=	6 asparagus spears, 7 to 8 baby carrots or carrot sticks, 1 ear of corn, or 3 spears broccoli
½ cup chopped fresh vegetables	=	3 regular ice cubes
1 cup chopped fresh leafy greens	=	4 lettuce leaves
1 medium orange or apple, or 1 cup fruit or yogurt	=	Baseball

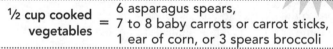

Source: National Center for Nutrition and Dietetics of The American Dietetic Association and its Foundation, ADAF, copyright 1998

Sweet Substitutions

There are several sugar substitutes on the market, and the best one to use is really a personal preference. However, we've found that some types of sweeteners work better in cooking than others.

Here's a list of the sweeteners we have used in this book and what they're called in the recipes.

- **Splenda:** "measures-like-sugar" calorie-free sweetener
- **Equal:** calorie-free sweetener with aspartame
- **Equal Spoonful:** "measures-like-sugar" calorie-free sweetener with aspartame
- **Brown Sugar Twin:** "measures-like-sugar" brown sugar calorie-free sweetener

Aspartame Safety

The Food and Drug Administration (FDA) approved the use of aspartame (sold under the trade names Equal and Nutrasweet) in all foods and beverages in 1996.

Both The American Dietetic Association and the American Diabetes Association consider FDA-approved sugar substitutes a safe part of a calorie- or carbohydrate-controlled diet.

Although this sweetener has come under a lot of scrutiny due to reports that it caused symptoms such as headaches, dizziness, nausea, memory loss, and seizures and was responsible for the increased incidence of brain tumors, there is no scientific research to support these complaints. None of the leading health organizations in the United States has found a causal relationship between aspartame and the adverse effects listed above.

Using sugar substitutes on a diabetic eating plan

When you love sweets and are trying to cut back on carbohydrate to help control your blood sugars, calorie-free sweeteners and sugar substitutes can help you enjoy sweet treats without adding carbohydrates that could increase your blood sugar.

In our diabetes-friendly recipes, you'll see that we use small amounts of a variety of sweeteners: calorie-free sweeteners, honey, fruit juices, and even real sugar.

More Options for Sweeteners

In addition to the calorie-free sweeteners in the chart on the next page, there are some other products that you can use to add sweetness to your recipes.

Equal Sugar Lite: This new product is a blend of sugar and calorie-free sweeteners and has half the calories and carbohydrate of granulated sugar (8 calories and 2 grams of carbohydrate per teaspoon). It measures cup-for-cup like sugar, and can be used in most recipes that call for sugar. It bakes, browns, and provides volume to baked goods better than some of the calorie-free sweeteners.

Stevia: This herbal sweetener is derived from the plant *stevia rebaudiana* and is said to be 100–300 times sweeter than granulated sugar. Stevia extract is available in health-food stores in bulk powdered form, liquid extract, and single-serving packets. One teaspoon of powdered stevia extract has 0 grams of carbohydrate and 0 calories. It's most often used in the powdered form and stirred into beverages. See the package instructions or contact the manufacturer for specific instructions on baking with stevia. Go to **www.nowfoods.com** for more information or to order.

Fructose: Fructose, or fruit sugar, is found naturally in fruits and fruit juices. Fructose is really not better or worse for you than sucrose (table sugar). They are both simple sugars and are broken down by the body in essentially the same way. Fructose is 1.5 times sweeter than sucrose, so a slightly smaller amount provides the same level of sweetness. It's also added to certain foods as high-fructose corn syrup or a crystalline form. Crystalline fructose is available in packaged form and can usually be found on the supermarket shelves near the other sweeteners. High-fructose corn syrup is used by food manufacturers in a wide variety of products.

Fructose is not better or worse for you than table sugar. They are both simple sugars and are broken down by the body in the same way.

Sugar Substitute Guide

Types of Sugar Substitutes	Brand Names*
Measured like sugar, these sugar substitutes can be used in most recipes in place of sugar. Use the same amount of sugar substitute as you would use of sugar.	Splenda
	Equal Spoonful
	Sugar Twin
	DiabetiSweet
These sugar substitutes are in a more concentrated form, so you don't use as much of these as you would use of sugar in order to get the same sweetness.	Equal for Recipes
	Equal Packets
	Sweet 'N Low
	Sweet One
Liquid sugar substitutes blend easily with other ingredients and work well in sauces and marinades.	Sweet 'N Low
	Sweet-10

*This list includes the sugar substitutes that we use most often in our Test Kitchens. It is not an all-inclusive list and is not meant as an endorsement of any particular product.

Description	Amount to equal ½ cup sugar
Contains sucralose, a modified sugar molecule that isn't absorbed by the body; no aftertaste; extremely heat stable; also available in packets	½ cup
Contains aspartame; no aftertaste; loses some sweetness in high heat	½ cup
Contains saccharin; some aftertaste; heat stable	½ cup
Contains a combination of acesulfame-K (Sunette) and isomalt; no aftertaste; looks like sugar; heat stable	½ cup
Contains aspartame; no aftertaste; the bulk form of Equal packets; loses some sweetness in high heat	3½ teaspoons
Contains aspartame; no aftertaste; same as Equal for Recipes, but in packets; loses some sweetness in high heat	12 packets
Contains saccharin; some aftertaste; available in bulk form or in packets; heat stable	1 tablespoon or 12 packets
Contains acesulfame-K (Sunette); no aftertaste; heat stable	12 packets
Contains saccharin; some aftertaste; heat stable	1 tablespoon
Contains saccharin; some aftertaste; heat stable	1 tablespoon

5 Dine for Pleasure

A diabetic meal plan does not sentence you to cooking all of your meals at home. You may be traveling for work or pleasure, or just in the mood for dinner out on the town. And then there are the holidays: Thanksgiving at Grandma's, the office Christmas party, the Fourth of July at the lake. Use the Restaurant Guide on pages 27 to 33 to help you make diabetes-wise choices the next time you are eating out. If you find holiday meals and parties a challenge, see the Holiday Party Strategies on page 34. Instead of approaching dining out with thoughts of deprivation, arm yourself with information so you may return to the pleasures of the table. If you're entertaining, turn to the Holiday Menu Planner on page 37 for ten festive menus using the recipes in this book.

Let's Go Out to Eat

Following your diabetic eating plan when you're traveling, or simply out and about in town, is easy when you keep these strategies in mind. We've rated each type of restaurant based on the variety of low-carb items on the menu (see the middle column of the chart). No restaurant is really off-limits; some are just more of a challenge than others. Look under "Strategies" for specific information about what to order when you go into that type of restaurant. If you can, map out your restaurant plan of action. That way, you can fit those restaurant meals into your whole day's eating plan. If you're not sure what's on the menu at a specific restaurant, call ahead to ask or request a menu. Many restaurants post their menus online.

If the restaurant portion seems bigger than you need, choose an appetizer portion, split the meal with a dining companion, or ask for a box to take a portion of the meal home. Or ask if you can order from the senior citizens' menu or the children's menu.

Menu Cues

In general, if you're looking for lower-fat items on the menu, look for these key terms: baked, braised, broiled, cooked in its own juices, grilled, poached, roasted, steamed, stir-fried.

Because the following words usually indicate a high-fat food, avoid menu items that include the following terms: au gratin, batter-fried, breaded, buttered, creamed, crispy, deep-fried, double crust, en croute, pan-fried, pastry, rich, sautéed, scalloped, with gravy, with thick sauce.

Restaurant Guide

Type of Restaurant	Variety of Diabetes-Friendly Menu Items	Strategies for Making Diabetes-Friendly Selections
Fast-Food Burgers	limited	■ Many fast-food restaurants now sell low-carb items such as burgers wrapped in lettuce instead of a bun. If not, just order a burger and take off the bun. ■ Order a grilled chicken sandwich and remove the bun. ■ Order a salad. ■ If you order a sugar-free soft drink, make sure that's what you get. Sometimes the servers get confused, or the lines get crossed in the soda machines. ■ Leave off the fries.
Fast-Food Chicken	limited	■ Order grilled or rotisserie chicken if they have it on the menu. ■ Order breasts (white meat) instead of thighs and drumsticks (dark meat) because white meat is lower in fat than dark. ■ Remove the breading from fried chicken if that is all they have. ■ Generally, the coleslaw has added sugar, so it's best to avoid the slaw and order a salad. ■ Order green beans instead of sweet baked beans.

Type of Restaurant	Variety of Diabetes-Friendly Menu Items	Strategies for Making Diabetes-Friendly Selections
Pizza	limited	■ If you're eating pizza, you're eating carbs unless you eat only the toppings. But you can reduce your carbs by eating thin-crust rather than thick. ■ Order a salad.
Casual Family-Style	good selection	■ If you're ordering soup, make sure that it's one without a lot of high-carb ingredients such as pasta, rice, or potatoes. ■ Order a main-dish salad such as a Cobb Salad or Chicken Caesar Salad. ■ If you're going to the salad bar, steer clear of the macaroni salads and sweet fruit salads. Leave off the crackers and the croutons. ■ Ask for a salad or steamed vegetables instead of a baked potato or fries.
Steak & Seafood	good selection	■ Instead of a baked potato or fries, request steamed vegetables. ■ Ask about the sauce that comes on any meat to make sure it's not a sweet sauce or glaze. ■ Order a salad and request that they leave off the croutons. ■ Order grilled or broiled meats and seafood with savory seasonings instead of sweet sauces, marinades, and glazes.

Type of Restaurant	Variety of Diabetes-Friendly Menu Items	Strategies for Making Diabetes-Friendly Selections
Asian-Style	limited	■ Order steamed spring rolls instead of fried egg rolls. ■ Since the rice is usually served separately, it's not hard to leave it off and just eat the meat and vegetables in a stir-fry. ■ If you do have rice, order plain rice instead of fried because the plain rice is lower in fat and sodium. ■ Pay attention to portion size. Even if you're eating a meat and vegetable stir-fry and leaving off the rice, stir-fry mixtures are often thickened with cornstarch, so the carbohydrate content may be higher than you think. ■ Order individual stir-fry items instead of combination plates with fried rice and egg rolls. (Egg rolls have about 25 grams of carbohydrate per roll.) ■ Eat only small amounts of dipping sauces such as plum or ginger sauce; they generally have a good bit of sugar. ■ Avoid items with "sweet and sour" in the title. The meat, poultry, or fish in these items is typically breaded and deep-fat fried. ■ If you want a bite of something sweet, eat the fortune cookie. One cookie has 30 calories, about 6 grams of carbohydrate, and less than 1 gram of fat.

Type of Restaurant	Variety of Diabetes-Friendly Menu Items	Strategies for Making Diabetes-Friendly Selections
Italian	limited	■ Go easy on the bread and dipping oil that is served before the meal. ■ Select menu items that aren't pasta dishes. If it's a dish such as veal piccata that is served with pasta, request that the pasta be left off. ■ Keep in mind that all Italian food isn't pasta. If you're eating at a restaurant that specializes in northern Italian cuisine, there may be plenty of selections that feature meat, poultry, or seafood in a tomato-based sauce, but not served over pasta. Many Italian restaurants feature traditional bean and vegetable dishes. ■ Order a fresh garden salad, "insalata," to round out your meal. Ask for oil and vinegar dressing on the side. ■ Read the menu description carefully, or ask your server to describe the dish. ■ Tomato sauces often have a little sugar added; ask the server to describe the sweetness of the tomato sauce at that particular restaurant. ■ Pasta is often served as a side dish; ask the server if there are other side dish options such as a vegetable, soup, or salad.

Type of Restaurant	Variety of Diabetes-Friendly Menu Items	Strategies for Making Diabetes-Friendly Selections
Mexican	limited	■ Order a low-fat appetizer such as gazpacho (cold tomato soup), black bean soup without sour cream, or jícama and salsa.
		■ Ask the server not to bring the basket of chips to the table. Or move to the end of the table as far away from the chips as you can.
		■ Order fajitas and don't eat the tortillas.
		■ Order soft tacos instead of crispy because the crispy ones are fried.
		■ Order a taco salad, but don't eat the fried tortilla shell.
		■ Order guacamole and sour cream on the side so you can control the amount you eat.
		■ Look for these menu cues—words that identify items that may be lower in fat: asada (grilled), mole sauce (chile-chocolate sauce), served with salsa verde (green sauce), simmered, tomato sauce, picante, topped with lettuce and tomato, Veracruz-style (tomato sauce), with chiles, wrapped in a soft tortilla.
		■ Keep the beans. Although beans have carbohydrate, it's complex carbohydrate and very high in fiber.
		■ Steer clear of the margaritas—they're high in sugar.
		■ Choose baked or stir-fried entrées such as enchiladas or fajitas instead of fried items such as chile relleños, chimichangas, or flautas.

Type of Restaurant	Variety of Diabetes-Friendly Menu Items	Strategies for Making Diabetes-Friendly Selections
Breakfast	good selection	■ Order eggs (fried, poached, scrambled) or egg dishes such as omelets or frittatas. If you're trying to cut down on fat and/or cholesterol, order egg items made with an egg substitute or egg whites if that choice is available. ■ Order bacon or sausage as a side item instead of potatoes or grits. ■ Request whole wheat toast. ■ Order fresh fruit instead of fruit juice, or tomato juice instead of orange juice. ■ If you don't want eggs, you can order oatmeal or whole-grain bran cereal. ■ Avoid sweet pastries and doughnuts. ■ Avoid pancakes and waffles unless there is a whole-grain choice. ■ Request sugar-free syrup or sugar-free jelly.

Type of Restaurant	Variety of Diabetes-Friendly Menu Items	Strategies for Making Diabetes-Friendly Selections
Delicatessen	limited	■ Order a sandwich on 100-percent whole wheat or whole-grain bread. ■ Order a sandwich with sandwich-sliced bread rather than a hoagie roll, submarine roll, bagel, or bun. ■ Ask for a salad or fruit side dish instead of chips (or some delis may have soy chips as another option). ■ Request a plain or spicy mustard instead of honey mustard. ■ Request dill pickles rather than sweet pickle relish. ■ Plain meats and cheeses may be slightly lower in carbohydrate than chicken or tuna salad, especially if the salad contains sweet pickle relish. ■ If you're ordering soup, order chili or a vegetable-based soup without potatoes. ■ Ask if the coleslaw has a lot of added sugar. Some slaws are much sweeter than others. Some delis will substitute shredded lettuce for slaw if you ask. ■ Order a Chef's Salad with deli meats instead of a sandwich.

Holiday Party Strategies

During the holidays, it can be a challenge to maintain blood sugar control because of the seasonal emphasis on big meals, parties, and abundant sweets. But with a little bit of planning and foresight, you can enjoy the holiday season while making good decisions about your diabetes care. Whether you are the host or the guest, here are some strategies for making wise choices and eating well without giving up your social life.

Plan Ahead for Parties

- If a meal will be served, call the host to find out what time the meal will be served so that you can plan when to take your insulin.

- Depending on your insulin dose and schedule, you might be able to eat your evening snack at your usual dinner time, and then eat your meal at the time you usually have your snack.

- If a meal will not be served, eat your regular meal before you go to the party. Then you won't be hungry and tempted to overindulge in the snacks and sweets.

- Don't skip meals during the day to "save up" for overeating at the party.

- Keep a glass of water, sparkling water, or sugar-free soft drink in your hand at all times. It's harder to eat when one hand is busy.

Nibbling on a few nuts can help fill you up without causing a rise in blood sugar. Although nuts are not low in fat, they contain monounsaturated fat—a type of fat that protects against heart disease.

- Don't stand next to the serving table all night. Move to another room. Enjoy conversation. When your mouth is busy talking, it's not busy eating.

- Offer to bring a low-fat, low-sugar dish to the party.

- Fill up on low-calorie, high-fiber foods like fresh vegetables and fruits. But go easy on the vegetable dip and cheese on the fruit and cheese platter because they are high in fat.

- Keep the fat content of your regular meals especially low during the holidays to balance the extra fat from party food.

- If you must have something sweet, go ahead and have a little taste and allow for the extra carbohydrate in your meal plan. Plain cookies or cake (such as shortbread cookies or pound cake) are better choices than those with sugary icing or frosting.

- Steer clear of the holiday punch or cider unless you know it's sugar-free. Even if it's a fruit juice-based beverage, fruit juice is all carbohydrate.

- If you drink alcohol, drink in moderation (two drinks a day for men and one for women). One drink equals a 5-ounce glass of wine, a 12-ounce light beer, or 1½ ounces of 80-proof liquor.

- Choose low-sugar or sugar-free mixers such as diet soft drinks, diet tonic water, club soda, seltzer, or water.

- If you are drinking alcohol, be sure to eat some food as well because alcohol can lower blood glucose levels.

Party Picks
Choose these low-fat, low-sugar party foods.

Fruit
Apple wedges
Grapes
Pear slices
Pineapple cubes
Strawberries

Vegetables
Broccoli florets
Carrot sticks
Cauliflower florets
Celery sticks
Cherry tomatoes
Squash slices

Breads
Breadsticks
French bread
Low-fat potato
  chips
Low-fat tortilla
  chips
Melba rounds
Pita bread wedges
Plain crackers
Plain rolls
Pretzels
Whole-grain crackers

Dips
Black Bean Dip
Salsa

**Meats, Poultry,
& Seafood**
Boiled shrimp
Lean roast beef
Pork tenderloin
Turkey

(continued on next page)

Focus on Fun

Another way to keep your blood sugars in control during the holidays is to take some of the focus away from food and add some other activities to your holiday gatherings. Entertainment such as a storyteller or a musician allows an opportunity to move away from the food table for a while. Here are some other suggestions for alternate party activities:

- sing carols around the piano
- go caroling in the neighborhood
- ask any musicians in the group to bring their instruments and invite them to play
- exchange gag gifts
- share stories of holiday memories
- address cards to nursing home residents, hospital patients, or members of the armed services
- wrap toys for needy children
- collect canned goods for a local food bank
- play charades or any group game
- watch a holiday classic movie

Get Moving

If you cannot maintain your normal exercise schedule, try to get some type of physical activity, even if it's extra walking while you're shopping at the mall. Instead of driving around the neighborhood to view the holiday lights, take a walk. Tramp around a tree farm to find the perfect tree. Seize any opportunity you can to be moving instead of sitting at the table.

Holiday Hospitality Tips

Whether you have diabetes, or you're entertaining for people who do, here are some tips that will make you a great host.

- Have plenty of sugar-free drinks available.
- Make a special sugar-free dessert or purchase a carton of no-sugar-added ice cream.
- Let guests know which dishes do not have sugar if it's not obvious.
- Include a fresh vegetable tray or fruit and cheese platter on your menu.
- If you're serving dinner, let guests know what time you plan to serve so that those on insulin can plan when to take their injection.
- Serve flavored coffee with dessert. It's easier to pass up a high-sugar dessert if you have a sweet-tasting cup of coffee to savor.
- Have a place in the house other than the food table where people can gather.

Achieve Balance

The fact is, the holidays are special times filled with activities and events that may only happen once a year. It's okay not to be perfect. Relax and take one day at a time. If one day gets a little out of control, resolve to start again the next day with more healthy choices. Many people find that a slight break from the normal routine is helpful in avoiding ruts. A few days off may offer a time for renewal and a new sense of motivation.

Holiday Menu Planner

Use the recipe chapters of the *All-New Complete Step-by-Step Diabetic Cookbook* to plan festive holiday meals for your family and friends. Just because you or a family member has diabetes doesn't mean that you can't enjoy good food during the holidays. And we guarantee that these tried-and-true, kitchen-tested recipes will be enjoyed by everyone at the table.

Holiday Helpers

Don't be overwhelmed by figuring out what to cook and serve when you have company. Keep these menu tips in mind when you're planning meals for special holidays.

Use convenience foods

Take advantage of the many choices of prepared and packaged healthy foods that are on the market instead of feeling pressure to prepare everything from scratch. Here are just a few examples: whole wheat rolls; sugar-free and reduced-sugar pies, cakes, and cookies from the bakery; prechopped/sliced vegetables and prepackaged salads from the produce section; frozen vegetables and fruit; and roasted chicken, roasted turkey, or ham from the deli.

Simplify the menu

Every meal does not have to feature multiple dishes. Sometimes a one-dish meal or two or three memorable dishes are more satisfying than a huge array of food.

Select quick and easy dishes

A time-saving strategy is to select one labor-intensive recipe, and add easy side dishes to round out the meal. Look for the ready in __ minutes tags on the recipes throughout this book for recipes that are ready in under 30 minutes.

Get ahead with make-aheads

Prepare a dish ahead of time and store it in the freezer or refrigerator, then just reheat it when you need it. Look for the make-ahead tags on recipes throughout the book, or look for the make-ahead entry in the Recipe Index for a complete list.

Favor the Familiar

There's no need to experiment with challenging, gourmet-style healthy recipes during the holidays. Often with a few simple substitutions (see charts on page 19 and 24), you can lighten up some of your family favorites.

New Year's Day Brunch
serves 6
*Ring in a healthy and happy new year with a hearty brunch menu that's
mostly make-ahead.*

Spicy Tomato Sippers (page 44),
Sausage-Egg Casserole (page 169),
Zippy Garlic-Cheese Grits (page 282),
Fresh Fruit Salad (page 206),
Sage and Cheese Biscuits (page 76)

Super Bowl Celebration
serves 12
*No matter which teams are playing, all fans will cheer for
these crowd-pleasing dishes.*

Speedy Salsa (page 53), baked tortilla chips,
Hearty Sausage-Bean Chili (page 314),
Chile-Cheese Corn Bread (page 86),
Fudgy Cream Cheese Brownies (page 339)

For more low-fat,
low-sugar munchies,
see "Party Picks"
on page 35.

Valentine's Day Dinner
serves 2
*Show your special sweetie how much you care with this
elegant, heart-healthy dinner for two.*

Grapefruit and Greens (page 209),
Artichoke Veal Chops (page 157),
Garlic-Lemon Pasta (page 288),
Tiramisù (page 353)

Note: Recipe yields do not all exactly match the number of menu servings. Some recipes
will need to be doubled, and for others you will have extra portions.

Springtime Celebration

serves 8

Welcome spring with a special dinner featuring flavors that are as fresh and clean as the season itself.

Parslied Leg of Lamb (page 160),
New Potatoes with Chives (page 279), roasted asparagus,
Quick Yeast Rolls (page 92),
Lemon Cheesecake (page 335)

Mother's Day Brunch

serves 6

Give Mom the day off and surprise her with this casually elegant brunch.

Artichoke Quiche (page 124),
Asparagus with Mock Hollandaise Sauce (page 261),
Blueberry Muffins (page 81),
Frosted Cappuccino (page 45)

Fourth of July Barbecue

serves 8

What's a Fourth of July without barbecue, coleslaw, and homemade ice cream? You'll need to supply the fireworks.

Barbecue Pork Sandwiches (page 258),
Garden Pasta Salad (page 227), **Vinaigrette Coleslaw** (page 215),
Three-Bean Salad (page 217),
Homemade Peach Ice Cream (page 324),
watermelon slices

Football Tailgating Fare

serves 10-12

Show your team spirit with a portable menu that you can serve from the tailgate of your vehicle or a folding table in the stadium parking lot.

Spicy Snack Mix (page 61),
Black Bean Dip (page 58), **Spicy Tortilla Chips** (page 62),
Roast Beef Wraps (page 248),
Jalapeño Potato Salad (page 226),
Chocolate-Cereal Bars (page 338)

Thanksgiving Feast

serves 8

*Gather 'round the table with family and friends to enjoy
a classic Thanksgiving meal.*

roasted turkey breast,
Sausage-Corn Bread Dressing (page 281),
Orange Sweet Potatoes (page 280),
Broccoli-Cheese Casserole (page 263),
Holiday Cranberry Salad (page 208), whole wheat rolls,
Apple Pie (page 341)

Holiday Dinner Party

serves 9

Celebrate the season with this festive and elegant entertaining menu.

Orange-Pecan Mixed Green Salad (page 210),
Beef Tenderloin with Horseradish Sauce (page 153),
Roasted-Garlic Mashed Potatoes (page 277),
steamed broccoli, French bread,
Mocha Trifle (page 357)

If you want to serve
wine with dinner, a
standard 750-milliliter
bottle contains about
five servings of wine.

Open-House Appetizer Buffet

serves 20

*Invite neighbors over for a cup of cheer and an assortment
of hearty appetizers and suitable sweets.*

Marinated Cheese Appetizers (page 64),
assorted crackers and breadsticks, **Creamy Pineapple Dip** (page 55),
apple and pear slices, **Hot Crabmeat Dip** (page 60),
Mexican Pinwheels (page 65),
Chocolate-Peppermint Cookies (page 336),
Holiday Hot Fruit Punch (page 51)

Note: Recipe yields do not all exactly match the number of menu servings. Some recipes will
need to be doubled, and for others you will have extra portions.

beverages and snacks

Orange-Pineapple Slush

3   cups ice cubes
1   cup orange juice
½   cup pineapple juice
¼   cup lemon juice
3   tablespoons "measures-like-sugar" calorie-free sweetener

Combine all ingredients in a blender or food processor; process on high speed until smooth and frothy.

Serve immediately. **Yield:** 4 servings (serving size: 1 cup).

Per Serving:

Calories 57	**Fiber** 0.2g
Fat 0.1g (sat 0.0g)	**Cholesterol** 0mg
Protein 0.6g	**Sodium** 13mg
Carbohydrate 14.3g	**Exchange:** 1 Fruit

Instead of using two different containers of juice, you can use a bottle or can of pineapple-orange juice.

Watermelon-Berry Slush

4   cups cubed seeded watermelon
1   (10-ounce) package frozen raspberries in light syrup
1   (11-ounce) bottle sparkling water

Place watermelon cubes in a single layer in a shallow pan; freeze until firm.

Remove watermelon from freezer; let stand 5 minutes. Drop watermelon through food processor chute with processor running; process until smooth. Add chunks of frozen raspberries alternately with sparkling water; processing until mixture is smooth.

Serve immediately. **Yield:** 5 servings (serving size: 1 cup).

Per Serving:

Calories 72	**Fiber** 2.7g
Fat 0.5g (sat 0.3g)	**Cholesterol** 0mg
Protein 0.7g	**Sodium** 18mg
Carbohydrate 16.9g	**Exchange:** 1 Fruit

This is a great recipe to make when you have half of a watermelon left over. Or you can substitute containers of cubed watermelon from the produce section of the supermarket.

Spicy Tomato Sippers

2¾ cups no-salt-added tomato juice
2 tablespoons lime juice
2 teaspoons low-sodium Worcestershire sauce
1 teaspoon prepared horseradish
½ teaspoon celery salt
¼ teaspoon hot sauce
Lime slices (optional)

Combine first 6 ingredients in a small pitcher; stir well. Cover and chill thoroughly.

Garnish with lime slices, if desired. **Yield:** 3 servings (serving size: 1 cup).

Per Serving:

Calories 51	**Fiber** 0.9g
Fat 0.0g (sat 0.0g)	**Cholesterol** 0mg
Protein 2.3g	**Sodium** 390mg
Carbohydrate 12.9g	**Exchanges:** 2 Vegetable

For an even spicier drink, increase the hot sauce to ½ teaspoon.

Frosted Cappuccino

2   cups brewed espresso (or very strong brewed coffee),
        chilled
2   cups vanilla no-added-sugar, fat-free ice cream
½   teaspoon vanilla extract
Ground cinnamon (optional)

Combine first 3 ingredients in a blender; process until smooth.
Pour into glasses. Sprinkle each serving with cinnamon, if desired.

Serve immediately. **Yield:** 4 servings (serving size: 1 cup).

Per Serving:

Calories 94	**Fiber** 1.0g
Fat 0.0g (sat 0.0g)	**Cholesterol** 0mg
Protein 4.1g	**Sodium** 78mg
Carbohydrate 21.6g	**Exchanges:** 1½ Starch

Create the sweet taste and texture of a luxuriously rich coffee beverage without the sugar and fat.

make-ahead

Pink Tulip Punch

1   (12-ounce) package frozen unsweetened raspberries, thawed
2   ripe bananas, peeled and sliced
2   (12-ounce) cans frozen orange-pineapple-apple juice concentrate, thawed
2   cups water
1   (32-ounce) bottle berry-flavored sparkling mineral water, chilled

Place raspberries in a blender; process until smooth. Pour raspberry puree through a wire-mesh strainer into a bowl, discarding pulp and seeds remaining in strainer. Return strained puree to blender. Add sliced banana and 1 can juice concentrate; process until smooth.

Pour mixture into a large freezer-proof container. Stir in remaining 1 can juice concentrate and 2 cups water. Cover and freeze 4 hours or until slushy.

To serve, transfer juice mixture to a small punch bowl. Stir in mineral water, and serve immediately. **Yield:** 12 servings (serving size: 1 cup).

Per Serving:

Calories 122	**Fiber** 3.2g
Fat 0.4g (sat 0.0g)	**Cholesterol** 0mg
Protein 1.8g	**Sodium** 18mg
Carbohydrate 29.4g	**Exchanges:** 2 Fruit

make-ahead

Citrus Punch

4   cups water
3   cups pineapple juice
½   cup lemon juice
¼   cup "measures-like-sugar" calorie-free sweetener
1   (6-ounce) can frozen orange juice concentrate
3   (12-ounce) cans sugar-free lemon-lime carbonated beverage,
        chilled
Lime slices (optional)

Combine first 5 ingredients in a large bowl; cover and chill.

To serve, stir in carbonated beverage. Serve immediately over ice. Garnish with lime slices, if desired. **Yield:** 13 servings (serving size: 1 cup).

Per Serving:

Calories 59	**Fiber** 0.2g
Fat 0.1g (sat 0.0g)	**Cholesterol** 0mg
Protein 0.5g	**Sodium** 19mg
Carbohydrate 14.6g	**Exchange:** 1 Fruit

If you're having a party, combine all of the juices and water a day or two before and refrigerate. Stir in the carbonated beverage just before serving.

Sugar-Free Cocoa Mix

2⅓ cups instant nonfat dry milk
⅓ cup unsweetened cocoa
⅓ cup "measures-like-sugar" calorie-free sweetener
Miniature marshmallows (optional)
Sugar-free candy canes (optional)

Combine first 3 ingredients in a large bowl; stir well. Store in an air-tight container.

To serve, spoon ¼ cup cocoa mix into each mug. Add 1 cup boiling water, and stir well. Top with miniature marshmallows or sugar-free candy canes, if desired (marshmallows and candy canes not included in analysis). **Yield:** 12 servings (serving size: 1 cup).

Per Serving:

Calories 62	**Fiber** 0.8g
Fat 0.4g (sat 0.3g)	**Cholesterol** 2mg
Protein 5.1g	**Sodium** 73mg
Carbohydrate 13.5g	**Exchange:** 1 Skim Milk

If you're not a milk drinker, hot cocoa is a great way to add calcium to your diet. One serving of this sugar-free cocoa has 166 milligrams of calcium. Most adults need 1,000 milligrams per day.

Holiday Tea Mix

1¼ cups "measures-like-sugar" calorie-free sweetener
1 (1.8-ounce) container sugar-free orange drink mix
   (such as sugar-free Tang)
1 (0.45-ounce) package sugar-free lemonade mix
¾ cup unsweetened instant tea without lemon
1 teaspoon ground cloves
2 teaspoons ground cinnamon

Combine all ingredients in a large bowl; stir well. Store in an airtight container.

To serve, spoon 2 teaspoons tea mix into each cup. Add ¾ cup boiling water, and stir well. **Yield:** 54 servings (serving size: ¾ cup).

Per Serving:

Calories 8	**Fiber** 0.0g
Fat 0.0g (sat 0.0g)	**Cholesterol** 0mg
Protein 0.1g	**Sodium** 7mg
Carbohydrate 1.7g	**Exchange:** Free

Mulled Cider Supreme

4½ cups apple cider
1 cup water
2 tablespoons "measures-like-sugar" brown sugar calorie-free
   sweetener (such as Brown Sugar Twin)
2 (3-inch) cinnamon sticks
5 whole cloves
3 whole allspice
1 (2-inch) piece peeled fresh ginger

Combine first 3 ingredients in a saucepan, stirring well.

Place cinnamon sticks and remaining 3 ingredients on a 6-inch square of cheesecloth; tie with string. Add spice bag to cider mixture.

Bring to a simmer over medium-high heat, stirring occasionally. Reduce heat to low, and cook, uncovered, 15 minutes, stirring occasionally. Discard spice bag. Pour into individual mugs, and serve warm. **Yield:** 5 servings (serving size: 1 cup).

Per Serving:

Calories 109	**Fiber** 0.4g
Fat 0.2g (sat 0.0g)	**Cholesterol** 0mg
Protein 0.1g	**Sodium** 13mg
Carbohydrate 27.1g	**Exchanges:** 2 Fruit

Holiday Hot Fruit Punch

1   (46-ounce) can apple juice
1   teaspoon ground nutmeg
1   (3-inch) cinnamon stick
2   teaspoons whole cloves
2   medium oranges, quartered
1   (46-ounce) can pineapple juice
1   (46-ounce) can orange juice
¼   cup "measures-like-sugar" calorie-free sweetener
Fresh orange slices (optional)
Additional cinnamon sticks (optional)

Combine first 3 ingredients in a Dutch oven; bring to a boil. Cover, reduce heat, and simmer 20 minutes, stirring occasionally.

Insert cloves into rinds of orange quarters. Add pineapple juice, orange juice, and sweetener to apple juice mixture; stir well. Add orange quarters. Cook 5 minutes or until mixture is thoroughly heated. (Do not boil.)

Remove and discard orange quarters and cinnamon stick. Serve warm. If desired, garnish with orange slices or cinnamon sticks. **Yield:** 23 servings (serving size: ¾ cup).

Per Serving:

Calories 91	**Fiber** 0.3g
Fat 0.2g (sat 0.0g)	**Cholesterol** 0mg
Protein 0.6g	**Sodium** 6mg
Carbohydrate 22.1g	**Exchanges:** 1½ Fruit

Hot Cranberry Cocktail

1   tablespoon whole cloves
2   teaspoons whole allspice
4   cups pineapple juice
1   (48-ounce) bottle low-calorie cranberry juice drink

Cut a 6-inch square of cheesecloth; place cloves and allspice in center, and tie with string.

Combine spice bag, pineapple juice, and cranberry juice in a large saucepan. Bring to a boil; cover, reduce heat, and simmer 5 minutes. Remove and discard spice bag. Serve warm. **Yield:** 10 servings (serving size: 1 cup).

Per Serving:

Calories 80	**Fiber** 0.1g
Fat 0.1g (sat 0.0g)	**Cholesterol** 0mg
Protein 0.3g	**Sodium** 46mg
Carbohydrate 20.0g	**Exchange:** 1 Fruit

Speedy Salsa

1   (10-ounce) can diced tomatoes and green chiles, undrained
1   (14½-ounce) can no-salt-added stewed tomatoes, undrained
1   teaspoon pepper
1   garlic clove

Combine all ingredients in a blender; process 30 seconds, stopping once to scrape down sides.

Serve with baked tortilla chips (chips not included in analysis). **Yield:** 3 cups (serving size: 1 tablespoon).

Per Serving:

Calories 3

Fat 0.0g (sat 0.0g)

Protein 0.1g

Carbohydrate 0.8g

Fiber 0.1g

Cholesterol 0mg

Sodium 21mg

Exchange: Free

If you've got a minute, you've got time to make this spunky salsa. Four ingredients and a blender are all it takes.

Fiesta Onion Salsa

1   cup chopped onion (about 1 large)
¾   cup chopped tomato (about 1 medium)
1   (4.5-ounce) can chopped green chiles, drained
3   tablespoons sliced ripe olives
2   tablespoons white wine vinegar
¼   teaspoon salt
¼   teaspoon Worcestershire sauce
⅛   teaspoon ground cumin
⅛   teaspoon pepper
⅛   teaspoon hot sauce

Combine all ingredients in a medium bowl; cover and chill at least 2 hours.

Serve with baked tortilla chips (chips not included in analysis). **Yield:** 2 cups (serving size: 1 tablespoon).

Per Serving:

Calories 5	**Fiber** 0.2g
Fat 0.2g (sat 0.0g)	**Cholesterol** 0mg
Protein 0.1g	**Sodium** 45mg
Carbohydrate 0.9g	**Exchange:** Free

This salsa is also great on grilled chicken and fish.

Creamy Pineapple Dip

1   cup lemon low-fat yogurt
3   tablespoons frozen pineapple juice concentrate
1   tablespoon fat-free sour cream

Combine all ingredients in a small bowl; stir well. Cover and chill at least 25 minutes.

Stir just before serving. Serve with assorted fresh fruit (fruit not included in analysis).

Store remaining dip in an airtight container in the refrigerator up to 5 days. **Yield:** 1¼ cups (serving size: 1 tablespoon).

Per Serving:

Calories 22	**Fiber** 0.0g
Fat 0.1g (sat 0.1g)	**Cholesterol** 0mg
Protein 0.5g	**Sodium** 9mg
Carbohydrate 4.7g	**Exchange:** Free (up to 2 tablespoons)

Be sure to use a low-fat yogurt that has been sweetened with Splenda® or Nutrasweet® instead of sugar.

Orange Dip

1 (8-ounce) carton vanilla low-fat yogurt
3 tablespoons tub-style light cream cheese, softened
1 (11-ounce) can mandarin oranges in light syrup, drained
  and chopped
1 teaspoon "measures-like-sugar" calorie-free sweetener
2 teaspoons lime juice

Spoon yogurt onto several layers of heavy-duty paper towels, spreading to ½-inch thickness. Cover with additional paper towels; let stand 5 minutes.

Scrape yogurt into a bowl, using a rubber spatula. Add cream cheese and remaining ingredients, stirring well until blended.

Serve with fresh fruit, such as apple or pear slices, strawberries, or pineapple chunks (fruit not included in analysis). **Yield:** 1 cup (serving size: 1 tablespoon).

Per Serving:

Calories 23   **Fiber** 0.0g
Fat 0.6g (sat 0.3g) **Cholesterol** 2mg
Protein 0.9g   **Sodium** 22mg
Carbohydrate 3.6g   **Exchange:** Free (up to 3 tablespoons)

ready in **30** minutes

Swiss-Onion Dip

1   (10-ounce) package frozen chopped onion, thawed
2   cups (8 ounces) shredded reduced-fat Swiss cheese
1   cup fat-free mayonnaise
1   tablespoon coarse-grained Dijon mustard
⅛   teaspoon pepper

Preheat oven to 325°.

Drain onion on paper towels.

Combine onion and remaining ingredients in a 1-quart baking dish. Bake at 325° for 25 minutes or until bubbly and lightly browned.

Serve with low-fat crackers (crackers not included in analysis). **Yield:** 2¼ cups (serving size: 1 tablespoon).

Per Serving:

Calories 28	**Fiber** 0.0g
Fat 1.1g (sat 0.6g)	**Cholesterol** 4mg
Protein 2.3g	**Sodium** 103mg
Carbohydrate 2.1g	**Exchange:** Free (up to 3 tablespoons)

Black Bean Dip

1	(15-ounce) can black beans, drained
1	(8-ounce) can no-salt-added tomato sauce
½	cup (2 ounces) shredded reduced-fat sharp Cheddar cheese
1	teaspoon chili powder

Combine beans and tomato sauce in a small saucepan; bring to a boil over medium heat, stirring occasionally. Remove from heat.

Mash beans with a potato masher or back of a spoon. Add cheese and chili powder; cook, stirring constantly, until cheese melts.

Serve dip warm with toasted pita chips or fresh vegetables (chips and vegetables not included in analysis). **Yield:** 2 cups (serving size: 1 tablespoon).

Per Serving:

Calories 19	Fiber 0.5g
Fat 0.4g (sat 0.2g)	Cholesterol 1mg
Protein 1.3g	Sodium 37mg
Carbohydrate 2.6g	Exchange: Free (up to 4 tablespoons)

If you're on a low-sodium diet, make this spicy dip with no-salt-added beans and serve it with unsalted chips or fresh vegetables.

Artichoke and Green Chile Dip

⅔ cup fat-free mayonnaise
½ cup plain low-fat yogurt
1 (14-ounce) can artichoke hearts, drained and chopped
1 (4.5-ounce) can chopped green chiles, drained
½ cup grated fresh Parmesan cheese, divided
¼ teaspoon garlic powder
¼ teaspoon hot sauce
Cooking spray
Fresh green chile slices (optional)

Preheat oven to 350°.

Combine mayonnaise and yogurt in a medium bowl, stirring until smooth. Add artichoke, chopped chiles, 6 tablespoons Parmesan cheese, garlic powder, and hot sauce, stirring well.

Spoon mixture into a 1-quart baking dish coated with cooking spray. Bake, uncovered, at 350° for 25 minutes.

Sprinkle with remaining 2 tablespoons Parmesan cheese. Turn oven temperature to broil, and cook 1 to 2 minutes or until lightly browned.

Garnish with green chile slices, if desired. Serve with Melba toast rounds or breadsticks (rounds and breadsticks not included in analysis). **Yield:** 2¾ cups (serving size: 1 tablespoon).

Per Serving:

Calories 13	**Fiber** 0.1g
Fat 0.4g (sat 0.2g)	**Cholesterol** 1mg
Protein 0.7g	**Sodium** 78mg
Carbohydrate 1.7g	**Exchange:** Free (up to 4 tablespoons)

Hot Crabmeat Dip

2	(8-ounce) packages ⅓-less-fat cream cheese
½	cup fat-free mayonnaise
¼	cup grated onion
½	teaspoon garlic powder
¼	teaspoon salt
½	teaspoon pepper
3	tablespoons dry white wine
2	teaspoons prepared mustard
2	teaspoons prepared horseradish
½	pound lump crabmeat, drained and shell pieces removed
2	tablespoons chopped fresh chives
2	tablespoons chopped fresh parsley

Combine first 9 ingredients in a medium saucepan, stir well. Cook over low heat, stirring constantly, until cream cheese melts and mixture is smooth.

Stir in crabmeat and remaining ingredients. Transfer to a chafing dish, and keep warm.

Serve with low-fat crackers (crackers not included in analysis). **Yield:** 3½ cups (serving size: 1 tablespoon).

Per Serving:

Calories 25	**Fiber** 0.1g
Fat 1.5g (sat 0.8g)	**Cholesterol** 9mg
Protein 1.7g	**Sodium** 97mg
Carbohydrate 1.2g	**Exchange:** Free (up to 4 tablespoons)

Spicy Snack Mix

1½ cups bite-size crispy corn squares
1½ cups bite-size crispy rice squares
1½ cups bite-size crispy wheat squares
¾ cup small unsalted pretzels
¼ cup unsalted dry roasted peanuts
¼ cup fat-free margarine, melted
2 tablespoons low-sodium soy sauce
1½ teaspoons chili powder
½ teaspoon garlic powder
¼ teaspoon ground red pepper

Preheat oven to 300°.

Combine first 5 ingredients in a large heavy-duty zip-top plastic bag. Combine margarine and remaining 4 ingredients; pour over cereal mixture. Seal bag; shake well to coat.

Place cereal mixture on a 15- x 10-inch jelly-roll pan. Bake at 300° for 18 to 20 minutes or until lightly browned, stirring occasionally. Remove from oven; let cool completely.

Store snack mix in an airtight container. **Yield:** 10 servings (serving size: ½ cup).

Per Serving:

Calories 59	**Fiber** 0.6g
Fat 0.6g (sat 0.1g)	**Cholesterol** 0mg
Protein 1.3g	**Sodium** 223mg
Carbohydrate 11.6g	**Exchange:** 1 Starch

Spicy Tortilla Chips

12   (6-inch) corn tortillas
½   cup lime juice
¼   cup water
½   teaspoon garlic powder
¼   teaspoon salt
⅛   teaspoon ground cumin
⅛   teaspoon ground red pepper

Preheat oven to 350°.

Cut each tortilla into 4 wedges. Combine lime juice and water. Dip wedges in lime juice mixture; drain on paper towels. Arrange wedges in a single layer on a large baking sheet.

Combine garlic powder and remaining 3 ingredients; sprinkle evenly over wedges. Bake at 350° for 12 to 14 minutes or until crisp. Transfer chips to wire racks; cool completely.

Store chips in an airtight container. **Yield:** 12 servings (serving size: 4 chips).

Per Serving:

Calories 60	**Fiber** 1.3g
Fat 0.6g (sat 0.1g)	**Cholesterol** 0mg
Protein 1.5g	**Sodium** 89mg
Carbohydrate 12.7g	**Exchange:** 1 Starch

make-ahead

Pineapple Cheese Ball

¾   cup (3 ounces) shredded fat-free sharp Cheddar cheese
½   cup finely chopped green bell pepper
2   teaspoons grated onion
1   (8-ounce) can crushed pineapple in juice, well drained
½   (8-ounce) package ⅓-less-fat cream cheese, softened
½   (8-ounce) package fat-free cream cheese, softened
⅔   cup chopped fresh parsley

Combine first 6 ingredients in a medium bowl. Cover and chill 30 minutes.

Shape cheese mixture into a ball; roll in chopped parsley, coating thoroughly. Cover and chill at least 3 hours.

Serve with Melba toast rounds or low-fat crackers (rounds and crackers not included in analysis). **Yield:** 2¼ cups (serving size: 1 tablespoon).

Per Serving:

Calories 17	Fiber 0.1g
Fat 0.8g (sat 0.5g)	Cholesterol 3mg
Protein 1.6g	Sodium 49mg
Carbohydrate 0.9g	Exchange: Free (up to 4 tablespoons)

We tested this cheese ball using only fat-free cream cheese, but found that a combination of fat-free and reduced-fat cream cheese produced a creamier dip.

Marinated Cheese Appetizers

1   (8-ounce) block part-skim mozzarella cheese
1   (8-ounce) block reduced-fat Cheddar cheese
1   cup fat-free Italian dressing
¼   teaspoon freshly ground black pepper
1   (12-ounce) French baguette
Fresh basil leaves (optional)

Cut cheeses into ¼-inch-thick slices; place slices in a 13- x 9-inch dish, overlapping slightly.

Combine dressing and pepper; pour over cheese. Cover and chill 8 hours.

Preheat oven to 350°.

Cut baguette into ¼-inch-thick slices. Place on baking sheets. Bake at 350° for 8 to 10 minutes or until lightly toasted, turning once.

Drain cheeses. Place 1 cheese slice on each bread slice. Garnish with fresh basil, if desired. **Yield:** 44 appetizers (serving size: 1 appetizer).

Per Serving:

Calories 52	Fiber 0.1g
Fat 2.0g (sat 1.2g)	Cholesterol 7mg
Protein 3.5g	Sodium 163mg
Carbohydrate 5.2g	Exchange: ½ Medium-Fat Meat

To make ahead, marinate the cheese overnight in the refrigerator. Toast the bread a day ahead, and store it at room temperature. Assemble the appetizers right before serving.

Mexican Pinwheels

1   (8-ounce) package fat-free cream cheese, softened
½   cup fat-free sour cream
1   cup (4 ounces) shredded reduced-fat sharp Cheddar cheese
⅓   cup chopped green onions
¼   teaspoon salt-free herb-and-spice blend
1   (4.5-ounce) can chopped green chiles, drained
1   (2¼-ounce) can sliced ripe olives, drained
1   garlic clove, pressed
8   (8-inch) flour tortillas

Beat cream cheese and sour cream with a mixer at medium speed until smooth. Stir in Cheddar cheese and next 5 ingredients. Spread cheese mixture evenly over each tortilla; roll up tortillas. Wrap each separately in plastic wrap. Chill up to 8 hours.

To serve, unwrap each roll, and cut into 8 slices. Secure pinwheels with wooden picks, if desired. **Yield:** 32 servings (serving size: 2 pinwheels).

Per Serving:

Calories 52
Fat 1.6g (sat 0.5g)
Protein 3.1g
Carbohydrate 6.0g

Fiber 0.4g
Cholesterol 4mg
Sodium 181mg
Exchange: ½ Starch

ready in **15** minutes

Pizza Bites

¾ cup (3 ounces) shredded part-skim mozzarella cheese
⅓ cup grated fresh Parmesan cheese
1 (14-ounce) package mini English muffins
⅓ cup chopped Canadian bacon
⅓ cup chopped green bell pepper

Preheat oven to 400°.

Combine mozzarella and Parmesan cheeses; set aside.

Cut each muffin in half horizontally and place on an ungreased baking sheet. Sprinkle bacon, green bell pepper, and cheese mixture evenly on muffin halves.

Bake at 400° for 10 to 12 minutes or until lightly browned.

Serve warm. **Yield:** 2 dozen (serving size: 1 appetizer).

Per Serving:

Calories 56	**Fiber** 0.0g
Fat 1.2g (sat 0.7g)	**Cholesterol** 5mg
Protein 3.5g	**Sodium** 147mg
Carbohydrate 7.8g	**Exchanges:** ½ Starch, ½ Lean Meat

breads

Cinnamon French Toast

½   cup egg substitute
½   cup fat-free milk
½   to ¾ teaspoon ground cinnamon
Cooking spray
1   tablespoon plus 1 teaspoon reduced-calorie margarine,
     divided
4   (1⅓-ounce) slices whole wheat bread

Combine first 3 ingredients in a shallow bowl, stirring well with a wire whisk.

Coat a nonstick skillet with cooking spray. Add 1 teaspoon margarine; place over medium heat until margarine melts.

Dip 1 bread slice into egg substitute mixture. Place coated bread in skillet; cook until browned and crisp on each side, turning once. Repeat procedure with remaining margarine, bread, and egg substitute mixture. Serve immediately. **Yield:** 4 servings (serving size: 1 slice).

Per Serving:

Calories 141	**Fiber** 3.1g
Fat 4.4g (sat 0.4g)	**Cholesterol** 1mg
Protein 7.1g	**Sodium** 248mg
Carbohydrate 21.2g	**Exchanges:** 1½ Starch, 1 Fat

Cheesy French Bread

1½ cups (6 ounces) shredded reduced-fat Monterey Jack cheese
½   cup light mayonnaise
1½ teaspoons dried parsley flakes
1   (16-ounce) loaf French bread, cut in half horizontally

Preheat oven to 350°.

Combine first 3 ingredients. Spread on cut sides of bread; place on a baking sheet.

Bake at 350° for 10 to 15 minutes or until cheese is melted.

Slice into equal portions, and serve warm. **Yield:** 16 servings (serving size: 1 slice).

Per Serving:

Calories 134	**Fiber** 0.6g
Fat 4.6g (sat 1.7g)	**Cholesterol** 10mg
Protein 5.8g	**Sodium** 288mg
Carbohydrate 16.4g	**Exchanges:** 1 Starch, ½ High-Fat Meat

Herbed Garlic Bread

¼ cup reduced-calorie margarine, softened
1½ tablespoons grated fresh Parmesan cheese
2 teaspoons minced fresh parsley
2 teaspoons minced fresh basil
¼ teaspoon garlic powder
12 (¾-inch-thick) slices French bread

Preheat oven to 400°.

Combine first 5 ingredients in a small bowl; stir well. Spread mixture evenly on 1 side of bread slices.

Wrap bread in aluminum foil, and bake at 400° for 15 minutes.

Remove bread from foil, and serve warm. **Yield:** 12 servings (serving size: 1 slice).

Per Serving:

Calories 103	**Fiber** 0.7g
Fat 3.0g (sat 0.5g)	**Cholesterol** 1mg
Protein 2.6g	**Sodium** 203mg
Carbohydrate 15.8g	**Exchanges:** 1 Starch, ½ Fat

Get the flavor of commercial garlic bread but with a lot less fat. Begin with plain French bread and spread with our low-fat cheese-herb mixture.

Sesame-Garlic French Braid

1   (11-ounce) can refrigerated French bread dough
Cooking spray
2   garlic cloves, thinly sliced
1½ tablespoons reduced-calorie margarine, melted
2   teaspoons sesame seeds

Preheat oven to 350°.

Unroll dough; cut into 3 equal pieces. Shape each portion into a rope. Place ropes on a baking sheet coated with cooking spray; (do not stretch). Braid ropes; pinch loose ends to seal. Insert garlic slices evenly into braid. Brush melted margarine over braid, and sprinkle with sesame seeds.

Bake braid at 350° for 25 minutes or until loaf sounds hollow when tapped. Remove from baking sheet immediately. Serve warm. **Yield:** 10 servings (serving size: ¹⁄₁₀ of loaf).

Per Serving:

Calories 86	**Fiber** 0.3g
Fat 2.2g (sat 0.7g)	**Cholesterol** 0mg
Protein 3.1g	**Sodium** 212mg
Carbohydrate 13.7g	**Exchange:** 1 Starch

Onion-Sesame Rolls

1½ tablespoons grated Parmesan cheese
1   tablespoon instant minced onion
½   teaspoon garlic powder
1   (13.8-ounce) can refrigerated pizza crust dough
Butter-flavored cooking spray
2   tablespoons fat-free Italian dressing
1   tablespoon sesame seeds

Preheat oven to 400°.

Combine first 3 ingredients; set cheese mixture aside.

Unroll pizza dough, and pat into a 10- x 8-inch rectangle. Coat dough with cooking spray, and brush with dressing. Sprinkle cheese mixture over dough, leaving a ½-inch border. Roll up, jelly-roll fashion, starting with short side; pinch seam to seal.

Cut into 10 (1-inch-thick) slices, and place on an ungreased baking sheet. Coat tops of rolls with cooking spray, and sprinkle with sesame seeds.

Bake at 400° for 10 to 12 minutes or until rolls are lightly browned. **Yield:** 10 servings (serving size: 1 roll).

Per Serving:

Calories 115	**Fiber** 0.6g
Fat 2.0g (sat 0.1g)	**Cholesterol** 1mg
Protein 4.0g	**Sodium** 304mg
Carbohydrate 19.4g	**Exchanges:** 1½ Starch

Sour Cream Rolls

2¼ cups low-fat baking mix (such as reduced-fat Bisquick),
     divided
1   (8-ounce) carton fat-free sour cream
½   cup reduced-calorie margarine, melted
Cooking spray

Preheat oven to 350°.

Combine 2 cups baking mix, sour cream, and margarine, stirring well.

Sprinkle remaining ¼ cup baking mix on a flat surface. Drop dough by level tablespoonfuls onto surface, and roll into balls. Place 3 balls into each of 12 muffin cups coated with cooking spray.

Bake at 350° for 20 minutes or until rolls are golden.
Serve warm. **Yield:** 1 dozen (serving size: 1 roll).

Per Serving:

Calories 140	**Fiber** 0.2g
Fat 6.5g (sat 1.0g)	**Cholesterol** 0mg
Protein 2.7g	**Sodium** 345mg
Carbohydrate 17.0g	**Exchanges:** 1 Starch, 1 Fat

Italian Biscuit Knots

2   cups plus 2 tablespoons low-fat baking mix (such as reduced-
      fat Bisquick), divided
1½ teaspoons dried Italian seasoning
¾   cup fat-free milk
1   tablespoon fat-free Italian dressing

Preheat oven to 400°.

Combine 2 cups baking mix and Italian seasoning, stirring well.
Add milk; stir with a fork just until dry ingredients are moistened.

Sprinkle remaining 2 tablespoons baking mix evenly over work surface.
Turn dough out onto floured surface. Divide dough into 12 equal
portions. (Dough will be very soft.) Roll each portion of dough into
an 8-inch rope; tie each rope into a loose knot. Place knots on a
baking sheet. Brush Italian dressing evenly over knots.

Bake at 400° for 12 minutes or until golden. Serve warm. **Yield:** 1 dozen
(serving size: 1 knot).

Per Serving:

Calories 87	**Fiber** 0.3g
Fat 1.4g (sat 0.3g)	**Cholesterol** 0mg
Protein 2.2g	**Sodium** 267mg
Carbohydrate 16.1g	**Exchange:** 1 Starch

Cheddar Drop Biscuits

2 cups low-fat baking mix (such as reduced-fat Bisquick)
½ cup (2 ounces) shredded reduced-fat sharp Cheddar cheese
¾ cup fat-free milk
Cooking spray
2 tablespoons reduced-calorie margarine, melted
¼ teaspoon garlic powder
½ teaspoon dried parsley flakes, crushed

Preheat oven to 450°.

Combine baking mix and cheese in a bowl; make a well in center of mixture. Add milk, stirring just until dry ingredients are moistened.

Drop dough by rounded tablespoonfuls, 2 inches apart, onto a baking sheet coated with cooking spray. Bake at 450° for 8 to 10 minutes or until biscuits are golden.

Combine margarine, garlic powder, and parsley flakes; brush over warm biscuits, and serve immediately. **Yield:** 1 dozen (serving size: 1 biscuit).

Per Serving:

Calories 106	**Fiber** 0.3g
Fat 3.5g (sat 1.0g)	**Cholesterol** 3mg
Protein 3.4g	**Sodium** 291mg
Carbohydrate 15.0g	**Exchanges:** 1 Starch, ½ Fat

Low-fat baking mix is a handy item to keep in your pantry so that you can always whip up "homemade" biscuits and rolls for breakfast or supper.

Sage and Cheese Biscuits

1   cup all-purpose flour
1½   teaspoons baking powder
¼   teaspoon salt
1   teaspoon ground sage
⅛   teaspoon freshly ground black pepper
2   tablespoons margarine or butter
⅓   cup fat-free evaporated milk
2   tablespoons (½ ounce) shredded reduced-fat Monterey Jack
       cheese
1½   teaspoons all-purpose flour

Preheat oven to 450°.

Combine first 5 ingredients in a large bowl; cut in margarine with a pastry blender until mixture resembles coarse meal. Add milk and cheese, stirring just until dry ingredients are moistened.

Sprinkle 1½ teaspoons flour over work surface. Turn dough out onto floured surface, and knead 10 to 12 times. Roll dough to ½-inch thickness; cut into rounds using a 2-inch biscuit cutter.

Place rounds on an ungreased baking sheet. Bake at 450° for 8 to 10 minutes or until biscuits are golden. Serve warm. **Yield:** 8 servings (serving size: 1 biscuit).

Per Serving:

Calories 93	**Fiber** 0.4g
Fat 3.4g (sat 0.8g)	**Cholesterol** 2mg
Protein 2.8g	**Sodium** 189mg
Carbohydrate 12.7g	**Exchanges:** 1 Starch, ½ Fat

For baking success, use this method to correctly measure flour: Fluff the flour with a fork, lightly spoon it into a dry measuring cup, and level with a straight edge.

Scones

1½ cups all-purpose flour
2   teaspoons baking powder
½   teaspoon baking soda
3   tablespoons margarine or butter
⅓   cup nonfat buttermilk
3   tablespoons brown sugar
1   teaspoon vanilla extract
1   large egg, lightly beaten

Preheat oven to 400°.

Combine first 3 ingredients in a medium bowl; cut in margarine with a pastry blender until mixture resembles coarse meal.

Combine buttermilk and remaining 3 ingredients in a medium bowl, stirring well with a wire whisk. Add buttermilk mixture to flour mixture, stirring just until dry ingredients are moistened.

Turn dough out onto a lightly floured surface, and knead lightly for 30 seconds. Divide dough in half, and pat each half into a ¾-inch-thick circle. Cut each circle into 6 wedges. Place wedges on an ungreased baking sheet. Bake at 400° for 15 to 18 minutes or until lightly browned. Serve warm. **Yield:** 1 dozen (serving size: 1 wedge).

Per Serving:

Calories 106	**Fiber** 0.4g
Fat 3.0g (sat 1.0g)	**Cholesterol** 18mg
Protein 2.0g	**Sodium** 181mg
Carbohydrate 16.0g	**Exchanges:** 1 Starch, ½ Fat

Brown sugar helps make these scones tender as well as sweet. Even with real sugar, each wedge has only 16 grams of carbohydrate.

Applesauce Pancakes

1	cup all-purpose flour
1	teaspoon baking soda
⅛	teaspoon salt
2	tablespoons toasted wheat germ
1	cup nonfat buttermilk
¼	cup unsweetened applesauce
2	teaspoons vegetable oil
1	large egg, lightly beaten

Cooking spray
Sugar-free maple syrup (optional)
Fresh fruit slices (optional)

Combine first 4 ingredients in a medium bowl; make a well in center of mixture. Combine buttermilk and next 3 ingredients. Add buttermilk mixture to dry ingredients, stirring just until dry ingredients are moistened.

Heat a nonstick griddle or nonstick skillet coated with cooking spray over medium heat. For each pancake, pour ¼ cup batter onto hot griddle, spreading to a 5-inch circle. Cook pancakes until tops are covered with bubbles and edges look cooked; turn pancakes, and cook other side.

Serve with maple syrup and fresh fruit, if desired (syrup and fruit not included in analysis). **Yield:** 10 servings (serving size: 1 pancake).

Per Serving:

Calories 74	**Fiber** 0.6g
Fat 1.8g (sat 0.4g)	**Cholesterol** 22mg
Protein 3.0g	**Sodium** 143mg
Carbohydrate 11.5g	**Exchange:** 1 Starch

One tablespoon of sugar-free maple syrup has 8 calories and 3 grams of carbohydrate.

ready in **20** minutes

Yogurt-Pecan Waffles

Cooking spray
1 cup all-purpose flour
1 teaspoon baking powder
½ teaspoon baking soda
¼ teaspoon salt
1 cup plus 2 tablespoons plain fat-free yogurt
¼ cup egg substitute
2 tablespoons reduced-calorie margarine, melted
2 tablespoons finely chopped pecans, toasted
Sugar-free maple syrup (optional)

Coat an 8-inch waffle iron with cooking spray and preheat.

Combine flour and next 3 ingredients in a medium bowl. Combine yogurt, egg substitute, and margarine; add to dry ingredients, beating well with a mixer at medium speed. Stir in pecans.

Pour 1 cup batter onto hot waffle iron, spreading batter to edges. Bake 4 to 5 minutes or until steaming stops. Cut each waffle into 4 squares. Serve with maple syrup, if desired (syrup not included in analysis). **Yield:** 8 servings (serving size: 1 four-inch waffle).

Per Serving:

Calories 112	**Fiber** 0.6g
Fat 3.9g (sat 0.2g)	**Cholesterol** 1mg
Protein 4.4g	**Sodium** 215mg
Carbohydrate 15.1g	**Exchanges:** 1 Starch, 1 Fat

One of the best ways to bring out the flavor of nuts is to toast them. Just place any kind of whole or chopped nuts in a shallow pan or on a baking sheet, and bake at 350° for 6 to 8 minutes. Be sure to watch them carefully; they can go from toasted to burned very quickly.

Overnight Bran Muffins

4   cups (6 ounces) wheat bran flakes cereal with raisins
2½ cups all-purpose flour
1½ teaspoons baking soda
1   teaspoon salt
1   cup mixed dried fruit
½   cup "measures-like-sugar" calorie-free sweetener
2   cups nonfat buttermilk
¼   cup vegetable oil
2   large eggs, lightly beaten
Cooking spray

Combine first 6 ingredients in a large bowl; make a well in center of mixture. Combine buttermilk, oil, and eggs; add to dry ingredients, stirring just until dry ingredients are moistened. Cover and chill at least 8 hours.

Preheat oven to 400°.

Spoon batter into 24 muffin cups coated with cooking spray, filling about three-fourths full. Bake at 400° for 14 to 15 minutes or until golden. Remove muffins from pans immediately, and serve warm. **Yield:** 2 dozen (serving size: 1 muffin).

Per Serving:

Calories 126	**Fiber** 1.9g
Fat 3.2g (sat 0.5g)	**Cholesterol** 18mg
Protein 3.1g	**Sodium** 227mg
Carbohydrate 22.0g	**Exchanges:** 1½ Starch, ½ Fat

You can make this muffin batter ahead and store it in the refrigerator up to three days.

Blueberry Muffins

1¾ cups all-purpose flour
3 tablespoons sugar
3 tablespoons "measures-like-sugar" calorie-free sweetener
2 teaspoons baking powder
¼ teaspoon salt
½ teaspoon ground allspice
1 cup fresh or frozen blueberries, thawed and drained
¾ cup fat-free milk
¼ cup vegetable oil
1 large egg, lightly beaten
1 teaspoon grated lemon rind
1 teaspoon grated orange rind
1 teaspoon vanilla extract
Cooking spray

Preheat oven to 400°.

Combine first 6 ingredients in a medium bowl; add blueberries, and toss to coat. Make a well in center of flour mixture. Combine milk and next 5 ingredients; add to flour mixture, stirring just until dry ingredients are moistened.

Spoon batter into 12 muffin cups coated with cooking spray, filling two-thirds full. Bake at 400° for 20 to 25 minutes or until golden. Remove muffins from pans immediately, and cool on wire racks. **Yield:** 1 dozen (serving size: 1 muffin).

Per Serving:

Calories 142	**Fiber** 1.1g
Fat 5.5g (sat 1.0g)	**Cholesterol** 19mg
Protein 3.0g	**Sodium** 145mg
Carbohydrate 20.3g	**Exchanges:** 1 Starch, ½ Fruit, 1 Fat

Applesauce-Bran Muffins

2½   cups all-purpose flour
¼   cup sugar
¼   cup "measures-like-sugar" calorie-free sweetener
1½   teaspoons baking soda
½   teaspoon salt
2   cups nonfat buttermilk
¼   cup fat-free milk
½   cup egg substitute
½   cup unsweetened applesauce
3   cups unprocessed wheat bran
Cooking spray

Preheat oven to 400°.

Combine first 5 ingredients in a large bowl. Make a well in center of mixture, and set aside. Combine buttermilk and next 3 ingredients, stirring well with a wire whisk. Stir in bran; let stand 5 minutes.

Add bran mixture to flour mixture, stirring just until dry ingredients are moistened.

Spoon batter evenly into 24 muffin cups coated with cooking spray, filling three-fourths full. Bake at 400° for 22 to 24 minutes or until golden. Remove muffins from pans immediately, and cool on wire racks. **Yield:** 2 dozen (serving size: 1 muffin).

Per Serving:

Calories 88	**Fiber** 3.6g
Fat 0.7g (sat 0.1g)	**Cholesterol** 1mg
Protein 3.8g	**Sodium** 158mg
Carbohydrate 18.9g	**Exchange:** 1 Starch

Carrot-Pineapple-Bran Muffins

1¾ cups all-purpose flour
¼ cup sugar
1 teaspoon baking powder
1 teaspoon baking soda
1 teaspoon ground cinnamon
¾ cup fat-free milk
1 large egg, lightly beaten
1 (8-ounce) can crushed pineapple in juice, undrained
2 tablespoons margarine or butter, melted
1 cup wheat bran flakes cereal
1 cup shredded carrot
2 tablespoons water
Cooking spray

Preheat oven to 350°.

Combine first 5 ingredients in a large bowl. Make a well in center of mixture, and set aside. Combine milk and next 3 ingredients, stirring well. Stir in cereal; let stand 5 minutes.

Place carrot and water in a small saucepan. Cover and bring to a boil; reduce heat, and cook 1 to 2 minutes or until carrot is tender. Drain and set aside.

Add cereal mixture to flour mixture; add carrot, and stir just until dry ingredients are moistened. Spoon batter evenly into 18 muffin cups coated with cooking spray, filling two-thirds full. Bake at 350° for 20 to 22 minutes or until golden. Remove muffins from pans immediately, and cool on wire racks. **Yield:** 18 servings (serving size: 1 muffin).

Per Serving:

Calories 88	**Fiber** 0.7g
Fat 1.9g (sat 0.4g)	**Cholesterol** 12mg
Protein 2.1g	**Sodium** 109mg
Carbohydrate 15.8g	**Exchange:** 1 Starch

Cornmeal Muffins

1   cup yellow cornmeal
1   cup all-purpose flour
2   teaspoons baking powder
1   teaspoon baking soda
½   teaspoon salt
2   teaspoons "measures-like-sugar" calorie-free sweetener
1½ cups nonfat buttermilk
¼   cup egg substitute
3   tablespoons vegetable oil
Cooking spray

Preheat oven to 425°.

Combine first 6 ingredients in a bowl; make a well in center of mixture. Combine buttermilk, egg substitute, and oil; add to dry ingredients, stirring just until dry ingredients are moistened.

Spoon batter into 12 muffin cups coated with cooking spray, filling three-fourths full. Bake at 425° for 14 minutes or until golden. Remove muffins from pans immediately, and serve warm. **Yield:** 1 dozen (serving size: 1 muffin).

Per Serving:

Calories 124	**Fiber** 0.9g
Fat 4.0g (sat 0.7g)	**Cholesterol** 1mg
Protein 3.6g	**Sodium** 262mg
Carbohydrate 18.2g	**Exchanges:** 1 Starch, 1 Fat

Baked Hush Puppies

1 cup yellow cornmeal
1 cup all-purpose flour
1 tablespoon baking powder
1 teaspoon "measures-like-sugar" calorie-free sweetener
1 teaspoon salt
⅛ teaspoon ground red pepper
2 large eggs, lightly beaten
¾ cup fat-free milk
¼ cup vegetable oil
½ cup finely chopped onion
Cooking spray

Preheat oven to 425°.

Combine first 6 ingredients in a large bowl; make a well in center of mixture. Combine eggs and next 3 ingredients, stirring well; add to dry ingredients, stirring just until dry ingredients are moistened.

Coat 36 miniature (1¾-inch) muffin cups with cooking spray. Spoon about 1 tablespoon batter into each muffin cup (cups will be about three-fourths full).

Bake at 425° for 15 minutes or until done. Remove from pans immediately, and serve warm. **Yield:** 3 dozen (serving size: 1 hush puppy).

Per Serving:

Calories 56	**Fiber** 0.4g
Fat 2.9g (sat 0.4g)	**Cholesterol** 10mg
Protein 1.1g	**Sodium** 112mg
Carbohydrate 6.2g	**Exchanges:** ½ Starch, ½ Fat

Chile-Cheese Corn Bread

1	cup yellow cornmeal
1	cup all-purpose flour
1	tablespoon plus 1 teaspoon baking powder
¼	teaspoon salt
¼	cup nonfat dry milk powder
1	tablespoon "measures-like-sugar" calorie-free sweetener
1	cup water
½	cup egg substitute
2	tablespoons vegetable oil
¾	cup (3 ounces) shredded reduced-fat Cheddar cheese
1	(4.5-ounce) can chopped green chiles, drained

Cooking spray

Preheat oven to 375°.

Combine first 6 ingredients in a medium bowl; make a well in center of mixture. Combine water, egg substitute, and oil; add to flour mixture, stirring just until dry ingredients are moistened. Stir in cheese and green chiles.

Pour batter into an 8-inch square baking dish coated with cooking spray. Bake at 375° for 30 minutes or until golden. Cut into squares, and serve warm. **Yield:** 16 servings (serving size: 1 square).

Per Serving:

Calories 105	**Fiber** 0.7g
Fat 3.0g (sat 0.9g)	**Cholesterol** 4mg
Protein 4.6g	**Sodium** 227mg
Carbohydrate 14.7g	**Exchanges:** 1 Starch, ½ Fat

Spoonbread

1½ cups boiling water
1   cup cornmeal
¾   teaspoon salt
2   tablespoons reduced-calorie margarine
1   cup fat-free milk
1   large egg, separated
1   teaspoon baking powder
1   large egg white
Cooking spray

Preheat oven to 375°.

Pour boiling water over cornmeal gradually, stirring until smooth. Add salt and margarine, stirring until blended; cool 10 minutes. Stir in milk, egg yolk, and baking powder.

Beat egg white with a mixer at high speed until stiff peaks form. Gently fold beaten egg white into cornmeal mixture. Pour mixture into a 1½-quart baking dish coated with cooking spray.

Bake at 375° for 45 minutes or until lightly browned. Serve immediately. **Yield:** 6 servings (serving size: 1 cup).

Per Serving:

Calories 125	**Fiber** 2.2g
Fat 4.2g (sat 0.4g)	**Cholesterol** 38mg
Protein 4.7g	**Sodium** 378mg
Carbohydrate 18.0g	**Exchanges:** 1 Starch, 1 Fat

If you grew up eating spoonbread in your grandmother's kitchen, this lightened version should bring back some happy memories.

Cumin Quick Bread

1½ cups all-purpose flour
2   tablespoons "measures-like-sugar" calorie-free sweetener
1   tablespoon baking powder
2   teaspoons ground cumin
½   teaspoon cumin seed, slightly crushed
¼   teaspoon dry mustard
¼   teaspoon salt
⅔   cup fat-free milk
⅓   cup egg substitute
2½ tablespoons vegetable oil
2   tablespoons picante sauce
Cooking spray

Preheat oven to 350°.

Combine first 7 ingredients in a medium bowl; make a well in center of mixture. Combine milk and next 3 ingredients; stir well. Add to flour mixture, stirring just until dry ingredients are moistened.

Spoon batter into an 8½- x 4½-inch loafpan coated with cooking spray. Bake at 350° for 40 minutes or until a wooden pick inserted in center comes out clean. Remove from pan, and let cool on a wire rack. **Yield:** 10 servings (serving size: 1 slice).

Per Serving:

Calories 115	**Fiber** 0.6g
Fat 3.9g (sat 0.5g)	**Cholesterol** 0mg
Protein 3.4g	**Sodium** 262mg
Carbohydrate 16.4g	**Exchanges:** 1 Starch, 1 Fat

Spiced Pumpkin Bread

2   cups sifted cake flour
2   teaspoons baking powder
¼   teaspoon baking soda
¼   teaspoon salt
½   cup firmly packed brown sugar
1   teaspoon ground cinnamon
¼   teaspoon ground ginger
¼   teaspoon ground cloves
1   cup canned pumpkin
¼   cup unsweetened applesauce
3   tablespoons vegetable oil
2   large eggs, lightly beaten
1   teaspoon vanilla extract
Cooking spray

Preheat oven to 350°.

Combine first 8 ingredients in a medium bowl; make a well in center of mixture. Combine pumpkin and next 4 ingredients; add to flour mixture, stirring just until dry ingredients are moistened.

Spoon batter into a 9- x 5-inch loafpan coated with cooking spray. Bake at 350° for 45 to 50 minutes or until a wooden pick inserted in center comes out clean. Cool in pan on a wire rack 10 minutes; remove loaf from pan, and let cool completely on wire rack. **Yield:** 18 servings (serving size: 1 slice).

Per Serving:

Calories 103	**Fiber** 1.0g
Fat 3.0g (sat 0.6g)	**Cholesterol** 25mg
Protein 1.9g	**Sodium** 115mg
Carbohydrate 17.2g	**Exchanges:** 1 Starch, ½ Fat

Caraway-Swiss Casserole Bread

1   (16-ounce) package hot roll mix
1⅓ cups warm water (100° to 110°)
1   cup (4 ounces) shredded reduced-fat Swiss cheese
¼   cup finely chopped onion
2   tablespoons margarine or butter, melted
1   tablespoon caraway seeds
1   teaspoon cracked black pepper
Cooking spray

Combine yeast packet from roll mix and warm water in a large bowl. Let stand 5 minutes. Add three-fourths of flour packet from roll mix, cheese, and next 4 ingredients. Beat with a mixer at low speed until blended. Stir in remaining flour from roll mix.

Scrape dough from sides of bowl. Cover and let rise in a warm place (85°), free from drafts, 30 minutes or until doubled in bulk. Stir dough 25 strokes.

Preheat oven to 350°.

Spoon dough into a 2-quart casserole dish coated with cooking spray. Bake at 350° for 45 to 50 minutes or until loaf is browned and sounds hollow when tapped. Cut into wedges, and serve warm. **Yield:** 14 servings (serving size: 1 wedge).

Per Serving:

Calories 160	**Fiber** 0.7g
Fat 4.4g (sat 1.1g)	**Cholesterol** 5mg
Protein 6.1g	**Sodium** 246mg
Carbohydrate 23.1g	**Exchanges:** 1½ Starch, 1 Fat

Monkey Bread

1   package active dry yeast
1   cup warm water (100° to 110°), divided
2¾ cups all-purpose flour
2   tablespoons sugar
¾   teaspoon salt
3   tablespoons reduced-calorie margarine, melted
Butter-flavored cooking spray

Combine yeast and ¼ cup warm water in a 1-cup liquid measuring cup; let stand 5 minutes. Combine yeast mixture, remaining ¾ cup warm water, flour, sugar, and salt in a large bowl; beat with a mixer at medium speed until well blended. Cover and chill at least 8 hours.

Punch dough down. Turn out onto a heavily floured surface, and knead 3 or 4 times. Shape dough into 36 (1-inch) balls.

Brush balls with melted margarine, and layer in a 12-cup Bundt pan coated with cooking spray. Cover and let rise in a warm place (85°), free from drafts, 40 to 45 minutes or until doubled in bulk.

Preheat oven to 350°.

Bake at 350° for 30 to 35 minutes or until golden. Serve warm. **Yield:** 18 servings (serving size: 2 balls).

Per Serving:

Calories 86	**Fiber** 0.6g
Fat 1.5g (sat 0.0g)	**Cholesterol** 0mg
Protein 2.1g	**Sodium** 116mg
Carbohydrate 16.1g	**Exchange:** 1 Starch

Quick Yeast Rolls

2   packages active dry yeast
½   cup warm water (100° to 110°)
1   cup fat-free milk
¼   cup egg substitute
2   tablespoons sugar
1   tablespoon vegetable oil
1½ teaspoons salt
4   cups all-purpose flour, divided
Butter-flavored cooking spray

Combine yeast and warm water in a 2-cup liquid measuring cup; let stand 5 minutes. Combine yeast mixture, milk, and next 4 ingredients in a large bowl. Gradually add 1 cup flour, stirring until smooth. Gradually stir in enough remaining flour to make a soft dough. Place in a bowl coated with cooking spray, turning to coat top, and let stand in a warm place (85°), free from drafts, 15 additional minutes.

Punch dough down; cover and let stand in a warm place (85°), free from drafts, 15 minutes.

Turn dough out onto a lightly floured surface; knead 3 or 4 times. Divide dough into 24 pieces; shape into balls. Place in 2 (9-inch) square pans or round pans coated with cooking spray, and let stand in a warm place (85°), free from drafts, 15 minutes.

Preheat oven to 400°.

Bake at 400° for 15 minutes or until golden. Serve warm. **Yield:** 2 dozen (serving size: 1 roll).

Per Serving:

Calories 92	**Fiber** 0.7g
Fat 0.8g (sat 0.2g)	**Cholesterol** 0mg
Protein 3.0g	**Sodium** 156mg
Carbohydrate 17.7g	**Exchange:** 1 Starch

fish and shellfish

ready in **15** minutes

Baked Striped Bass

4   (6-ounce) striped bass fillets (¾ inch thick)
Cooking spray
2   tablespoons light mayonnaise
1   teaspoon white wine Worcestershire sauce
½   teaspoon Old Bay seasoning
½   teaspoon lemon juice

Preheat oven to 450°.

Place fish in an 8-inch square baking dish coated with cooking spray. Combine mayonnaise and remaining 3 ingredients, stirring well. Brush mayonnaise mixture evenly over fish.

Bake, uncovered, at 450° for 8 to 10 minutes or until fish flakes easily when tested with a fork.

Transfer to a serving platter, and serve immediately. **Yield:** 4 servings (serving size: 1 fillet).

Per Serving:

Calories 195	**Fiber** 0.0g
Fat 6.6g (sat 1.4g)	**Cholesterol** 143mg
Protein 30.9g	**Sodium** 274mg
Carbohydrate 0.8g	**Exchanges:** 4 Very Lean Meat, ½ Fat

ready in **15** minutes

Pan-Fried Catfish

½   cup yellow cornmeal
1   teaspoon paprika
½   teaspoon pepper
¼   teaspoon salt
¼   teaspoon onion powder
¼   teaspoon ground celery seeds
¼   teaspoon dry mustard
4   (6-ounce) farm-raised catfish fillets
¼   cup fat-free milk
1   tablespoon vegetable oil

Combine first 7 ingredients. Dip fish in milk; dredge in cornmeal mixture.

Heat oil in a nonstick skillet over medium-high heat. Add fish; cook 3 minutes on each side or until fish flakes easily when tested with a fork.

Serve immediately. **Yield:** 4 servings (serving size: 1 fillet).

Per Serving:

Calories 332	**Fiber** 1.6g
Fat 16.9g (sat 3.6g)	**Cholesterol** 80mg
Protein 28.6g	**Sodium** 243mg
Carbohydrate 14.8g	**Exchanges:** 1 Starch, 4 Very Lean Meat, ½ Fat

Serve with Baked Hush Puppies (page 85) and Colorful Coleslaw (page 213).

Herbed Catfish Fillets

½   cup fine, dry breadcrumbs
¼   cup all-purpose flour
1   tablespoon chopped fresh parsley
1½ teaspoons chopped fresh dillweed
1½ teaspoons chopped fresh thyme
2   teaspoons chicken-flavored bouillon granules
1   teaspoon dried onion flakes
1   teaspoon paprika
¼   teaspoon garlic powder
4   (6-ounce) farm-raised catfish fillets
Butter-flavored cooking spray

Preheat oven to 400°.

Combine first 9 ingredients. Coat fish with cooking spray; dredge in breadcrumb mixture.

Place fish on rack of a broiler pan coated with cooking spray. Bake at 400° for 20 minutes or until fish flakes easily when tested with a fork.

Serve immediately. **Yield:** 4 servings (serving size: 1 fillet).

Per Serving:

Calories 292	**Fiber** 0.8g
Fat 13.4g (sat 3.1g)	**Cholesterol** 80mg
Protein 28.5g	**Sodium** 414mg
Carbohydrate 12.1g	**Exchanges:** 1 Starch, 4 Lean Meat

Easy Parmesan Flounder

4 (6-ounce) flounder fillets
Cooking spray
1 tablespoon lemon juice
¼ cup fat-free mayonnaise
3 tablespoons grated Parmesan cheese
1 tablespoon thinly sliced green onions
1 tablespoon reduced-calorie margarine, softened
⅛ teaspoon hot sauce

Preheat broiler.

Place fish on rack of a broiler pan coated with cooking spray; brush with lemon juice. Broil 5 to 6 minutes or until fish flakes easily when tested with a fork.

Combine mayonnaise and remaining 4 ingredients, stirring well. Spread mayonnaise mixture evenly over fish. Broil 1 minute or until lightly browned.

Serve immediately. **Yield:** 4 servings (serving size: 1 fillet).

Per Serving:

Calories 178	**Fiber** 0.4g
Fat 4.7g (sat 1.4g)	**Cholesterol** 85mg
Protein 29.9g	**Sodium** 335mg
Carbohydrate 2.6g	**Exchanges:** 4 Very Lean Meat, 1 Fat

If flounder isn't available, you can substitute sole or orange roughy.

Greek-Style Flounder

¼   cup lemon juice
1½   tablespoons balsamic vinegar
1   teaspoon dried oregano
1½   teaspoons olive oil
¼   teaspoon salt
⅛   teaspoon pepper
4   (6-ounce) flounder fillets
Cooking spray
3   tablespoons chopped fresh parsley

Preheat oven to 350°.

Combine first 6 ingredients in a small bowl.

Place fish in a 13- x 9-inch baking dish coated with cooking spray; pour lemon juice mixture over fish. Bake at 350° for 13 to 15 minutes or until fish flakes easily when tested with a fork.

Sprinkle with parsley, and serve immediately. **Yield:** 4 servings (serving size: 1 fillet).

Per Serving:

Calories 180	**Fiber** 0.3g
Fat 3.8g (sat 0.7g)	**Cholesterol** 82mg
Protein 32.3g	**Sodium** 287mg
Carbohydrate 2.6g	**Exchanges:** 5 Very Lean Meat

Peppered-Garlic Flounder

6   (6-ounce) flounder fillets
¼   cup low-sodium soy sauce
2   tablespoons minced garlic
1½ tablespoons lemon juice
2   teaspoons "measures-like-sugar" calorie-free sweetener
1   tablespoon mixed peppercorns, crushed
Cooking spray

Place fish in a shallow baking dish. Combine soy sauce and next 3 ingredients; pour over fish. Cover and marinate in refrigerator 30 minutes.

Preheat broiler.

Remove fish from marinade, and discard marinade. Sprinkle fish evenly with peppercorns, pressing firmly so peppercorns adhere to fish.

Place fish on rack of a broiler pan coated with cooking spray. Broil 8 to 10 minutes or until fish flakes easily when tested with a fork. Transfer to a serving platter. **Yield:** 6 servings (serving size: 1 fillet).

Per Serving:

Calories 170	**Fiber** 0.3g
Fat 2.3g (sat 0.5g)	**Cholesterol** 82mg
Protein 32.4g	**Sodium** 316mg
Carbohydrate 2.4g	**Exchanges:** 5 Very Lean Meat

Spicy Grilled Grouper

4   (6-ounce) grouper fillets
¼   cup lemon juice
1½ teaspoons chili powder
¼   teaspoon ground cumin
¼   teaspoon paprika
1   garlic clove, minced
Dash of ground red pepper
Cooking spray

Place fish in a shallow baking dish. Combine lemon juice and next 5 ingredients, stirring well; pour over fish. Cover and marinate in refrigerator 30 minutes.

Prepare grill.

Remove fish from marinade, reserving marinade. Place marinade in a small saucepan; bring to a boil, and set aside.

Place fish in a grill basket coated with cooking spray; grill 10 minutes on each side or until fish flakes easily when tested with a fork, basting often with reserved marinade. Serve immediately. **Yield:** 4 servings (serving size: 1 fillet).

Per Serving:

Calories 166	**Fiber** 0.5g
Fat 2.0g (sat 0.4g)	**Cholesterol** 63mg
Protein 33.2g	**Sodium** 101mg
Carbohydrate 2.2g	**Exchanges:** 5 Very Lean Meat

Hobo Fish Dinner

Cooking spray
1   teaspoon salt-free lemon-herb seasoning (such as Mrs. Dash)
½   teaspoon salt
½   teaspoon dried dillweed
4   small baking potatoes, thinly sliced
3   cups thinly sliced onion (about 2 medium)
1   cup thinly sliced carrot (about 2 medium)
4   (6-ounce) halibut fillets (or any firm white fish)

Preheat oven to 450°.

Coat 1 side of 4 (18-inch) squares of heavy-duty aluminum foil with cooking spray.

Combine seasoning, salt, and dillweed. Layer potato, onion, and carrot slices evenly in centers of coated foil squares. Sprinkle evenly with seasoning mixture. Place fish over vegetables. Fold foil over fish and vegetables; crimp edges to seal. Place packets on a baking sheet. Bake at 450° for 30 minutes. Serve immediately. **Yield:** 4 servings (serving size: 1 packet).

Per Serving:

Calories 370	**Fiber** 5.3g
Fat 4.2g (sat 0.7g)	**Cholesterol** 54mg
Protein 40.1g	**Sodium** 417
Carbohydrate 41.3g	**Exchanges:** 2 Starch, 2 Vegetable, 4 Very Lean Meat

Toss together a salad while the fish bakes and dinner is ready as soon as the fish comes out of the oven.

Sesame-Baked Orange Roughy

6   (6-ounce) orange roughy fillets
2   tablespoons water
1   teaspoon minced peeled fresh ginger
1   garlic clove, minced
½   teaspoon lemon juice
½   teaspoon low-sodium soy sauce
¼   teaspoon crushed red pepper
2   tablespoons sesame seeds, toasted
Cooking spray
¼   teaspoon paprika
Lemon wedges (optional)

Place fish in a heavy-duty zip-top plastic bag. Combine water and next 5 ingredients. Pour over fish. Seal bag, and turn to coat fish. Marinate in refrigerator 1 to 2 hours, turning once.

Preheat broiler.

Remove fish from marinade; discard marinade. Sprinkle both sides of each fillet with sesame seeds. Place fish on rack of a broiler pan coated with cooking spray. Broil 6 to 8 minutes or until fish flakes easily when tested with a fork.

Sprinkle fish evenly with paprika. Garnish with lemon wedges, if desired. **Yield:** 6 servings (serving size: 1 fillet).

Per Serving:

Calories 134	**Fiber** 0.5g
Fat 2.5g (sat 0.2g)	**Cholesterol** 34mg
Protein 25.5g	**Sodium** 116mg
Carbohydrate 0.9g	**Exchanges:** 4 Very Lean Meat

Steamed Orange Roughy with Herbs

½ cup fresh parsley sprigs
½ cup fresh chive sprigs
½ cup fresh thyme sprigs
½ cup fresh rosemary sprigs
4 (6-ounce) orange roughy fillets
Lemon wedges (optional)

Place a steamer basket over boiling water in Dutch oven. Place half of each herb in basket. Arrange fish over herbs in basket; top with remaining herbs.

Cover and steam 7 minutes or until fish flakes easily when tested with a fork. Remove and discard herbs.

Carefully transfer fish to a serving plate, and garnish with lemon wedges, if desired. **Yield:** 4 servings (serving size: 1 fillet).

Per Serving:

Calories 125	Fiber 0.8g
Fat 1.4g (sat 0.1g)	Cholesterol 34mg
Protein 25.4g	Sodium 110mg
Carbohydrate 1.4g	Exchanges: 4 Very Lean Meat

Use any combination of fresh herbs to infuse this fish with flavor. Squeeze some fresh lemon juice over the fish before serving, and you won't miss salt.

Zesty Baked Salmon

4   (6-ounce) salmon fillets
Cooking spray
2   tablespoons chopped green onions
1   tablespoon low-fat mayonnaise
1   tablespoon plain fat-free yogurt
1   teaspoon lemon pepper
¼   teaspoon salt
¼   teaspoon dry mustard
Chopped green onions (optional)
Lemon wedges (optional)

Preheat oven to 425°.

Place fish, skin side down, in a baking dish coated with cooking spray. Bake at 425° for 18 minutes or until fish flakes easily when tested with a fork.

Combine 2 tablespoons green onions and next 5 ingredients; spread evenly over fish. Bake 2 additional minutes or until sauce is bubbly.

Serve immediately. If desired, sprinkle with additional chopped green onions, and garnish with lemon wedges. **Yield:** 4 servings (serving size: 1 fillet).

Per Serving:

Calories 282	**Fiber** 0.1g
Fat 13.4g (sat 3.1g)	**Cholesterol** 87mg
Protein 36.4g	**Sodium** 293mg
Carbohydrate 1.6g	**Exchanges:** 5 Lean Meat

Because it has a higher fat content than many other kinds of fish, salmon stays moist and flavorful even if it's slightly overdone. It's a great choice if you're not used to cooking fish.

Poached Salmon
with Horseradish Sauce

¼ cup fat-free mayonnaise
¼ cup plain fat-free yogurt
2 teaspoons prepared horseradish
1½ teaspoons chopped fresh or frozen chives
1½ teaspoons lemon juice
4 cups water
1 teaspoon peppercorns
1 lemon, sliced
1 carrot, sliced
1 celery stalk, sliced
4 (6-ounce) salmon fillets
Lemon wedges (optional)
Fresh celery leaves (optional)

Combine first 5 ingredients. Cover and chill.

Combine water and next 4 ingredients in a large skillet; bring to a boil over medium heat. Cover, reduce heat, and simmer 10 minutes. Add salmon to skillet; cover and simmer 10 minutes.

Remove skillet from heat; let stand, covered, 8 minutes. Remove fish from skillet. Discard liquid and vegetables.

Serve with horseradish mixture. If desired, garnish with lemon wedges and celery leaves. **Yield:** 4 servings (serving size: 1 fillet and 2 tablespoons sauce).

Per Serving:

Calories 292	**Fiber** 0.5g
Fat 13.5g (sat 3.2g)	**Cholesterol** 89mg
Protein 36.9g	**Sodium** 216mg
Carbohydrate 3.8g	**Exchanges:** 5 Lean Meat

ready in **30** minutes

Creole Red Snapper

1   tablespoon olive oil
¼   cup chopped onion
¼   cup chopped green bell pepper
1   garlic clove, minced
1   (14½-ounce) can no-salt-added whole tomatoes, undrained
      and chopped
2   teaspoons low-sodium Worcestershire sauce
2   teaspoons red wine vinegar
½   teaspoon dried basil
¼   teaspoon salt
¼   teaspoon freshly ground black pepper
Dash of hot sauce
4   (6-ounce) red snapper fillets
Fresh basil sprigs (optional)

Heat oil in a large nonstick skillet over medium-high heat until hot.
Add onion, green bell pepper, and garlic; sauté until tender.

Add tomatoes and next 6 ingredients. Bring to a boil; add fillets,
spooning tomato mixture over fish. Reduce heat; cover and simmer
12 minutes or until fish flakes easily when tested with a fork.

Garnish with basil sprigs, if desired, and serve immediately. **Yield:**
4 servings (serving size: 1 fillet and ¼ of tomato mixture).

Per Serving:

Calories 228	**Fiber** 1.4g
Fat 5.8g (sat 1.0g)	**Cholesterol** 63mg
Protein 36.1g	**Sodium** 269mg
Carbohydrate 6.5g	**Exchanges:** 1 Vegetable, 5 Very Lean Meat

Italian Red Snapper

4	(6-ounce) red snapper fillets
¼	cup dry white wine or low-sodium chicken broth
¼	cup lemon juice
½	teaspoon dried oregano
½	teaspoon dried basil
¼	teaspoon salt
¼	teaspoon pepper
4	garlic cloves, minced
1	(14½-ounce) can no-salt-added diced tomatoes, drained

Preheat oven to 350°.

Place fish in an 11- x 7-inch baking dish. Combine wine and next 6 ingredients, stirring well. Pour wine mixture and tomato over fish.

Bake, uncovered, at 350° for 25 minutes or until fish flakes easily when tested with a fork. **Yield:** 4 servings (serving size: 1 fillet).

Per Serving:

Calories 193	**Fiber** 0.9g
Fat 2.4g (sat 0.5g)	**Cholesterol** 63mg
Protein 36.0g	**Sodium** 300mg
Carbohydrate 5.4g	**Exchanges:** 1 Vegetable, 5 Very Lean Meat

Spoon the flavorful tomato mixture evenly over the fish when you serve it.

Soy-Lime Grilled Tuna

4   (6-ounce) tuna steaks (1 inch thick)
½   cup lime juice
¼   cup low-sodium soy sauce
1   teaspoon minced peeled fresh ginger
½   teaspoon crushed red pepper
Cooking spray

Place fish in a heavy-duty zip-top plastic bag. Combine lime juice and next 3 ingredients, stirring well. Pour lime juice mixture over fish. Seal bag, turning to coat fish. Marinate in refrigerator 30 minutes, turning once.

Prepare grill.

Remove fish from marinade; reserve marinade. Place marinade in a small saucepan; bring to a boil, and set aside.

Place fish on grill rack coated with cooking spray; grill, covered, 4 to 5 minutes on each side or until fish flakes easily when tested with a fork, basting often with reserved marinade. Remove from grill, and serve immediately. **Yield:** 4 servings (serving size: 1 steak).

Per Serving:

Calories 263	**Fiber** 0.3g
Fat 8.4g (sat 2.2g)	**Cholesterol** 65mg
Protein 40.7g	**Sodium** 600mg
Carbohydrate 4.4g	**Exchanges:** ½ Fruit, 6 Very Lean Meat

Grilled Trout

2   tablespoons herb-flavored or plain vegetable oil
¼   cup lemon juice
½   teaspoon salt
4   (6-ounce) trout fillets
4   sprigs fresh tarragon
1   lemon, sliced
Cooking spray

Combine first 3 ingredients in a small bowl, stirring well with a wire whisk.

Place fish in a 13- x 9-inch baking dish. Pour oil mixture over fish. Top fish evenly with tarragon and lemon slices. Cover and marinate in refrigerator 2 hours.

Prepare grill.

Place fish in a grill basket coated with cooking spray. Grill, covered, 5 to 7 minutes on each side or until fish flakes easily when tested with a fork. **Yield:** 4 servings (serving size: 1 fillet).

Per Serving:

Calories 304	**Fiber** 1.3g
Fat 16.3g (sat 3.7g)	**Cholesterol** 100mg
Protein 35.9g	**Sodium** 351mg
Carbohydrate 4.3g	**Exchanges:** 5 Lean Meat, ½ Fat

Substitute any fresh herb for the tarragon in this recipe.

Seasoned Crab Cakes

1½ cups soft breadcrumbs
2   tablespoons chopped green onions
2   tablespoons chopped red bell pepper
2   tablespoons fat-free mayonnaise
1   tablespoon finely chopped fresh parsley
½   teaspoon dry mustard
¼   teaspoon ground red pepper
1   large egg white
1   pound lump crabmeat, drained and shell pieces removed
Butter-flavored cooking spray
1   teaspoon vegetable oil
Lemon wedges (optional)

Combine first 8 ingredients; stir well. Add crabmeat, stirring gently. Shape mixture into 4 patties.

Coat a large nonstick skillet with cooking spray; add oil. Place over medium heat until hot. Add patties; cook 5 minutes on each side or until lightly browned.

Serve immediately. Garnish with lemon wedges, if desired. **Yield:** 4 servings (serving size: 1 crab cake).

Per Serving:

Calories 168	**Fiber** 0.8g
Fat 3.2g (sat 0.5g)	**Cholesterol** 68mg
Protein 22.2g	**Sodium** 525mg
Carbohydrate 11.2g	**Exchanges:** 1 Starch, 3 Very Lean Meat

Steamed Clams

3   dozen fresh cherrystone clams
¾   cup water
⅓   cup dry white wine or low-sodium chicken broth
1   tablespoon Old Bay seasoning
½   teaspoon ground white pepper
Lemon wedges (optional)

Scrub clams thoroughly, discarding any that are cracked or open.

Combine water and next 3 ingredients in a large Dutch oven; bring to a boil. Add clams; cover, reduce heat, and simmer 10 to 12 minutes or until clams open. Remove and discard any unopened clams. Remove remaining clams with a slotted spoon, reserving liquid, if desired.

Serve clams immediately. If desired, serve with reserved liquid and lemon wedges. **Yield:** 2 servings (serving size: about 18 clams).

Per Serving:

Calories 197	**Fiber** 0.1g
Fat 2.5g (sat 0.3g)	**Cholesterol** 89mg
Protein 33.5g	**Sodium** 1,109mg
Carbohydrate 7.6g	**Exchanges:** ½ Starch; 4 Very Lean Meat

If you're on a low-sodium diet, omit the Old Bay seasoning and serve clams with lemon wedges to pump up the flavor.

Lemon-Sauced Scallops

¾ cup all-purpose flour
¼ teaspoon ground white pepper
1½ pounds fresh bay scallops
3 large egg whites, lightly beaten
Cooking spray
1 tablespoon plus 1 teaspoon reduced-calorie margarine,
    divided
⅔ cup dry white wine or low-sodium chicken broth
½ cup sliced green onions
¼ cup lemon juice
⅛ teaspoon salt

Combine flour and pepper in a shallow dish. Dip scallops in flour mixture; dip in egg white, and dip in flour mixture again.

Coat a nonstick skillet with cooking spray; add 2 teaspoons margarine. Place over medium-high heat until margarine melts. Add half of scallops; cook 6 minutes or until scallops are lightly browned, turning to brown all sides. Remove scallops from pan; set aside, and keep warm. Repeat with remaining margarine and scallops. Add wine and remaining 3 ingredients to pan; cook 3 minutes or until mixture reduces to ⅓ cup.

To serve, arrange scallops on a serving platter; top with sauce. **Yield:** 4 servings (serving size: about 5 ounces scallops and 1 tablespoon sauce).

Per Serving:

Calories 278	**Fiber** 1.0g
Fat 3.7g (sat 0.7g)	**Cholesterol** 57mg
Protein 34.5g	**Sodium** 454mg
Carbohydrate 24.7g	**Exchanges:** 1½ Starch, 4 Very Lean Meat

Scallop and Pasta Toss

Cooking spray
1   tablespoon reduced-calorie margarine
2   cups diagonally sliced celery
1   cup sliced mushrooms
½   cup sliced green onions (about 2 onions)
½   cup sliced carrot
2   garlic cloves, minced
¾   pound fresh bay scallops
2   tablespoons water
2   teaspoons white wine Worcestershire sauce
½   teaspoon ground ginger
¼   teaspoon salt
⅛   teaspoon pepper
4   cups cooked spinach linguine (cooked without salt or fat)

Coat a large nonstick skillet with cooking spray; add margarine.
Place over medium-high heat until margarine melts. Add celery and
next 4 ingredients; sauté until crisp-tender. Add scallops and next 5
ingredients; cook 5 to 7 minutes or until scallops are opaque, stirring
occasionally.

Place pasta in a large serving bowl; add scallop mixture, and toss
gently. Serve immediately. **Yield:** 4 servings (serving size: about 2 cups).

Per Serving:

Calories 323	**Fiber** 4.9g
Fat 5.0g (sat 0.7g)	**Cholesterol** 28mg
Protein 23.3g	**Sodium** 444mg
Carbohydrate 46.8g	**Exchanges:** 3 Starch, 2 Very Lean Meat

Barbecued Shrimp

24   unpeeled jumbo shrimp (about 1½ pounds)
Cooking spray
¼   cup chopped onion
½   cup ketchup
1   tablespoon dried rosemary
1   tablespoon dry mustard
1   tablespoon "measures-like-sugar" calorie-free sweetener
1   tablespoon white vinegar
¼   teaspoon garlic powder
Dash of hot sauce
4   lemon wedges

Peel and devein shrimp, leaving tails intact. Place shrimp in a large heavy-duty zip-top plastic bag. Set aside.

Coat a nonstick skillet with cooking spray; place over medium-high heat until hot. Add onion; sauté until tender. Stir in ketchup and next 6 ingredients; pour over shrimp. Seal bag; shake until shrimp is coated. Marinate in refrigerator 1 hour, turning once.

Prepare grill.

Thread shrimp evenly onto 8-inch skewers, running skewers through necks and tails. Place skewers on grill rack coated with cooking spray, and grill, covered, 3 to 4 minutes on each side or until shrimp are done.

Squeeze 1 lemon wedge over each skewer; serve immediately. **Yield:** 4 servings (serving size: 1 skewer).

Per Serving:

Calories 192	**Fiber** 1.1g
Fat 2.5g (sat 0.5g)	**Cholesterol** 252mg
Protein 28.5g	**Sodium** 628mg
Carbohydrate 13.3g	**Exchanges:** 1 Starch, 4 Very Lean Meat

Light Shrimp Curry

3   pounds unpeeled medium shrimp
Cooking spray
1   tablespoon margarine or butter
1   cup chopped onion
¼   cup minced jalapeño pepper (about 1 pepper)
2   tablespoons minced peeled fresh ginger
1   teaspoon minced garlic
2   tablespoons curry powder
2   (14½-ounce) cans no-salt-added stewed tomatoes, undrained
1   (8-ounce) carton plain fat-free yogurt
¼   teaspoon salt
¼   teaspoon ground white pepper
3   cups cooked long-grain rice
⅓   cup chopped green onions (about 1½ onions)

Peel and devein shrimp; set aside.

Coat a large nonstick skillet with cooking spray; add margarine. Place over medium-high heat until margarine melts. Add chopped onion, and sauté until tender. Stir in jalapeño pepper, ginger, and garlic; sauté 2 minutes. Add curry powder; sauté 2 minutes. Add tomatoes; cook over medium heat 5 minutes or until slightly thickened, stirring often. Stir in yogurt, salt, and white pepper. Add shrimp; bring to a boil. Reduce heat, and simmer 5 minutes or until shrimp are done.

Spoon mixture over rice; sprinkle with onions. Serve immediately.
Yield: 6 servings (serving size: ½ cup rice and ⅙ of shrimp mixture).

Per Serving:

Calories 331	**Fiber** 2.0g
Fat 4.5g (sat 0.8g)	**Cholesterol** 173mg
Protein 29.6g	**Sodium** 344mg
Carbohydrate 42.4g	**Exchanges:** 2 Starch, 2 Vegetable, 3 Very Lean Meat

To save time, you can buy shrimp that has already been peeled and deveined. You'll need 2¼ pounds peeled shrimp to equal 3 pounds unpeeled.

Lemon-Garlic Shrimp

3   pounds unpeeled large shrimp
Cooking spray
3   tablespoons minced onion
3   tablespoons minced fresh parsley
1½ teaspoons minced garlic
½   cup lemon juice
¼   cup fat-free Italian dressing
¼   cup water
¼   cup low-sodium soy sauce
½   teaspoon freshly ground black pepper

Peel and devein shrimp, leaving tails intact. Place shrimp in a large heavy-duty zip-top plastic bag. Set aside.

Coat a nonstick skillet with cooking spray; place over medium-high heat until hot. Add onion, parsley, and garlic; sauté until tender. Stir in lemon juice and remaining 4 ingredients. Pour mixture over shrimp; seal bag, turning to coat shrimp. Marinate in refrigerator 1 to 2 hours, turning occasionally.

Preheat broiler.

Remove shrimp from marinade, reserving marinade. Place marinade in a small saucepan; bring to a boil, and cook 1 minute. Broil shrimp 5 minutes or until shrimp are done, basting with marinade. Serve immediately with a slotted spoon. **Yield:** 6 servings (serving size: about 5 ounces shrimp).

Per Serving:

Calories 190	**Fiber** 0.4g
Fat 2.0g (sat 0.5g)	**Cholesterol** 336mg
Protein 36.9g	**Sodium** 849mg
Carbohydrate 4.5g	**Exchanges:** 5 Very Lean Meat

Spicy Shrimp Creole

Olive oil-flavored cooking spray
1   cup chopped onion (about 1 medium)
1   cup chopped green bell pepper (about 1 medium)
½   teaspoon crushed red pepper
6   garlic cloves, minced
2   (14½-ounce) cans Cajun-style stewed tomatoes, undrained
¾   pound peeled and deveined medium shrimp
2½ cups cooked long-grain rice

Coat a nonstick skillet with cooking spray; place over medium-high heat until hot. Add onion and next 3 ingredients; sauté until tender. Add tomatoes. Bring to a boil; reduce heat, and simmer, uncovered, 10 minutes, stirring occasionally. Add shrimp. Cover and cook 5 minutes or until shrimp are done.

To serve, spoon shrimp mixture over rice. **Yield:** 5 servings (serving size: 1½ cups shrimp and ½ cup rice).

Per Serving:

Calories 247	**Fiber** 2.2g
Fat 1.6g (sat 0.3g)	**Cholesterol** 103mg
Protein 18.1g	**Sodium** 521mg
Carbohydrate 34.6g	**Exchanges:** 2 Starch, 1 Vegetable, 2 Very Lean Meat

Quick Paella

1   dozen fresh mussels
2½ cups canned low-sodium chicken broth
1   cup uncooked converted rice
1   tablespoon curry powder
¼   teaspoon salt
1   cup frozen English peas
2   (8-ounce) packages chunk-style lobster-flavored seafood
     product
1   (7½-ounce) jar diced pimientos, drained

Remove beards on mussels, and scrub shells with a brush. Discard opened, cracked, or heavy mussels (they're filled with sand). Set aside.

Pour broth into a large saucepan, and bring to a boil; add rice, curry powder, and salt. Cover, reduce heat, and simmer 15 minutes. Add mussels, peas, seafood, and pimiento; cook 5 additional minutes or until mussels open and rice is tender. Discard unopened mussels. Serve immediately. **Yield:** 6 servings (serving size: ⅙ of mixture).

Per Serving:

Calories 232	**Fiber** 1.7g
Fat 1.5g (sat 0.4g)	**Cholesterol** 8mg
Protein 13.2g	**Sodium** 697mg
Carbohydrate 40.4g	**Exchanges:** 2½ Starch, 1 Very Lean Meat

Use converted (parboiled) rice in this recipe so your rice won't be gummy.

meatless
main dishes

Vegetable Frittata

1	cup egg substitute
1	tablespoon fat-free milk
¼	teaspoon dried oregano
⅛	teaspoon garlic powder
⅛	teaspoon salt
⅛	teaspoon black pepper

Cooking spray

¼	cup chopped red bell pepper
¼	cup chopped broccoli florets
2	mushrooms, sliced
¼	cup alfalfa sprouts
½	cup (2 ounces) shredded reduced-fat Swiss cheese

Combine first 6 ingredients; set aside.

Coat a small nonstick skillet with cooking spray, and place over medium-high heat until hot. Add red bell pepper, broccoli, and mushrooms; sauté until tender.

Add egg mixture to pan; cover and cook over medium-low heat 8 to 10 minutes or until set. Remove from heat; top frittata with alfalfa sprouts, and sprinkle with cheese. Cover and let stand 3 to 5 minutes or until cheese melts. Cut into 4 wedges, and serve immediately. **Yield:** 2 servings (serving size: 2 wedges).

Per Serving:

Calories 162	**Fiber** 0.8g
Fat 5.5g (sat 2.8g)	**Cholesterol** 18mg
Protein 22.6g	**Sodium** 372mg
Carbohydrate 5.0g	**Exchanges:** 1 Vegetable, 3 Very Lean Meat

Garden-Fresh Puffy Omelets

½   cup egg substitute
2   tablespoons fat-free milk
1½ teaspoons minced fresh dillweed
¼   teaspoon salt
⅛   teaspoon pepper
4   large egg whites
1   tablespoon all-purpose flour
Cooking spray
½   cup alfalfa sprouts
1   tomato, thinly sliced
1½ tablespoons grated fresh Parmesan cheese

Combine first 5 ingredients in a large bowl; set aside.

Beat egg whites with a mixer at high speed until soft peaks form; add flour, beating until stiff peaks form. Fold egg white into egg substitute mixture.

Coat a 6-inch nonstick skillet with cooking spray; place over medium heat until hot. Pour half of egg white mixture into pan, spreading evenly. Cover and cook 5 minutes or until center is set. Layer half each of alfalfa sprouts, tomato, and cheese over half of omelet. Loosen omelet with spatula; fold in half. Slide omelet onto a plate. Repeat procedure with remaining egg white mixture, sprouts, tomato, and cheese. Serve immediately. **Yield:** 2 servings (serving size: 1 omelet).

Per Serving:

Calories 155	**Fiber** 1.7g
Fat 3.9g (sat 1.9g)	**Cholesterol** 8mg
Protein 19.0g	**Sodium** 677mg
Carbohydrate 11.1g	**Exchanges:** 2 Vegetable, 2 Lean Meat

Potato-Cheddar Omelets

Cooking spray
1   cup shredded unpeeled round red potato (about ½ pound potatoes)
½   cup chopped zucchini
½   cup chopped red bell pepper
¼   cup sliced green onions (about 1 onion)
1½ cups egg substitute
¼   cup fat-free milk
½   teaspoon minced fresh oregano
¼   teaspoon black pepper
⅛   teaspoon salt
½   cup (2 ounces) shredded reduced-fat Cheddar cheese

Coat a 10-inch nonstick skillet with cooking spray; place over medium-high heat until hot. Add potato and next 3 ingredients; sauté 7 minutes or until tender. Remove from pan; set aside. Wipe pan with a paper towel. Combine egg substitute and next 4 ingredients, stirring well.

Coat pan with cooking spray; place over medium-high heat until hot. Pour half of egg mixture into pan. As mixture begins to cook, lift edges with a spatula, and tilt pan to allow uncooked portion to flow underneath. When set, spoon half of vegetables over half of omelet. Sprinkle vegetables with half of cheese. Loosen with spatula; fold in half. Cook 1 to 2 minutes or until cheese begins to melt. Slide onto a plate, cut in half, and keep warm. Repeat with remaining ingredients. Serve immediately. **Yield:** 4 servings (serving size: ½ omelet).

Per Serving:

Calories 136	**Fiber** 1.4g
Fat 3.1g (sat 1.6g)	**Cholesterol** 9mg
Protein 15.2g	**Sodium** 326mg
Carbohydrate 11.8g	**Exchanges:** 2 Vegetable, 2 Very Lean Meat

ready in **20** minutes

Spinach-Mushroom Omelet

Butter-flavored cooking spray
1   cup sliced mushrooms
1   tablespoon chopped green onions
3   cups loosely packed fresh spinach, coarsely chopped
2   tablespoons tub-style light cream cheese, softened
½   cup egg substitute
1   large egg
⅛   teaspoon salt
⅛   teaspoon pepper
2   tablespoons (½ ounce) shredded reduced-fat Cheddar cheese

Coat a 10-inch nonstick skillet with cooking spray; place over medium-high heat until hot. Add mushrooms and onions; sauté until tender. Remove from pan; set aside.

Add spinach to pan; sauté until spinach wilts. Remove from heat; stir in cream cheese. Remove from pan, and keep warm. Wipe pan with a paper towel. Combine egg substitute and next 3 ingredients, stirring well.

Coat pan with cooking spray; place over medium heat until hot. Pour egg mixture into pan. As mixture begins to cook, lift edges with a spatula, and tilt pan to allow uncooked portion to flow underneath. When set, spoon mushroom mixture, spinach mixture, and Cheddar cheese over half of omelet. Loosen with spatula, and fold in half. Cook 1 to 2 minutes or until cheese begins to melt. Slide onto a plate; cut in half. Serve immediately. **Yield:** 2 servings (serving size: ½ omelet).

Per Serving:

Calories 145	Fiber 2.5g
Fat 7.0g (sat 3.1g)	Cholesterol 123mg
Protein 15.0g	Sodium 440mg
Carbohydrate 6.2g	Exchanges: 1 Vegetable, 2 Lean Meat

Artichoke Quiche

2   cups cooked long-grain rice
¾   cup (3 ounces) shredded reduced-fat sharp Cheddar cheese,
          divided
¾   cup egg substitute, divided
1   teaspoon dried dillweed
½   teaspoon salt
1   small garlic clove, crushed
Cooking spray
1   (14-ounce) can quartered artichoke hearts, drained
¾   cup fat-free milk
¼   cup sliced green onions
1   tablespoon Dijon mustard
¼   teaspoon ground white pepper
Green onion strips (optional)

Preheat oven to 350°.

Combine rice, ¼ cup cheese, ¼ cup egg substitute, dillweed, salt, and garlic; press into a 9-inch pieplate coated with cooking spray. Bake at 350° for 5 minutes.

Arrange artichoke quarters on bottom of rice crust; sprinkle evenly with remaining ½ cup cheese. Combine remaining ½ cup egg substitute, milk, and next 3 ingredients; pour over cheese.

Bake at 350° for 50 minutes or until set. Let stand 5 minutes; cut into wedges. Garnish with green onion strips, if desired. **Yield:** 6 servings (serving size: 1 wedge).

Per Serving:

Calories 169	**Fiber** 0.4g
Fat 3.5g (sat 1.8g)	**Cholesterol** 11mg
Protein 10.4g	**Sodium** 490mg
Carbohydrate 23.1g	**Exchanges:** 1½ Starch, 1 Lean Meat

Cheese and Onion Quesadillas

Butter-flavored cooking spray
1   cup chopped onion (about 1 medium)
4   (8-inch) fat-free flour tortillas
1   cup (4 ounces) shredded reduced-fat sharp Cheddar cheese
½   teaspoon ground cumin
½   cup salsa
½   cup fat-free sour cream

Coat a large nonstick skillet with cooking spray; place over medium-high heat until hot. Add onion; sauté 5 minutes or until tender. Remove from pan. Wipe pan with a paper towel.

Coat pan with cooking spray; place over medium heat until hot. Place 1 tortilla in pan. Cook 1 minute or until bottom of tortilla is golden. Sprinkle one-fourth each of onion, cheese, and cumin over half of tortilla. Fold tortilla in half. Cook tortilla 1 minute on each side or until golden and cheese melts. Repeat procedure with remaining tortillas, onion, cheese, and cumin.

To serve, top each quesadilla with 2 tablespoons salsa and 2 tablespoons sour cream. **Yield:** 4 servings (serving size: 1 quesadilla).

Per Serving:

Calories 237	**Fiber** 2.2g
Fat 5.8g (sat 3.2g)	**Cholesterol** 19mg
Protein 14.0g	**Sodium** 650mg
Carbohydrate 31.4g	**Exchanges:** 2 Starch, 1 Medium-Fat Meat

Vegetable-Cheese Pie

4½ cups frozen shredded hash brown potatoes, thawed
1 cup (4 ounces) shredded reduced-fat Cheddar cheese
¼ cup finely chopped green bell pepper
¼ cup chopped tomato
3 tablespoons finely chopped onion
¾ cup fat-free milk
¾ cup egg substitute
½ teaspoon salt
¼ teaspoon black pepper
Cooking spray

Preheat oven to 350°.

Combine first 9 ingredients in a large bowl, stirring well. Pour mixture into a 9-inch pie plate coated with cooking spray.

Bake, uncovered, at 350° for 45 minutes or until a knife inserted in center comes out clean.

Let stand 10 minutes before cutting into wedges. **Yield:** 4 servings (serving size: 1 wedge).

Per Serving:

Calories 201	**Fiber** 0.9g
Fat 5.7g (sat 3.2g)	**Cholesterol** 19mg
Protein 15.9g	**Sodium** 603mg
Carbohydrate 21.3g	**Exchanges:** 1 Starch, 1 Vegetable, 2 Lean Meat

Keep a bag of shredded potatoes and a carton of egg substitute in the freezer so you can whip up this pie for a casual brunch or lunch. Vary the vegetables depending on what you have on hand.

Potato-Vegetable Pie

6   cups frozen mixed vegetables, thawed
1   (15-ounce) can kidney beans, rinsed and drained
2   (8-ounce) cans no-salt-added tomato sauce
1   (4-ounce) can sliced mushrooms, drained
1   teaspoon chili powder
1   teaspoon low-sodium Worcestershire sauce
½   teaspoon salt
½   teaspoon pepper
Butter-flavored cooking spray
1⅓   cups fat-free milk
2⅔   cups frozen mashed potatoes, thawed
½   cup fat-free sour cream
¼   teaspoon salt
Paprika

Preheat oven to 350°.

Combine first 8 ingredients in a large bowl; stir well. Spoon mixture into an 11- x 7-inch baking dish coated with cooking spray.

Heat milk in a medium saucepan over medium heat until very hot. (Do not boil.) Stir in potatoes; cook, stirring constantly, 5 minutes or until thickened. Stir in sour cream and ¼ teaspoon salt.

Spread potato mixture over vegetable mixture; sprinkle with paprika. Spray top with cooking spray. Bake at 350° for 40 minutes or until top is lightly browned. Serve immediately. **Yield:** 6 servings (serving size: 1⅓ cups).

Per Serving:

Calories 266	**Fiber** 7.9g
Fat 2.7g (sat 0.2g)	**Cholesterol** 3mg
Protein 13.5g	**Sodium** 641mg
Carbohydrate 48.0g	**Exchanges:** 3 Starch, 1 Vegetable, ½ Fat

Roasted Vegetable Pot Pie

2   (16-ounce) packages frozen stew vegetables, thawed
2   tablespoons fat-free Italian dressing
1   (25¾-ounce) jar fat-free chunky spaghetti sauce with
    mushrooms and sweet peppers
1   (15-ounce) can no-salt-added red kidney beans,
    rinsed and drained
1   (13.8-ounce) can refrigerated pizza crust dough
1   teaspoon fennel seeds

Preheat oven to 450°.

Combine vegetables and Italian dressing, tossing well. Spoon vegetable mixture onto a large baking sheet. Bake at 450° for 20 minutes or until vegetables are lightly browned, stirring once. Remove from oven. Reduce oven temperature to 375°.

Combine roasted vegetable mixture, spaghetti sauce, and kidney beans in a 13- x 9-inch baking dish, stirring well.

Unroll dough onto a work surface; sprinkle dough with fennel seeds. Roll dough to a 14- x 10-inch rectangle; place over vegetable mixture. Bake at 375° for 30 minutes or until lightly browned. **Yield:** 8 servings (serving size: ⅛ of pie).

Per Serving:

Calories 284	Fiber 7.5g
Fat 1.9g (sat 0.0g)	Cholesterol 0mg
Protein 9.7g	Sodium 769mg
Carbohydrate 54.1g	Exchanges: 3 Starch, 2 Vegetable

The fennel seeds add flavor to refrigerated pizza crust dough and make it a little more special.

Squash Parmesan

6   yellow squash
4   zucchini
2   large eggs, lightly beaten
¼   cup water
⅔   cup dry breadcrumbs
¾   cup grated Parmesan cheese, divided
⅓   cup minced fresh basil
¼   teaspoon crushed red pepper
3   garlic cloves, minced
2   teaspoons olive oil
Cooking spray
2   (15-ounce) cans no-salt-added crushed tomatoes, undrained

Preheat oven to 350°.

Cut each squash and zucchini lengthwise into 4 slices. Combine eggs and water, stirring well. Combine breadcrumbs, ½ cup cheese, basil, pepper, and garlic; stir. Brush vegetables with egg mixture. Dredge in breadcrumb mixture. Reserve remaining breadcrumb mixture.

Heat oil in a large nonstick skillet over medium-high heat. Add squash and zucchini to pan; cook 3 minutes on each side or until lightly browned. Layer squash and zucchini in a 13- x 9-inch baking dish coated with cooking spray. Pour tomatoes over squash and zucchini. Top with remaining breadcrumb mixture. Cover; bake at 350° for 35 minutes. Uncover; sprinkle with remaining cheese, and bake 25 minutes. Let stand 10 minutes. **Yield:** 6 servings (serving size: 1½ cups).

Per Serving:

Calories 233	**Fiber** 3.2g
Fat 8.5g (sat 3.6g)	**Cholesterol** 86mg
Protein 13.6g	**Sodium** 389mg
Carbohydrate 28.1g	**Exchanges:** 1 Starch, 2 Vegetable, 1 High-Fat Meat

Vegetable Burritos

Cooking spray
1   teaspoon olive oil
2   cups sliced mushrooms
½   cup chopped onion
½   cup chopped green bell pepper
1   garlic clove, pressed
¾   cup drained canned no-salt-added kidney beans
1   tablespoon chopped ripe olives
⅛   teaspoon black pepper
4   (8-inch) fat-free flour tortillas
¼   cup fat-free sour cream
¾   cup salsa, divided
½   cup (2 ounces) shredded reduced-fat sharp Cheddar cheese

Coat a large nonstick skillet with cooking spray; add oil. Place over medium-high heat until hot. Add mushrooms and next 3 ingredients; sauté until tender. Drain mixture, and transfer to a bowl. Add beans, olives, and black pepper, stirring well.

Spoon one-fourth of bean mixture down center of each tortilla. Top each with 1 tablespoon sour cream, 1 tablespoon salsa, and 2 tablespoons cheese; fold opposite sides over filling.

Wipe skillet with a paper towel. Coat pan with cooking spray; place over medium-high heat until hot. Place burritos, seam sides down, in pan; cook 1 minute on each side or until lightly browned. Serve with remaining ½ cup salsa. **Yield:** 4 servings (serving size: 1 burrito and 2 tablespoons salsa).

Per Serving:

Calories 251	**Fiber** 4.4g
Fat 4.7g (sat 1.9g)	**Cholesterol** 9mg
Protein 12.8g	**Sodium** 607mg
Carbohydrate 30.1g	**Exchanges:** 2 Starch, 1 Medium-Fat Meat

Seasoned Vegetable Tacos

1½ cups frozen whole-kernel corn, thawed
1   cup chopped zucchini (about 1 medium)
1   cup shredded carrot
1   (15-ounce) can no-salt-added kidney beans, rinsed and
      drained
2   teaspoons chili powder
½   teaspoon garlic powder
½   teaspoon onion powder
¼   teaspoon salt
¼   teaspoon ground oregano
¼   teaspoon "measures-like-sugar" calorie-free sweetener
½   cup water
4   cups shredded iceberg lettuce
8   corn taco shells
1   cup chopped tomato (about 1 medium)
1   cup (4 ounces) shredded reduced-fat Cheddar cheese
½   cup fat-free sour cream
½   cup salsa

Combine first 11 ingredients in a large nonstick skillet; bring to a boil. Cook, uncovered, 5 minutes or until vegetables are tender.

Place ½ cup lettuce in each taco shell. Spoon ½ cup corn mixture into each. Top each with 2 tablespoons tomato, 2 tablespoons cheese, 1 tablespoon sour cream, and 1 tablespoon salsa. **Yield:** 8 servings (serving size: 1 taco).

Per Serving:

Calories 226	**Fiber** 5.3g
Fat 6.2g (sat 2.1g)	**Cholesterol** 9mg
Protein 12.8g	**Sodium** 303mg
Carbohydrate 32.1g	**Exchanges:** 2 Starch, 1 Medium-Fat Meat

Spicy Vegetarian Tostadas

1   (16-ounce) can red beans, rinsed, drained, and divided
1   (15-ounce) can no-salt-added whole-kernel corn, drained
1   (14½-ounce) can diced tomatoes and green chiles
½   cup chopped green bell pepper
½   cup chopped onion
1½   teaspoons chili powder
6   (6-inch) corn tortillas
3   cups shredded lettuce
2   medium tomatoes, chopped
¾   cup (3 ounces) shredded reduced-fat sharp Cheddar cheese
¾   cup plain fat-free yogurt

Preheat oven to 350°.

Place 1 cup beans in a shallow bowl, and mash with a fork. Place in a medium saucepan; add remaining beans, corn, and next 4 ingredients. Bring to a boil; cover, reduce heat, and simmer 10 minutes. Uncover and cook until thickened and bubbly, stirring occasionally. Set aside, and keep warm.

Place tortillas in a single layer on a baking sheet; bake at 350° for 10 minutes or until crisp.

Spread bean mixture evenly on tortillas. Top with lettuce, chopped tomato, and cheese. Top each with 2 tablespoons yogurt. **Yield:** 6 servings (serving size: 1 tostada).

Per Serving:

Calories 271	**Fiber** 9.0g
Fat 4.0g (sat 2.0g)	**Cholesterol** 8mg
Protein 15.0g	**Sodium** 526mg
Carbohydrate 48.0g	**Exchanges:** 2½ Starch, 2 Vegetable, ½ High-Fat Meat

Spinach Lasagna

9	uncooked lasagna noodles
2	cups 1% low-fat cottage cheese
½	cup egg substitute
2	(10-ounce) packages frozen chopped spinach, thawed and drained
1	(25¾-ounce) jar fat-free spaghetti sauce with mushrooms
2	cups (8 ounces) shredded part-skim mozzarella cheese
¼	cup plus 2 tablespoons grated Parmesan cheese

Preheat oven to 350°.

Cook lasagna noodles according to package directions, omitting salt and fat; drain well. Combine cottage cheese, egg substitute, and spinach in a medium bowl; stir well.

Spread ½ cup spaghetti sauce in a 13- x 9-inch baking dish. Place 3 noodles over sauce; spoon one-third of spinach mixture over noodles. Top with one-third of remaining spaghetti sauce, ½ cup mozzarella cheese, and 2 tablespoons Parmesan cheese. Repeat procedure twice. Top with remaining ½ cup mozzarella cheese.

Bake, uncovered, at 350° for 30 to 35 minutes or until thoroughly heated. Let stand 10 minutes before serving. **Yield:** 8 servings (serving size: ⅛ of lasagna).

Per Serving:

Calories 278	**Fiber** 3.6g
Fat 6.9g (sat 4.1g)	**Cholesterol** 22mg
Protein 23.6g	**Sodium** 803mg
Carbohydrate 30.2g	**Exchanges:** 2 Starch, 2½ Lean Meat

You can assemble the lasagna a day ahead. Just cover and refrigerate it after you've topped it with cheese. Let the dish come to room temperature before baking.

Vegetable Lasagna

1 (14½-ounce) can stewed tomatoes, undrained
1½ cups fat-free, no-salt-added pasta sauce
2 cups fat-free cottage cheese
½ cup grated Parmesan cheese
¼ teaspoon pepper
Cooking spray
9 uncooked lasagna noodles
3 zucchini, trimmed and shredded
6 (1-ounce) slices provolone cheese, cut into strips

Preheat oven to 350°.

Combine tomatoes and pasta sauce; stir well. Combine cottage cheese, Parmesan cheese, and pepper; stir well.

Spoon one-third tomato mixture into bottom of a 13- x 9-inch baking dish coated with cooking spray. Place 3 noodles over tomato mixture; top with one-third zucchini and one-third cheese mixture. Top with 2 slices provolone. Repeat layers twice with remaining ingredients.

Cover and bake at 350° for 45 minutes. Uncover, and bake 15 additional minutes. Let stand 15 minutes before serving. **Yield:** 8 servings (serving size: ⅛ of lasagna).

Per Serving:

Calories 308	**Fiber** 2.3g
Fat 8.5g (sat 5.1g)	**Cholesterol** 23mg
Protein 22.4g	**Sodium** 783mg
Carbohydrate 35.7g	**Exchanges:** 2 Starch, 1 Vegetable, 2 Medium-Fat Meat

This recipe saves you a little time because you assemble it with uncooked noodles. To make ahead, cover and refrigerate unbaked lasagna. Bring to room temperature, and bake as directed.

Black Bean Lasagna Rolls

8   uncooked lasagna noodles
1   cup (4 ounces) shredded reduced-fat Monterey Jack cheese
1   (15-ounce) carton part-skim ricotta cheese
1   (4.5-ounce) can chopped green chiles, drained
½   teaspoon chili powder
⅛   teaspoon salt
2   cups drained canned no-salt-added black beans
Cooking spray
1   (15½-ounce) jar no-salt-added salsa
Fresh cilantro sprigs (optional)

Preheat oven to 350°.

Cook lasagna noodles according to package directions, omitting salt and fat; drain well.

Combine cheeses and next 3 ingredients, stirring well. Spread cheese mixture over 1 side of each noodle. Spoon black beans evenly over cheese mixture. Roll up noodles, jelly-roll fashion, beginning at narrow ends.

Place lasagna rolls, seam sides down, in an 11- x 7-inch baking dish coated with cooking spray. Cover and bake at 350° for 25 minutes or until thoroughly heated.

To serve, spoon salsa evenly over rolls, and garnish with cilantro sprigs, if desired. **Yield:** 8 servings (serving size: 1 roll).

Per Serving:

Calories 295	**Fiber** 2.8g
Fat 7.8g (sat 4.3g)	**Cholesterol** 26mg
Protein 18.8g	**Sodium** 387mg
Carbohydrate 37.8g	**Exchanges:** 2 Starch, 1 Vegetable, 2 Lean Meat

Spinach Manicotti

8   uncooked manicotti shells
1½ cups part-skim ricotta cheese
1   cup (4 ounces) shredded part-skim mozzarella cheese
⅓   cup grated Parmesan cheese
1   tablespoon chopped fresh parsley
¼   teaspoon pepper
1   (10-ounce) package frozen chopped spinach, thawed
        and drained
1   large egg, lightly beaten
1   large egg white
Olive oil-flavored cooking spray
2½ cups marinara sauce

Preheat oven to 350°.

Cook pasta according to package directions, omitting salt and fat.
Drain and rinse.

Combine ricotta cheese and next 7 ingredients in a medium bowl,
stirring well. Spoon mixture evenly into pasta shells. Place shells in an
11- x 7-inch baking dish coated with cooking spray. Spoon marinara
sauce evenly over shells. Bake, covered, at 350° for 20 minutes or until
thoroughly heated. **Yield:** 8 servings (serving size: 1 stuffed shell).

Per Serving:

Calories 243	**Fiber** 2.2g
Fat 9.8g (sat 4.8g)	**Cholesterol** 48mg
Protein 15.7g	**Sodium** 572mg
Carbohydrate 23.7g	**Exchanges:** 1 Starch, 2 Vegetable, 1 High-Fat Meat

Sun-Dried Tomato Pizza

12	sun-dried tomatoes (packed without oil)
¾	cup boiling water
3	garlic cloves
½	cup coarsely chopped fresh basil or parsley
⅛	teaspoon pepper
1	(10-ounce) thin-crust Italian bread shell (such as Boboli)
¾	cup ⅓-less-fat cream cheese, softened
3	tablespoons grated fresh Parmesan cheese

Preheat oven to 450°.

Combine tomatoes and boiling water; let stand 10 minutes. Drain. With food processor running, drop garlic through food chute; process 3 seconds. Add basil and pepper; process until minced. Add tomatoes, 1 at a time, through food chute; process until minced.

Place bread shell on an ungreased baking sheet. Spread cream cheese over shell. Spoon tomato mixture over cream cheese, covering cheese completely. Bake at 450° for 5 minutes; sprinkle with Parmesan cheese. Bake 3 additional minutes or until cheese melts. Cut into 4 wedges. **Yield:** 4 servings (serving size: 1 wedge).

Per Serving:

Calories 310	**Fiber** 1.3g
Fat 12.7g (sat 6.2g)	**Cholesterol** 34mg
Protein 15.4g	**Sodium** 745mg
Carbohydrate 34.6g	**Exchanges:** 2 Starch, 1 Vegetable, 1 Medium-Fat Meat, 1 Fat

An unopened package of sun-dried tomatoes can be stored in the pantry up to one year; an opened package will keep for three months.

Thin-Crust Vegetable Pizza

1   (6½-ounce) package pizza crust mix
⅓   cup yellow cornmeal
⅔   cup hot water
Cooking spray
1   teaspoon vegetable oil
1   large onion, sliced
1   small yellow squash, sliced
1½ teaspoons salt-free herb-and-spice blend
¼   teaspoon salt
2   tablespoons fat-free Italian dressing
1   tomato, cut into 6 slices
1½ cups (6 ounces) shredded reduced-fat sharp Cheddar cheese

Preheat oven to 450°.

Combine pizza crust mix and cornmeal; add ⅔ cup water, stirring well. Shape dough into a ball; cover and let stand 5 minutes. Pat dough into a 14- x 11-inch rectangle on a large baking sheet coated with cooking spray. Bake at 450° for 5 minutes.

Coat a large nonstick skillet with cooking spray; add oil. Place over medium-high heat until hot. Add onion and squash; sauté 10 minutes or until vegetables are tender. Stir in herb blend and salt.

Brush crust with dressing; top with onion mixture and tomato slices. Sprinkle with cheese. Bake at 450° for 10 minutes or until crust is golden and cheese melts. **Yield:** 6 servings (serving size: ⅙ of pizza).

Per Serving:

Calories 260	**Fiber** 2.6g
Fat 7.3g (sat 3.3g)	**Cholesterol** 19mg
Protein 13.4g	**Sodium** 529mg
Carbohydrate 14.2g	**Exchanges:** 1 Starch, 1½ Medium-Fat Meat

Three-Pepper Pizza

¼   teaspoon Italian seasoning
⅓   cup tomato paste
¼   cup water
1   (12-inch) prebaked refrigerated pizza crust
1   cup (4 ounces) shredded part-skim mozzarella cheese
1½ cups diced green, red, and yellow bell pepper (about 3 small
       peppers)
½   onion, chopped

Preheat oven to 450°.

Combine seasoning, tomato paste, and water in a small bowl; stir well. Spread over pizza crust. Top evenly with cheese. Sprinkle bell pepper and onion evenly over cheese.

Bake at 450° for 10 to 12 minutes or until cheese melts. Cut into 6 wedges, and serve. **Yield**: 6 servings (serving size: 1 wedge).

Per Serving:

Calories 236	**Fiber** 2.1g
Fat 6.1g (sat 2.0g)	**Cholesterol** 10mg
Protein 10.3g	**Sodium** 352mg
Carbohydrate 36.2g	**Exchanges:** 2 Starch, 1 Vegetable, ½ High-Fat Meat

Bell peppers come in an assortment of colors: green, red, yellow, orange, brown, and purple. The color depends on variety and ripeness. When peppers are picked before they reach maturity, they are green. But when left on the vine a little longer, a pepper ripens and changes color, depending on its variety.

ready in **30** minutes

Pizza Pockets

Butter-flavored cooking spray
1   cup chopped zucchini (about 1 small)
½   cup chopped red bell pepper (about ½ medium)
½   cup coarsely chopped mushrooms
2½ cups pasta sauce, divided
1   (13.8-ounce) can refrigerated pizza crust dough
1   cup (4 ounces) shredded part-skim mozzarella cheese

Preheat oven to 400°.

Coat a large nonstick skillet with cooking spray; place over medium-high heat until hot. Add zucchini, red bell pepper, and mushrooms. Sauté 5 minutes. Stir in ½ cup pasta sauce; set aside.

Roll dough into a 15- x 10-inch rectangle; cut into 4 (7½- x 5-inch) rectangles.

Spoon one-fourth of vegetable mixture onto 1 end of each rectangle; sprinkle evenly with mozzarella cheese. Fold rectangles in half over filling; press edges together with a fork.

Coat tops with cooking spray, and place on a large baking sheet coated with cooking spray. Bake at 400° for 12 minutes or until golden. Serve with remaining 2 cups warm sauce. **Yield:** 4 servings (serving size: 1 pocket plus ½ cup sauce).

Per Serving:

Calories 406	**Fiber** 1.8g
Fat 9.5g (sat 2.9g)	**Cholesterol** 16mg
Protein 18.9g	**Sodium** 1,250mg
Carbohydrate 64.6g	**Exchanges:** 4 Starch, 1 Vegetable, 1 High-Fat Meat

meats

Mexican Pizza

1   (13.8-ounce) can refrigerated pizza crust dough
Cooking spray
½   teaspoon garlic pepper
¾   pound lean ground round
¼   cup chopped onion
1   jalapeño pepper, seeded and minced
¼   teaspoon salt
¼   teaspoon ground cumin
1   cup no-salt-added tomato sauce
¾   cup chopped seeded tomato
1   medium-size green bell pepper, sliced into rings
3   tablespoons sliced ripe olives
1   cup (4 ounces) shredded reduced-fat Monterey Jack cheese

Preheat oven to 425°.

Pat dough into a 13- x 9-inch rectangle on a baking sheet coated with cooking spray. Sprinkle with garlic pepper. Bake at 425° for 8 to 10 minutes or until bottom of dough is crisp.

Coat a large nonstick skillet with cooking spray; place over medium heat until hot. Add meat and next 4 ingredients; cook until meat is browned, stirring until it crumbles. Drain.

Combine tomato sauce and chopped tomato. Spread over crust, leaving a ½-inch border around edges. Top with meat mixture, bell pepper, and olives. Sprinkle with cheese. Bake at 425° for 5 to 7 minutes or until cheese melts. **Yield:** 6 servings (serving size: ⅙ of pizza).

Per Serving:

Calories 343	**Fiber** 2.3g
Fat 10.5g (sat 4.1g)	**Cholesterol** 46mg
Protein 24.4g	**Sodium** 801mg
Carbohydrate 37.5g	**Exchanges:** 2 Starch, 2 Vegetable, 2 Medium-Fat Meat

Individual Meat Loaves

½   pound lean ground round
¼   cup egg substitute
2   tablespoons chopped onion
1   tablespoon soft breadcrumbs
1   tablespoon chopped fresh parsley
¼   teaspoon garlic powder
¼   teaspoon low-sodium Worcestershire sauce
Dash of salt
3   tablespoons ketchup, divided
Cooking spray

Preheat oven to 350°.

Combine first 8 ingredients plus 1 tablespoon ketchup in a medium bowl, stirring well. Shape mixture into 2 (5½-inch) loaves. Place loaves on a rack in a roasting pan coated with cooking spray. Spread 1 tablespoon ketchup over each loaf.

Bake at 350° for 1 hour. Remove from oven; let stand 5 minutes before serving. **Yield:** 2 servings (serving size: 1 loaf).

Per Serving:

Calories 224	**Fiber** 0.6g
Fat 7.5g (sat 2.6g)	**Cholesterol** 71mg
Protein 28.5g	**Sodium** 545mg
Carbohydrate 10.2g	**Exchanges:** ½ Starch, 4 Lean Meat

You'll need to make your own soft breadcrumbs. Tear 1 slice of bread into pieces, place in a blender or food processor. Pulse about 5 times. Store extra crumbs in an airtight container in the freezer.

Beefy-Tortilla Pie

Cooking spray
5 (6-inch) flour tortillas
½ pound ground round
1 (4.5-ounce) can chopped green chiles, drained
1 small onion, chopped
½ cup (2 ounces) shredded reduced-fat sharp Cheddar cheese
¾ cup egg substitute
½ cup fat-free milk
3 tablespoons all-purpose flour
½ teaspoon baking powder
½ teaspoon chili powder

Preheat oven to 350°.

Coat bottom and sides of a 9-inch pieplate with cooking spray and line with tortillas. Set aside.

Cook meat, chiles, and onion in a large nonstick skillet over medium heat until meat is browned, stirring until it crumbles. Drain. Add cheese; stir well. Spoon meat mixture into prepared dish.

Combine egg substitute and remaining 4 ingredients in a large bowl; beat with a wire whisk until well blended. Pour egg mixture over beef mixture. Bake at 350° for 45 minutes or until set. Cut into wedges, and serve warm. **Yield:** 6 servings (serving size: 1 wedge).

Per Serving:

Calories 228	**Fiber** 1.8g
Fat 6.3g (sat 2.2g)	**Cholesterol** 30mg
Protein 18.0g	**Sodium** 548mg
Carbohydrate 24.1g	**Exchanges:** 1½ Starch, 2 Lean Meat

Marinated Flank Steak

1   (1-pound) flank steak
2½ teaspoons prepared mustard
1½ tablespoons dry red wine
1½ tablespoons low-sodium soy sauce
1½ tablespoons lemon juice
1½ tablespoons low-sodium Worcestershire sauce
Cooking spray

Make shallow cuts in steak diagonally across grain at 1-inch intervals. Brush both sides of steak with mustard. Place steaks in a large shallow dish.

Combine wine and next 3 ingredients; pour over steak. Cover and marinate in refrigerator 8 to 12 hours, turning steak occasionally.

Preheat broiler.

Remove steak from marinade, reserving marinade. Place reserved marinade in a small saucepan; bring to a boil. Remove from heat, and set aside.

Place steak on rack of a broiler pan coated with cooking spray. Broil 5 to 7 minutes on each side or to desired degree of doneness, basting with reserved marinade. Cut steak diagonally across grain into thin slices. **Yield:** 4 servings (serving size: 3 ounces).

Per Serving:

Calories 226	**Fiber** 0.0g
Fat 13.2g (sat 5.6g)	**Cholesterol** 61mg
Protein 22.3g	**Sodium** 277mg
Carbohydrate 1.8g	**Exchanges:** 3 Medium-Fat Meat

Grilled Flank Steak with Corn Salsa

1 cup frozen corn, thawed
½ cup drained canned black beans
½ cup finely chopped red bell pepper
1 jalapeño pepper, seeded and finely chopped
1 garlic clove, crushed
2 tablespoons fresh lime juice
2 teaspoons chopped fresh cilantro
2¼ teaspoons black pepper, divided
1 pound flank steak
½ cup dry red wine
¼ cup fresh lemon juice
3 garlic cloves, crushed
2 tablespoons chopped onion
2 tablespoons Worcestershire sauce
Cooking spray

Combine corn, beans, bell pepper, jalapeño, 1 garlic clove, lime juice, cilantro, and ¼ teaspoon black pepper. Cover and chill 8 hours.

Sprinkle steak with remaining 2 teaspoons black pepper, and place in a heavy-duty zip-top plastic bag. Combine wine and next 4 ingredients; pour over steak. Seal bag; marinate in refrigerator 8 hours.

Prepare grill.

Remove steak from bag; discard marinade. Place steak on grill rack coated with cooking spray; grill, covered, 7 minutes on each side or to desired degree of doneness. Remove from grill; cut into thin slices. Serve with corn salsa. **Yield:** 4 servings (serving size: 3 ounces steak and about ½ cup salsa).

Per Serving:

Calories 297	**Fiber** 2.4g
Fat 13.0g (sat 5.6g)	**Cholesterol** 60mg
Protein 25.4g	**Sodium** 213mg
Carbohydrate 18.3g	**Exchanges:** 1 Starch, 3 Medium-Fat Meat

Smothered Steak

1   (1½-pound) lean boneless round tip steak
3   tablespoons all-purpose flour
¼   teaspoon pepper
1   (14½-ounce) can no-salt-added stewed tomatoes, undrained
1   (10-ounce) package frozen chopped onion, celery, and bell
      pepper blend, thawed
3   tablespoons low-sodium Worcestershire sauce
1   tablespoon red wine vinegar
¼   teaspoon salt
3   cups cooked long-grain rice

Trim fat from steak; cut steak into 1½-inch pieces. Place steak in a 4-quart electric slow cooker. Add flour and pepper; toss. Add tomato and next 4 ingredients; stir well.

Cover with lid; cook on high-heat setting for 1 hour. Reduce heat setting to low; and cook 7 hours or until steak is tender, stirring once. To serve, spoon meat mixture evenly over rice. **Yield:** 6 servings (serving size: ⅙ of meat mixture and ½ cup rice).

Per Serving:

Calories 312	**Fiber** 0.6g
Fat 5.1g (sat 1.8g)	**Cholesterol** 68mg
Protein 27.9g	**Sodium** 225mg
Carbohydrate 36.5g	**Exchanges:** 2 Starch, 1 Vegetable, 3 Very Lean Meat

Using an electric slow cooker is like having a personal chef, but cheaper. Just throw some ingredients into the pot, go to work, and come home to a hot meal.

Simple Beef Stroganoff

¾   pound lean boneless top sirloin steak
Cooking spray
½   cup sliced onion
1   pound mushrooms, sliced
¼   cup dry white wine or less-sodium beef broth
¼   teaspoon salt
¼   teaspoon freshly ground black pepper
1   (10¾-ounce) can condensed reduced-fat, reduced-sodium
       cream of mushroom soup, undiluted
½   cup fat-free sour cream
4½ cups cooked egg noodles

Trim fat from steak; cut steak into thin slices. Coat a nonstick skillet with cooking spray; place over medium-high heat until hot. Add steak; sauté 5 minutes. Add onion and mushrooms; sauté 5 minutes. Reduce heat to medium-low. Add wine, salt, and pepper; cook 2 minutes.

Combine soup and sour cream; stir into steak mixture. Cook until thoroughly heated. To serve, spoon meat mixture evenly over noodles. **Yield:** 6 servings (serving size: ⅙ of meat mixture and ¾ cup noodles).

Per Serving:

Calories 307	**Fiber** 4.1g
Fat 6.3g (sat 1.9g)	**Cholesterol** 78mg
Protein 21.7g	**Sodium** 357mg
Carbohydrate 40.2g	**Exchanges:** 2½ Starch, 2 Lean Meat

Cook the noodles while you're cooking the meat mixture so that everything is ready at the same time.

Grilled Sirloin
with Red Pepper Puree

1   (1-pound) lean boneless beef sirloin steak (about ¾ inch thick)
¼   teaspoon salt
¼   teaspoon black pepper
Cooking spray
1   (7-ounce) jar roasted red bell peppers, undrained
⅓   cup chopped green onions
2   tablespoons dry white wine or water
1   teaspoon beef-flavored bouillon granules

Prepare grill.

Trim excess fat from steak; sprinkle with salt and black pepper. Place steak on grill rack coated with cooking spray; grill, uncovered, 8 minutes on each side or until desired degree of doneness. Set aside; keep warm.

Place peppers and liquid, green onions, wine, and bouillon granules in a skillet; bring to a boil. Cover, reduce heat, and simmer 15 minutes. Cool sightly.

Transfer pepper mixture to a blender; process until pureed. Strain mixture, discarding liquid; return puree to pan to heat thoroughly.

Cut steak into 4 equal portions, and place on a serving plate. Spoon red pepper puree over each portion. **Yield:** 4 servings (serving size: 3 ounces steak and ¼ of pepper puree).

Per Serving:

Calories 186	**Fiber** 0.2g
Fat 6.5g (sat 2.5g)	**Cholesterol** 76mg
Protein 26.5g	**Sodium** 474mg
Carbohydrate 3.8g	**Exchanges:** 1 Vegetable, 3 Lean Meat

Steak with Ale

1   (1½-pound) lean boneless top sirloin steak, trimmed
½   cup finely chopped onion
½   cup boiling water
½   cup flat pale ale or light beer
1   tablespoon brown sugar
1   tablespoon red wine vinegar
1   teaspoon dried thyme
1   teaspoon beef-flavored bouillon granules
Cooking spray
Fresh thyme sprigs (optional)

Place steak in a shallow dish; set aside. Combine chopped onion and next 6 ingredients in a blender; process until smooth. Reserve ½ cup ale mixture, and refrigerate. Pour remaining ale mixture over steak; turn to coat. Cover and marinate in refrigerator at least 8 hours, turning occasionally.

Prepare grill.

Remove steak from marinade; discard marinade. Place steak on grill rack coated with cooking spray; grill, covered, 5 to 6 minutes on each side or to desired degree of doneness, basting frequently with reserved ½ cup ale mixture. Garnish with thyme, if desired. **Yield:** 6 servings (serving size: 3 ounces).

Per Serving:

Calories 177	**Fiber** 0.2g
Fat 6.3g (sat 2.4g)	**Cholesterol** 76mg
Protein 26.0g	**Sodium** 110mg
Carbohydrate 2.3g	**Exchanges:** 4 Very Lean Meat

Beef and Pepper Stir-Fry

1	pound lean, boneless sirloin steak
1	teaspoon olive oil
2	garlic cloves, minced
½	teaspoon dried basil
½	teaspoon black pepper
¼	teaspoon salt
3	medium-size green bell peppers, seeded and cut into ¼-inch-wide strips
1	tablespoon balsamic vinegar
2	cups cooked long-grain rice

Trim fat from steak. Slice steak diagonally across grain into ¼-inch-thick strips. Cut strips into 2-inch pieces; set aside.

Add oil to a large nonstick skillet, and place over medium-high heat until hot. Add meat, garlic, and next 3 ingredients; cook 4 minutes, stirring often. Remove from pan, and set aside.

Add bell pepper strips to pan; cook 6 minutes or until tender, stirring often. Return meat to pan, and add vinegar. Cook 2 minutes or until thoroughly heated. Spoon meat mixture over rice. **Yield:** 4 servings (serving size: ¼ of meat mixture and ½ cup rice).

Per Serving:

Calories 279	**Fiber** 3.0g
Fat 7.7g (sat 2.4g)	**Cholesterol** 69mg
Protein 26.8g	**Sodium** 221mg
Carbohydrate 24.5g	**Exchanges:** 1 Starch, 1 Vegetable, 3 Lean Meat

Beef Kebabs

1   (1-pound) beef tenderloin
2   teaspoons Worcestershire sauce
1   medium-size green bell pepper, cut into 20 squares
10   cherry tomatoes
10   small mushrooms
2   small yellow squash, cut into 10 slices
⅛   teaspoon black pepper
Cooking spray
¼   teaspoon salt

Prepare grill.

Cut meat into 20 (¾-inch) cubes. Sprinkle Worcestershire sauce over meat. Thread meat, bell pepper, tomatoes, mushrooms, and squash alternately onto 5 (12-inch) skewers. Sprinkle evenly with black pepper.

Place kebabs on grill rack coated with cooking spray; grill, uncovered, 10 minutes or to desired degree of doneness, turning once. Sprinkle evenly with salt. **Yield:** 5 servings (serving size: 1 kebab).

Per Serving:

Calories 172	**Fiber** 2.0g
Fat 7.1g (sat 3.0g)	**Cholesterol** 52mg
Protein 21.2g	**Sodium** 187mg
Carbohydrate 7.4g	**Exchanges:** 1 Vegetable, 3 Lean Meat

If using wooden skewers, be sure to soak them in water 30 minutes before threading to keep them from burning during grilling.

Beef Tenderloin
with Horseradish Sauce

1   (8-ounce) carton fat-free sour cream
¼   cup minced fresh parsley
¼   cup prepared horseradish
1   teaspoon white wine Worcestershire sauce
⅛   teaspoon pepper
1   (2-pound) beef tenderloin
Cooking spray
½   teaspoon salt-free lemon-herb seasoning (such as Mrs. Dash)

Combine first 5 ingredients. Cover and chill at least 1 hour.

Preheat oven to 500°.

Trim fat from tenderloin. Place tenderloin on a rack in a roasting pan coated with cooking spray; sprinkle lemon-herb seasoning over tenderloin. Insert a meat thermometer into thickest part of tenderloin, if desired. Bake at 500° for 35 minutes or until thermometer registers 145° (medium-rare) or 160° (medium). Let stand 10 minutes before slicing. Serve with horseradish sauce. **Yield:** 8 servings (serving size: 3 ounces beef and 2 tablespoons sauce).

Per Serving:

Calories 155	**Fiber** 0.2g
Fat 6.0g (sat 2.3g)	**Cholesterol** 54mg
Protein 20.2g	**Sodium** 75mg
Carbohydrate 3.1g	**Exchanges:** 3 Lean Meat

Fruited Cider Roast

1   (3½-pound) lean boneless top round roast
¼   teaspoon salt
¼   teaspoon pepper
Cooking spray
6   cups apple cider
3   cups cider vinegar
1   (6-ounce) package dried apricot halves, chopped
½   cup raisins
¼   cup "measures-like-sugar" brown sugar calorie-free sweetener
       (such as Brown Sugar Twin)
¼   teaspoon ground allspice

Trim fat from roast. Sprinkle roast with salt and pepper. Coat a large Dutch oven with cooking spray; place over medium-high heat until hot. Add roast, and cook until browned on all sides.

Combine cider and vinegar; pour over roast. Bring to a boil; cover, reduce heat, and simmer 3 to 3½ hours or until roast is tender. Transfer roast to a serving platter; set aside, and keep warm.

Skim fat from pan juices. Reserve 2 cups juices; discard remaining juices. Return 2 cups juices to pan; add apricots and remaining 3 ingredients. Cook over medium-high heat 10 minutes, stirring often. Serve fruit mixture with roast. **Yield:** 12 servings (serving size: 3 ounces roast and about 3 tablespoons fruit mixture).

Per Serving:

Calories 239	**Fiber** 1.6g
Fat 5.6g (sat 1.9g)	**Cholesterol** 73mg
Protein 28.4g	**Sodium** 111mg
Carbohydrate 18.9g	**Exchanges:** 1 Fruit, 4 Very Lean Meat

Picante Pot Roast

1   (4-pound) lean bottom round roast
Cooking spray
1   tablespoon chili powder
1¼ teaspoons ground cumin
1   teaspoon "measures-like-sugar" calorie-free sweetener
½   teaspoon dried whole oregano
¼   teaspoon ground red pepper
2   medium onions, cut into ¼-inch-thick slices
1   (8-ounce) can no-salt-added tomato sauce
2   cups picante sauce
½   cup water

Trim fat from roast. Coat a Dutch oven with cooking spray; place over medium-high heat until hot. Add roast; cook, turning occasionally, until browned on all sides. Combine chili powder and next 4 ingredients; sprinkle over roast. Add remaining ingredients, and bring to a boil. Cover, reduce heat, and simmer 4½ to 5 hours or until roast is tender.

Transfer roast to a serving platter; serve with sauce mixture. **Yield:** 16 servings (serving size: 3 ounces roast and about ⅓ cup sauce).

Per Serving:

Calories 166	**Fiber** 0.7g
Fat 4.1g (sat 1.5g)	**Cholesterol** 56mg
Protein 22.9g	**Sodium** 397mg
Carbohydrate 5.0g	**Exchanges:** 1 Vegetable, 3 Very Lean Meat

Veal Cordon Bleu

8   veal cutlets (about 1 pound)
½   teaspoon freshly ground black pepper
2   (¾-ounce) slices fat-free Swiss cheese
1   (1-ounce) slice lean cooked ham
2   tablespoons all-purpose flour
¼   cup plus 2 tablespoons egg substitute
½   cup dry breadcrumbs
Cooking spray
1   tablespoon reduced-calorie margarine
Fresh parsley sprigs (optional)
Lemon slices (optional)

Preheat oven to 375°.

Place cutlets between 2 sheets of wax paper, and flatten to ⅛-inch thickness. Sprinkle 4 cutlets with pepper. Cut each cheese slice in half; place 1 half-slice in center of each peppered cutlet. Cut ham slice into 4 pieces; place evenly on top of cheese. Place remaining 4 cutlets over ham; pound edges to seal.

Dredge cutlets in flour. Dip in egg substitute; dredge in breadcrumbs. Coat a large nonstick skillet with cooking spray; add margarine. Place over medium-high heat until margarine melts. Add cutlets; cook 2 minutes on each side or until lightly browned.

Place cutlets in an 11- x 7-inch baking dish coated with cooking spray. Bake, uncovered, at 375° for 20 minutes. Garnish with parsley sprigs and lemon slices, if desired. **Yield:** 4 servings (serving size: 1 cutlet).

Per Serving:

Calories 245	**Fiber** 0.5g
Fat 7.0g (sat 1.9g)	**Cholesterol** 98mg
Protein 31.1g	**Sodium** 489mg
Carbohydrate 12.7g	**Exchanges:** 1 Starch, 4 Lean Meat

Artichoke Veal Chops

4   (6-ounce) lean veal loin chops (¾ inch thick)
1   teaspoon cracked black pepper
Cooking spray
⅓   cup sliced green bell pepper
¾   cup sliced orange, red, and yellow bell pepper
⅓   cup canned fat-free, less-sodium chicken broth
¼   teaspoon dried whole thyme
2   garlic cloves, minced
1   (14-ounce) can artichoke hearts, drained and quartered
2   tablespoons chopped fresh parsley

Preheat oven to 350°.

Trim fat from veal chops. Rub cracked pepper over chops.

Coat a large ovenproof nonstick skillet with cooking spray, and place over medium-high heat until hot. Add chops, and cook 3 to 4 minutes on each side or until browned. Remove chops from pan; set aside. Wipe drippings from pan with a paper towel.

Place green bell pepper and next 4 ingredients in pan. Bring to a boil; reduce heat, and simmer 5 minutes. Stir in artichoke hearts. Return chops to pan, spooning artichoke mixture over veal chops. Cover and bake at 350° for 25 minutes or until veal is tender. Sprinkle with chopped parsley. **Yield:** 4 servings (serving size: 1 chop and ¼ of vegetable mixture).

Per Serving:

Calories 177	**Fiber** 1.5g
Fat 4.5g (sat 1.3g)	**Cholesterol** 91mg
Protein 25.3g	**Sodium** 285mg
Carbohydrate 8.9g	**Exchanges:** 2 Vegetable, 3 Very Lean Meat

We liked the vibrant color that the orange, red, and yellow bell peppers gave this dish, but you can use all one color of pepper, too.

Lamb Shish Kebabs

1   pound lean boneless lamb
⅓   cup lime juice
1   tablespoon grated onion
1½ teaspoons chili powder
1   teaspoon ground ginger
1   teaspoon ground turmeric
1   teaspoon minced garlic
2   tablespoons water
1½ teaspoons olive oil
2   medium onions
1   large green bell pepper, cut into 1-inch pieces
16 mushrooms
Cooking spray

Trim fat from lamb; cut lamb into 1¼-inch cubes. Place in a shallow dish. Combine lime juice and next 7 ingredients; pour over lamb. Cover and marinate in refrigerator at least 4 hours.

Prepare grill.

Cook 2 onions in boiling water to cover in a saucepan 10 minutes. Drain; cut each onion into 4 wedges. Remove lamb from marinade, reserving marinade. Place marinade in a saucepan, and bring to a boil. Remove from heat. Thread lamb, onion, green bell pepper, and mushrooms onto 8 (10-inch) skewers.

Place kebabs on grill rack coated with cooking spray; grill, covered, 13 to 15 minutes or until lamb is done, turning and basting frequently with reserved marinade. **Yield:** 4 servings (serving size: 2 kebabs).

Per Serving:

Calories 254	**Fiber** 3.6g
Fat 9.3g (sat 2.7g)	**Cholesterol** 76mg
Protein 27.1g	**Sodium** 75mg
Carbohydrate 16.5g	**Exchanges:** 3 Vegetable, 3 Lean Meat

Grilled Lamb Chops Dijon

2   (5-ounce) lean lamb loin chops (¾ inch thick)
2   tablespoons dry red wine
2   tablespoons water
1   tablespoon chopped garlic (about 1 large clove)
2   teaspoons dried rosemary, crushed
Cooking spray
2   tablespoons plain fat-free yogurt
1   teaspoon Dijon mustard
1   teaspoon capers
½   teaspoon lemon juice
⅛   teaspoon hot sauce

Trim fat from lamb chops; place chops in a small heavy-duty zip-top plastic bag. Combine wine and next 3 ingredients; pour over chops. Seal bag, and shake until chops are well coated. Marinate in refrigerator 8 hours, turning bag occasionally.

Prepare grill.

Remove chops from bag, discarding marinade. Place chops on grill rack coated with cooking spray; grill, covered, 10 minutes on each side or to desired degree of doneness. Transfer to serving plates, and keep warm.

Combine yogurt and remaining 4 ingredients, stirring well. Spoon yogurt mixture over chops. **Yield:** 2 servings (serving size: 1 chop and 1 tablespoon yogurt mixture).

Per Serving:

Calories 168	**Fiber** 0.2g
Fat 7.2g (sat 2.3g)	**Cholesterol** 63mg
Protein 20.9g	**Sodium** 256mg
Carbohydrate 2.4g	**Exchanges:** 3 Lean Meat

Parslied Leg of Lamb

1   cup chopped fresh parsley
½   cup chopped green onions (about 2 onions)
2   teaspoons grated orange rind
⅓   cup orange juice
1   tablespoon chopped hazelnuts or pecans
½   teaspoon pepper
1   (3½-pound) lean, boneless leg of lamb
Cooking spray

Combine first 6 ingredients in a blender or food processor; process until mixture forms a paste.

Trim fat from lamb, and place lamb in a shallow dish. Rub parsley mixture over lamb. Cover and marinate in refrigerator 8 hours.

Preheat oven to 325°.

Place lamb on a rack in a roasting pan coated with cooking spray. Insert a meat thermometer into thickest part of lamb, if desired. Bake, uncovered, at 325° for 1 hour and 45 minutes or until meat thermometer registers 145° (medium-rare) or desired degree of doneness.

Transfer lamb to a serving platter. Let stand 15 minutes before serving. **Yield:** 14 servings (serving size: about 3 ounces).

Per Serving:

Calories 155	**Fiber** 0.3g
Fat 6.5g (sat 2.1g)	**Cholesterol** 67mg
Protein 21.5g	**Sodium** 53mg
Carbohydrate 1.4g	**Exchanges:** 3 Lean Meat

Grilled Leg of Lamb

1   (3½-pound) lean boneless leg of lamb
¼   cup low-sodium soy sauce
3   tablespoons water
3   tablespoons Dijon mustard
2   tablespoons vegetable oil
2   teaspoons dried rosemary
2   teaspoons finely chopped garlic
1   teaspoon ground ginger
Cooking spray

Trim fat from lamb. Combine soy sauce and next 6 ingredients in a heavy-duty zip-top plastic bag. Add lamb; seal bag, and shake until lamb is well coated. Marinate in refrigerator 8 hours, turning bag occasionally.

Prepare grill.

Remove lamb from marinade, reserving marinade. Place marinade in a saucepan, and bring to a boil. Remove from heat. Place lamb on grill rack coated with cooking spray; grill, covered, 15 minutes on each side or until meat thermometer registers 145° (medium-rare) or desired degree of doneness, turning and basting occasionally with reserved marinade. **Yield:** 14 servings (serving size: about 3 ounces).

Per Serving:

Calories 188	**Fiber** 0.1g
Fat 8.8g (sat 2.8g)	**Cholesterol** 76mg
Protein 24.2g	**Sodium** 265mg
Carbohydrate 0.7g	**Exchanges:** 3 Lean Meat

Herbed Pork Chops

4   (4-ounce) boneless center-cut loin pork chops
        (¾ inch thick)
¼   cup dry breadcrumbs
1½   teaspoons dried parsley flakes
¼   teaspoon dried whole rosemary, crushed
⅛   teaspoon pepper
¼   cup Dijon mustard
Cooking spray

Trim fat from chops. Combine breadcrumbs and next 3 ingredients. Brush mustard over both sides of chops; dredge chops in bread-crumb mixture.

Coat a large nonstick skillet with cooking spray; place over medium-high heat until hot. Add chops; cook 4 to 6 minutes on each side or until tender. **Yield:** 4 servings (serving size: 1 chop).

Per Serving:

Calories 221   **Fiber** 0.3g
Fat 9.9g (sat 3.1g)   **Cholesterol** 68mg
Protein 24.3g   **Sodium** 564mg
Carbohydrate 5.7g   **Exchanges:** ½ Starch, 3 Lean Meat

You can use any combination of herbs you have on hand for these flavorful chops. In place of the rosemary, you might try oregano, basil, or thyme.

Skillet-Barbecued Pork Chops

4   (4-ounce) boneless center-cut loin pork chops
Cooking spray
¼   cup minced onion
1   tablespoon minced garlic (about 1 large clove)
1   cup water
½   cup no-salt-added tomato paste
3   tablespoons "measures-like-sugar" brown sugar calorie-free
    sweetener (such as Brown Sugar Twin)
3   tablespoons low-sodium soy sauce
1   tablespoon lemon juice
⅛   teaspoon salt

Trim fat from chops. Coat a small nonstick skillet with cooking spray, and place over medium-high heat until hot. Add pork chops, and cook 2 minutes on each side or until browned. Remove chops from pan. Wipe drippings from pan with a paper towel.

Coat pan with cooking spray; place over medium-high heat until hot. Add onion and garlic; sauté 1 minute. Add water and remaining 5 ingredients to pan; stir well. Return chops to pan; bring to a boil. Reduce heat, and simmer, uncovered, 20 minutes or until tender.

To serve, spoon sauce mixture over pork chops. **Yield:** 4 servings (serving size: 1 chop and about ⅓ cup sauce).

Per Serving:

Calories 243	**Fiber** 1.7g
Fat 11.1g (sat 3.7g)	**Cholesterol** 74mg
Protein 24.5g	**Sodium** 444mg
Carbohydrate 9.4g	**Exchanges:** ½ Starch, 3 Lean Meat

Easy Pork Parmesan

4   (4-ounce) boneless center-cut loin pork chops
⅓   cup dry breadcrumbs
2   tablespoons grated Parmesan cheese
¼   cup egg substitute
Cooking spray
1½   cups low-fat spaghetti sauce with garlic and herbs
½   cup (2 ounces) shredded reduced-fat mozzarella cheese

Preheat oven to 350°.

Trim fat from pork chops. Place chops between two sheets of heavy-duty plastic wrap, and flatten to ¼-inch thickness, using a meat mallet or rolling pin.

Combine breadcrumbs and Parmesan cheese in a small bowl. Dip chops in egg substitute; dredge in breadcrumb mixture.

Coat a large ovenproof nonstick skillet with cooking spray; place over medium heat until hot. Add chops, and cook 1 to 2 minutes on each side or until browned. Pour spaghetti sauce over chops. Cover and bake at 350° for 25 minutes or until chops are tender. Uncover; sprinkle with mozzarella cheese. Bake 5 additional minutes or until cheese melts. **Yield:** 4 servings (serving size: 1 chop).

Per Serving:

Calories 322	**Fiber** 2.0g
Fat 11.8g (sat 4.7g)	**Cholesterol** 79mg
Protein 34.6g	**Sodium** 614mg
Carbohydrate 17.1g	**Exchanges:** 1 Starch, 4 Lean Meat

Pork Marsala

1   (1-pound) pork tenderloin
¼   cup all-purpose flour
⅛   teaspoon salt
1   tablespoon margarine
¾   cup Marsala wine
1   teaspoon beef-flavored bouillon granules
¼   teaspoon freshly ground black pepper
3   cups cooked capellini

Trim fat from tenderloin; cut tenderloin into ½-inch-thick slices. Combine flour and salt in a heavy-duty zip-top plastic bag. Add tenderloin; seal bag, and shake until tenderloin is well coated.

Melt margarine in a nonstick skillet over medium heat. Add tenderloin; cook until browned, turning once. Remove from pan. Add wine, bouillon granules, and pepper to pan; bring to a boil. Reduce heat, and simmer, uncovered, 2 minutes. Return tenderloin to pan; cover and simmer 2 minutes or until sauce is thickened. Spoon pork mixture evenly over pasta. **Yield:** 4 servings (serving size: 3 ounces pork and ¾ cup pasta).

Per Serving:

Calories 340	**Fiber** 1.9g
Fat 6.6g (sat 1.7g)	**Cholesterol** 74mg
Protein 29.7g	**Sodium** 403mg
Carbohydrate 37.6g	**Exchanges:** 2½ Starch, 3 Lean Meat

You can use any type of thin pasta in place of the capellini—spaghetti, angel hair, or fettuccine. You'll need about 8 ounces of dry pasta to get 3 cups cooked. Cook the pasta according to package directions, omitting the salt and fat.

Indonesian Pork Tenderloin

1   (1-pound) pork tenderloin
2   tablespoons low-sodium soy sauce
2   tablespoons reduced-fat creamy peanut butter
1   teaspoon crushed red pepper
2   garlic cloves, minced
Cooking spray
¼   cup apricot spreadable fruit

Preheat oven to 375°.

Trim fat from tenderloin. Combine soy sauce and next 3 ingredients, stirring well. Spread soy sauce mixture over tenderloin.

Place tenderloin on a rack in a roasting pan coated with cooking spray. Insert meat thermometer into thickest part of tenderloin, if desired. Bake, uncovered, at 375° for 30 minutes. Brush tenderloin with apricot spread. Bake 10 additional minutes or until meat thermometer registers 160°, basting often with apricot spread. Let stand 10 minutes before slicing. **Yield:** 4 servings (serving size: 3 ounces).

Per Serving:

Calories 222	**Fiber** 0.5g
Fat 8.3g (sat 2.3g)	**Cholesterol** 79mg
Protein 26.6g	**Sodium** 285mg
Carbohydrate 8.0g	**Exchanges:** ½ Starch, 3 Lean Meat

Even though peanut butter is a high-fat food, the type of fat it contains is monounsaturated—a heart-healthy kind of fat.

Grilled Tenderloin with Cream Sauce

2   (¾-pound) pork tenderloins
Cooking spray
¾   cup 1% low-fat milk
1½ tablespoons all-purpose flour
3   tablespoons Dijon mustard
2   tablespoons dry white wine or low-sodium chicken broth
¼   cup fat-free sour cream
⅛   teaspoon pepper
Fresh rosemary sprigs (optional)

Prepare grill.

Insert a meat thermometer into thickest part of 1 tenderloin, if desired. Place tenderloins on grill rack coated with cooking spray. Grill, covered, 25 to 30 minutes or until meat thermometer registers 160°, turning occasionally.

Combine milk and flour in a saucepan, stirring until smooth. Cook over medium heat, stirring constantly, until thickened. Stir in mustard and wine; remove from heat. Stir in sour cream and pepper.

Cut tenderloins into ¼-inch-thick slices, and serve with cream sauce. Garnish with rosemary sprigs and serve with grilled vegetables, if desired. **Yield:** 6 servings (serving size: 3 ounces pork and about 2 tablespoons sauce).

Per Serving:

Calories 188	**Fiber** 0.1g
Fat 5.3g (sat 1.7g)	**Cholesterol** 86mg
Protein 28.1g	**Sodium** 307mg
Carbohydrate 4.3g	**Exchanges:** ½ Skim Milk, 3 Lean Meat

Peppercorn Pork Loin Roast

1   (2½-pound) lean, boneless pork loin roast
3   tablespoons Dijon mustard
1   tablespoon low-fat buttermilk
2   cups soft whole wheat breadcrumbs
2   tablespoons cracked black pepper
2   teaspoons whole assorted peppercorns, crushed
2   teaspoons chopped fresh thyme
¼   teaspoon salt
Cooking spray
Fresh thyme sprigs (optional)

Preheat oven to 325°.

Trim fat from roast. Combine mustard and buttermilk. Spread mustard mixture over roast.

Combine breadcrumbs and next 4 ingredients; press breadcrumb mixture evenly onto roast. Place roast on a rack in a roasting pan coated with cooking spray. Insert a meat thermometer into thickest part of roast, if desired. Bake at 325° for 2 hours or until meat thermometer registers 160°. Let stand 10 minutes before slicing. Garnish with thyme sprigs, if desired. **Yield:** 10 servings (serving size: 3 ounces).

Per Serving:

Calories 213	**Fiber** 0.8g
Fat 9.3g (sat 3.0g)	**Cholesterol** 68mg
Protein 24.8g	**Sodium** 323mg
Carbohydrate 6.4g	**Exchanges:** ½ Starch, 3 Lean Meat

make-ahead

Sausage-Egg Casserole

4   (1-inch) slices French bread, cubed
Cooking spray
¾   pound reduced-fat turkey and pork ground sausage
1   cup egg substitute
1½ cups fat-free milk
¾   cup (3 ounces) shredded reduced-fat Cheddar cheese
¼   teaspoon dry mustard
⅛   teaspoon ground red pepper

Preheat oven to 350°.

Place bread cubes in a 2-quart baking dish coated with cooking spray; set aside.

Cook sausage over medium heat until browned, stirring until it crumbles. Drain and pat dry with paper towels. Sprinkle sausage over bread cubes. Combine egg substitute and remaining ingredients; stir well. Pour egg mixture over sausage. Cover and chill 8 hours.

Bake, uncovered, at 350° for 50 minutes or until set. Serve immediately. **Yield:** 6 servings (serving size: ⅙ of casserole).

Per Serving:

Calories 290	**Fiber** 0.4g
Fat 15.0g (sat 5.9g)	**Cholesterol** 57mg
Protein 22.0g	**Sodium** 723mg
Carbohydrate 14.4g	**Exchanges:** 1 Starch, 3 Medium-Fat Meat

This hearty casserole is great for a brunch menu. Serve it with Zippy Garlic-Cheese Grits (page 282), Fresh Fruit Salad (page 206), and Spicy Tomato Sippers (page 44).

Ham and Grits Casserole

4 cups water
¼ teaspoon salt
1 cup uncooked quick-cooking grits
1 cup chopped reduced-fat, low-salt ham
3 tablespoons reduced-calorie margarine
1 teaspoon low-sodium Worcestershire sauce
1 cup egg substitute
Cooking spray
½ cup (2 ounces) shredded reduced-fat sharp Cheddar cheese

Preheat oven to 350°.

Combine 4 cups water and salt in a large saucepan; bring to a boil. Stir in grits; cover, reduce heat, and simmer 5 minutes or until grits are thickened, stirring occasionally. Remove from heat. Add ham, margarine, and Worcestershire sauce; stir until margarine melts. Gradually add egg substitute, stirring well.

Spoon grits mixture into an 11- x 7-inch baking dish coated with cooking spray. Bake at 350° for 45 minutes. Sprinkle with cheese. Bake 5 additional minutes or until cheese melts. Let stand 5 minutes before serving. **Yield:** 6 servings (serving size: 1 cup).

Per Serving:

Calories 221	**Fiber** 1.5g
Fat 7.1g (sat 2.4g)	**Cholesterol** 19mg
Protein 14.1g	**Sodium** 487mg
Carbohydrate 26.0g	**Exchanges:** 2 Starch, 1 Medium-Fat Meat

ready in **30** minutes

Red Beans and Rice

Cooking spray
6   ounces low-fat smoked sausage, thinly sliced
1   cup chopped onion
¾   cup chopped green bell pepper
1   garlic clove, minced
3   (16-ounce) cans red beans, drained
1   (14½-ounce) can no-salt-added stewed tomatoes, undrained
      and chopped
1½ cups water
1   (6-ounce) can no-salt-added tomato paste
¼   teaspoon dried oregano
¼   teaspoon dried thyme
¼   teaspoon hot sauce
1   bay leaf
4   cups cooked long-grain rice

Coat a Dutch oven with cooking spray. Place over medium-high heat until hot. Add sausage and next 3 ingredients; sauté until tender.

Add beans and next 7 ingredients; bring to a boil. Cover, reduce heat, and simmer 20 minutes or until thoroughly heated. Remove and discard bay leaf. To serve, spoon bean mixture evenly over rice. **Yield:** 8 servings (serving size: about 1 cup bean mixture and ½ cup rice).

Per Serving:

Calories 310	**Fiber** 5.7g
Fat 1.2g (sat 0.3g)	**Cholesterol** 9mg
Protein 15.9g	**Sodium** 448mg
Carbohydrate 59.2g	**Exchanges:** 4 Starch, ½ Lean Meat

Orange-Baked Ham

1   (2-pound) reduced-fat cooked ham
½   cup orange juice concentrate, thawed
¼   cup water
3   tablespoons "measures-like-sugar" brown sugar calorie-free
      sweetener (such as Brown Sugar Twin)
2   teaspoons white wine vinegar
1   teaspoon dry mustard
½   teaspoon grated orange rind
¼   teaspoon ground ginger
Cooking spray
2   tablespoons whole cloves

Score ham in a diamond design; place in a large heavy-duty zip-top plastic bag. Combine orange juice concentrate and next 6 ingredients; pour mixture over ham. Seal bag, and shake until ham is well coated. Marinate in refrigerator at least 8 hours, turning bag occasionally.

Preheat oven to 325°.

Remove ham from marinade, reserving marinade. Set aside ½ cup marinade; discard remaining marinade. Place ham on a rack in a roasting pan coated with cooking spray; stud with cloves by pushing the long clove ends into the scored intersections in the ham. Insert a meat thermometer into ham, if desired; brush ham lightly with reserved marinade. Cover; bake at 325° for 1½ hours or until thermometer registers 140°, basting occasionally with marinade. Serve warm or chilled. **Yield:** 16 servings (serving size: 2 ounces).

Per Serving:

Calories 99	**Fiber** 0.1g
Fat 3.2g (sat 1.0g)	**Cholesterol** 30mg
Protein 12.1g	**Sodium** 685mg
Carbohydrate 4.8g	**Exchanges:** 2 Lean Meat

poultry

Chicken Enchiladas

8   (6-inch) corn tortillas
Cooking spray
1½ tablespoons chopped onion
1½ tablespoons chopped fresh cilantro
1   jalapeño pepper, seeded and chopped
3   cups shredded cooked chicken breast
3   (10-ounce) cans enchilada sauce, divided
1½ cups (6 ounces) shredded reduced-fat sharp Cheddar cheese
½   cup diced tomato
⅓   cup sliced ripe olives
4   cups shredded iceberg lettuce

Preheat oven to 350°.

Wrap tortillas in aluminum foil; bake at 350° for 15 minutes. While tortillas bake, coat a large nonstick skillet with cooking spray; place over medium-high heat until hot. Add onion, cilantro, and jalapeño; sauté until onion is tender. Add chicken and 1 can enchilada sauce; cook 5 minutes.

Spoon chicken mixture evenly down centers of tortillas. Roll up tortillas; place, seam sides down, in a 13- x 9-inch baking dish. Heat remaining 2 cans enchilada sauce in a saucepan; pour over enchiladas, and top with cheese. Bake at 350° for 10 minutes or until enchiladas are thoroughly heated and cheese melts. Sprinkle evenly with tomato and olives. Serve over lettuce. **Yield:** 8 servings (serving size: 1 enchilada and ½ cup lettuce).

Per Serving:

Calories 272	**Fiber** 2.0g
Fat 9.7g (sat 3.1g)	**Cholesterol** 59mg
Protein 24.7g	**Sodium** 597mg
Carbohydrate 21.0g	**Exchanges:** 1 Starch, 1 Vegetable, 3 Lean Meat

ready in **15** minutes

Black Bean and Chicken Pizzas

2	cups shredded cooked chicken
1	teaspoon ground cumin
1	cup chunky salsa
4	(6-inch) Italian bread shells (such as Boboli)
1	(15-ounce) can no-salt-added black beans, rinsed and drained
¾	cup (3 ounces) shredded reduced-fat sharp Cheddar cheese
½	cup thinly sliced green onions (about 2 large)

Preheat oven to 450°.

Sprinkle chicken with cumin; toss well.

Spread salsa evenly over bread shells to within ½ inch of edges; arrange chicken over salsa. Layer beans over chicken; sprinkle with cheese. Place pizzas on a large ungreased baking sheet.

Bake at 450° for 10 minutes or until cheese melts. Sprinkle with green onions. Serve immediately. **Yield:** 4 servings (serving size: 1 pizza).

Per Serving:

Calories 437	**Fiber** 4.1g
Fat 10.3g (sat 4.2g)	**Cholesterol** 80mg
Protein 42.6g	**Sodium** 806mg
Carbohydrate 41.9g	**Exchanges:** 3 Starch, 4 Lean Meat

If you can't find no-salt-added black beans, use regular black beans and rinse them well. Rinsing and draining regular canned beans reduces the sodium content by 40 percent.

Chicken Dumpling Pie

3   cups chopped cooked chicken breast
2   cups frozen mixed vegetables, thawed and drained
2   (10¾-ounce) cans condensed reduced-fat, reduced-sodium
      cream of chicken soup, undiluted
1   (10½-ounce) can low-sodium chicken broth
½   teaspoon poultry seasoning
Cooking spray
2   cups low-fat baking mix (such as reduced-fat Bisquick)
1   cup fat-free milk
1   (8-ounce) carton low-fat sour cream

Preheat oven to 350°.

Combine first 5 ingredients in a large bowl, stirring well. Pour chicken mixture into a 13- x 9-inch baking dish coated with cooking spray.

Combine baking mix, milk, and sour cream in a medium bowl; spoon over chicken mixture.

Bake, uncovered, at 350° for 50 to 60 minutes or until topping is golden. Serve immediately. **Yield:** 8 servings (serving size: about 1½ cups).

Per Serving:

Calories 328	**Fiber** 2.2g
Fat 9.2g (sat 3.7g)	**Cholesterol** 61mg
Protein 22.8g	**Sodium** 740mg
Carbohydrate 36.0g	**Exchanges:** 2 Starch, 1 Vegetable, 2 Medium-Fat Meat

Wild Rice and Chicken Casserole

1   (4-ounce) package boil-in-bag long-grain and wild rice mix
1   (10¾-ounce) can condensed reduced-fat, reduced-sodium
       cream of mushroom soup, undiluted
¼   cup dry white wine or low-sodium chicken broth
Cooking spray
½   cup sliced mushrooms
½   cup sliced green onions
4   cups chopped cooked chicken breast
2   tablespoons chopped fresh parsley
¼   teaspoon salt
1   (2-ounce) jar diced pimiento, drained

Preheat oven to 350°.

Cook rice according to package directions, omitting seasoning packet. Combine soup and wine in a saucepan; cook over medium heat until heated.

Coat a small skillet with cooking spray; place over medium heat until hot. Add mushrooms and onions; sauté 2 to 3 minutes or until tender.

Combine rice, soup mixture, mushroom mixture, chicken, and remaining ingredients, stirring well. Spoon mixture into a 1½-quart baking dish coated with cooking spray. Bake at 350° for 15 minutes or until thoroughly heated. Serve immediately. **Yield:** 6 servings (serving size: 1 cup).

Per Serving:

Calories 260	**Fiber** 0.3g
Fat 4.6g (sat 1.4g)	**Cholesterol** 83mg
Protein 31.2g	**Sodium** 686mg
Carbohydrate 21.2g	**Exchanges:** 1 Starch, 1 Vegetable, 4 Very Lean Meat

Chicken Curry

1   teaspoon reduced-calorie margarine
Butter-flavored cooking spray
¼   cup chopped onion
½   cup low-sodium chicken broth
¼   cup fat-free milk
1   tablespoon all-purpose flour
1   teaspoon curry powder
1   cup chopped cooked chicken breast
1   tablespoon lemon juice
¼   teaspoon salt
1   cup cooked long-grain rice
¼   cup chopped peeled banana
2   tablespoons chopped green onions
1   tablespoon chutney
1   tablespoon chopped unsalted dry-roasted peanuts

Melt margarine in a medium nonstick skillet coated with cooking spray over medium-high heat. Add ¼ cup onion; sauté until tender.

Combine broth and next 3 ingredients; stir until smooth. Add to onion mixture. Cook over medium heat, stirring constantly, until thickened. Add chicken, lemon juice, and salt. Cook over medium heat 6 minutes or until thoroughly heated, stirring occasionally.

Spoon chicken mixture over rice. Top evenly with banana, green onions, chutney, and peanuts. **Yield:** 2 servings (serving size: ½ cup rice, ½ of chicken mixture, 2 tablespoons banana, 1 tablespoon green onions, ½ tablespoon chutney, and ½ tablespoon peanuts).

Per Serving:

Calories 381	**Fiber** 2.5g
Fat 8.0g (sat 1.3g)	**Cholesterol** 73mg
Protein 32.6g	**Sodium** 430mg
Carbohydrate 44.3g	**Exchanges:** 2 Starch, 1 Fruit, 4 Lean Meat

Salsa Chicken

6   (6-inch) corn tortillas
Cooking spray
2   cups chopped cooked chicken breast
½   cup salsa, divided
2   cups chopped onion (about 2 medium)
1   (4.5-ounce) can chopped green chiles, undrained
1   cup (4 ounces) shredded reduced-fat Monterey Jack cheese
½   cup fat-free sour cream, divided

Preheat oven to 350°.

Cut tortillas into ½-inch-wide strips. Place strips in a single layer on an ungreased baking sheet, and coat strips with cooking spray. Bake at 350° for 10 minutes or until crisp. Let cool.

Combine chicken and ¼ cup salsa in a large nonstick skillet. Bring to a boil over high heat. Reduce heat to medium-high, and cook 2 minutes, stirring occasionally. Remove from pan; wipe pan clean with a paper towel.

Coat pan with cooking spray; place over medium-high heat until hot. Add onion; sauté 2 minutes. Add green chiles; sauté 2 minutes. Add cheese and ¼ cup sour cream; stir until cheese melts.

To serve, arrange tortilla strips evenly on serving plates. Top strips evenly with chicken mixture. Spoon onion mixture evenly over chicken mixture. Top with salsa and sour cream. **Yield:** 4 servings (serving size: 18 tortilla strips, ½ cup chicken mixture, about ¾ cup onion mixture, 1 tablespoon salsa, and 1 tablespoon sour cream).

Per Serving:

Calories 333	**Fiber** 3.2g
Fat 9.2g (sat 4.0g)	**Cholesterol** 79mg
Protein 35.1g	**Sodium** 531mg
Carbohydrate 25.7g	**Exchanges:** 1½ Starch, 1 Vegetable, 4 Lean Meat

Sweet-and-Sour Chicken

2 tablespoons cornstarch
2 tablespoons "measures-like-sugar" calorie-free brown sugar sweetener (such as Brown Sugar Twin)
¾ teaspoon ground ginger
¼ teaspoon garlic powder
1½ cups pineapple juice
¼ cup rice wine vinegar
¼ cup low-sodium soy sauce
¼ cup reduced-calorie ketchup
1 tablespoon low-sodium Worcestershire sauce
Cooking spray
1¼ pounds skinless, boneless chicken breast halves, cut into 1-inch pieces
1 cup thinly sliced green bell pepper (about 1 large)
3 cups cooked long-grain rice

Combine first 9 ingredients; set aside.

Coat a large nonstick skillet with cooking spray; place over medium-high heat until hot. Add chicken; stir-fry 5 minutes. Add green bell pepper; stir-fry 2 minutes. Gradually stir cornstarch mixture into chicken mixture. Cook over medium heat, stirring constantly, until mixture is thickened and bubbly.

To serve, spoon ½ cup rice onto each plate; top evenly with chicken mixture. **Yield:** 6 servings (serving size: ⅙ of chicken mixture and ½ cup rice).

Per Serving:

Calories 265	**Fiber** 0.8g
Fat 1.7g (sat 0.3g)	**Cholesterol** 55mg
Protein 24.4g	**Sodium** 402mg
Carbohydrate 35.9g	**Exchanges:** 2 Starch, 1 Vegetable, 2 Very Lean Meat

Chicken Casserole

6   (8-ounce) skinless, bone-in chicken breast halves
4   cups water
1   teaspoon pepper
1   (10¾-ounce) can condensed reduced-fat, reduced-sodium
      cream of chicken soup, undiluted
1   (10¾-ounce) can condensed reduced-fat, reduced-sodium
      cream of celery soup, undiluted
1   (8-ounce) carton reduced-fat sour cream
½   teaspoon pepper
8   ounces reduced-fat oval-shaped buttery crackers, crushed
      (about 80 crackers)
Cooking spray
1   tablespoon margarine, melted

Combine first 3 ingredients in a large Dutch oven; bring to a boil.
Cover, reduce heat, and simmer 1 hour or until tender. Remove
chicken, and cool slightly.

Preheat oven to 325°.

Bone chicken; cut chicken into bite-size pieces. Combine chicken,
chicken soup, and next 3 ingredients, stirring well.

Place half of crushed crackers in an 11- x 7-inch baking dish coated
with cooking spray; spoon chicken mixture evenly over crackers.
Top with remaining crackers, and drizzle with margarine. Bake,
uncovered, at 325° for 35 minutes or until lightly browned. **Yield:**
8 servings (serving size: 1 cup).

Per Serving:

Calories 388	**Fiber** 0.7g
Fat 13.8g (sat 4.1g)	**Cholesterol** 91mg
Protein 33.0g	**Sodium** 518mg
Carbohydrate 30.2g	**Exchanges:** 2 Starch, 4 Lean Meat

Chicken-Sausage Jambalaya

¾   pound skinless, boneless chicken breast halves, cut into pieces
½   teaspoon black pepper
Olive oil-flavored cooking spray
1   teaspoon olive oil
10   ounces turkey breakfast sausage
2½ cups chopped onion (about 2 large)
2¼ cups chopped celery (about 6 stalks)
1¾ cups sliced green onions (about 7)
1   cup chopped green bell pepper (about 1 large)
2   garlic cloves, minced
2   chicken-flavored bouillon cubes
3⅓ cups hot water
3   tablespoons fat-free Italian dressing
1¼ cups uncooked long-grain rice

Sprinkle chicken with black pepper. Coat a Dutch oven with cooking spray; add oil. Place over medium-high heat until hot. Add chicken; sauté 3 minutes. Remove chicken; set aside.

Combine sausage and next 5 ingredients in pan. Cook over medium-high heat until sausage is browned. Stir in chicken.

Dissolve bouillon cubes in hot water; stir in dressing. Add to pan, and bring to a boil. Stir in rice. Cover, reduce heat, and simmer 20 minutes or until rice is tender and liquid is absorbed. Toss before serving. **Yield:** 6 servings (serving size: 1½ cups).

Per Serving:

Calories 345	**Fiber** 3.6g
Fat 7.5g (sat 1.2g)	**Cholesterol** 62mg
Protein 26.0g	**Sodium** 722mg
Carbohydrate 43.8g	**Exchanges:** 3 Starch, 3 Lean Meat

Chicken and Snow Pea Stir-Fry

Cooking spray
2   teaspoons vegetable oil, divided
¾   cup thinly sliced red bell pepper (about 1 medium)
¾   cup thinly sliced yellow bell pepper (about 1 medium)
6   ounces fresh snow pea pods
4   (6-ounce) skinless, boneless chicken breast halves, cut into
        thin strips
1   garlic clove, minced
1   cup low-sodium chicken broth
¼   cup low-sodium soy sauce
1   tablespoon plus 1 teaspoon cornstarch
3   tablespoons dry sherry
1   teaspoon grated peeled fresh ginger
¼   cup sesame seeds, toasted
3   cups hot cooked long-grain rice

Coat a large nonstick skillet with cooking spray. Add 1 teaspoon oil; place over medium-high heat until hot. Add peppers; stir-fry 2 minutes. Add snow peas; stir-fry 2 minutes. Remove from pan; keep warm.

Add remaining oil to pan. Add chicken and garlic; stir-fry 4 minutes or until chicken is lightly browned. Remove from pan.

Combine broth and next 4 ingredients; stir well. Add chicken, broth mixture, and sesame seeds to pan; cook 3 minutes or until mixture is thickened and bubbly, stirring frequently. Stir in vegetable mixture. To serve, spoon ¾ cup rice onto each plate; top evenly with chicken mixture. **Yield:** 4 servings (serving size: ¼ of chicken mixture and ¾ cup rice).

Per Serving:

Calories 467	**Fiber** 2.5g
Fat 11.0g (sat 1.4g)	**Cholesterol** 94mg
Protein 42.3g	**Sodium** 762mg
Carbohydrate 43.9g	**Exchanges:** 3 Starch, 4 Lean Meat

Sesame Chicken Tenders

2   large egg whites, lightly beaten
2   tablespoons low-sodium soy sauce
1   tablespoon honey
1   cup coarsely crushed cornflakes
2   tablespoons sesame seeds
½   teaspoon paprika
¼   teaspoon salt
¼   teaspoon pepper
1½ pounds chicken tenders
Cooking spray
Fat-free ranch dressing (optional)
Spicy mustard (optional)
Barbecue sauce (optional)

Preheat oven to 400°.

Combine first 3 ingredients in a medium bowl, stirring with a wire whisk. Combine next 5 ingredients in a small bowl.

Dip chicken in egg white mixture, and dredge in cereal mixture. Place chicken on a baking sheet coated with cooking spray. Bake at 400° for 23 to 25 minutes or until crispy and golden. Serve with fat-free ranch dressing, spicy mustard, or barbecue sauce, if desired (condiments not included in analysis). **Yield:** 4 servings (serving size: about 5 ounces chicken).

Per Serving:

Calories 319	**Fiber** 0.7g
Fat 6.3g (sat 1.4g)	**Cholesterol** 94mg
Protein 39.4g	**Sodium** 683mg
Carbohydrate 24.5g	**Exchanges:** 1½ Starch, 5 Very Lean Meat

Spicy Chicken Strips

4   (6-ounce) skinless, boneless chicken breast halves
1   (8-ounce) carton plain fat-free yogurt
2   tablespoons lemon juice
½   teaspoon chili powder
½   teaspoon garlic powder
¼   teaspoon ground cumin
1   cup crushed baked tortilla chips
Cooking spray

Cut chicken into 1-inch strips; set aside. Combine yogurt and next 4 ingredients in a medium bowl; stir well. Add chicken strips, and toss to coat. Cover and marinate in refrigerator 8 hours, stirring occasionally.

Preheat oven to 350°.

Remove chicken from marinade, discarding marinade. Dredge chicken strips in tortilla crumbs. Place chicken on a baking sheet coated with cooking spray. Bake at 350° for 35 minutes or until lightly browned and crisp. Serve immediately. **Yield:** 4 servings (serving size: about 5 ounces chicken).

Per Serving:

Calories 271	**Fiber** 1.0g
Fat 6.4g (sat 1.6g)	**Cholesterol** 95mg
Protein 37.0g	**Sodium** 261mg
Carbohydrate 14.5g	**Exchanges:** 1 Starch, 5 Very Lean Meat

If you don't care for spicy foods, just omit the chili powder and add an extra ¼ teaspoon of garlic powder. The chicken will still have good flavor from the garlic powder, cumin, and crushed chips.

Chicken Fajitas

2   pounds skinless, boneless chicken breasts
¼   cup white wine vinegar
¼   cup lime juice
2   tablespoons low-sodium Worcestershire sauce
2   tablespoons chopped onion
¼   teaspoon ground cumin
2   garlic cloves, minced
Cooking spray
8   (8-inch) flour tortillas
½   cup salsa
½   cup plain low-fat yogurt
1   (4.5-ounce) can chopped green chiles, drained

Place chicken between 2 sheets of heavy-duty plastic wrap; flatten to ¼-inch thickness, using a meat mallet or rolling pin. Place chicken in a 13- x 9-inch baking dish. Combine vinegar and next 5 ingredients; pour over chicken. Cover and refrigerate 4 hours.

Prepare grill.

Remove chicken from marinade; discard marinade. Place chicken on grill rack coated with cooking spray; grill, covered, 4 minutes on each side or until done. Remove chicken from grill; slice into strips.

Preheat oven to 325°.

Wrap tortillas in aluminum foil; bake at 325° for 15 minutes. Arrange chicken strips evenly down centers of tortillas; top with salsa, yogurt, and chiles. Roll up tortillas, and serve immediately. **Yield:** 8 servings (serving size: 1 tortilla, 3 ounces chicken, 1 tablespoon salsa, 1 tablespoon yogurt, and ½ tablespoon chiles).

Per Serving:

Calories 304	**Fiber** 1.9g
Fat 6.4g (sat 1.5g)	**Cholesterol** 73mg
Protein 31.3g	**Sodium** 347mg
Carbohydrate 28.3g	**Exchanges:** 2 Starch, 3 Lean Meat

Cashew Chicken

1	pound skinless, boneless chicken breasts, cut into strips
¼	cup orange juice
1	tablespoon plus 1 teaspoon cornstarch, divided
1	teaspoon vegetable oil
¼	cup chopped cashews
1	(8-ounce) can sliced water chestnuts, drained
1	cup chopped green bell pepper (about 1 large)
½	cup chopped green onions (about 2)
1	tablespoon minced fresh ginger
1	cup fat-free, less-sodium chicken broth
2	tablespoons low-sodium soy sauce
1	(11-ounce) can mandarin oranges in light syrup, drained
3	cups hot cooked brown rice

Combine chicken strips, orange juice, and 1 teaspoon cornstarch in a medium bowl; cover and chill 1 hour.

Heat oil in a nonstick skillet over medium heat. Add cashews; cook, stirring constantly, 30 seconds. Remove from pan; set aside. Add chicken mixture to pan. Cook, uncovered, over medium-high heat 8 minutes or until chicken is lightly browned, stirring constantly. Add water chestnuts and next 3 ingredients; cook 5 minutes.

Combine broth, soy sauce, and 1 tablespoon cornstarch; add to chicken mixture. Bring to a boil; reduce heat, and cook, stirring constantly, until thickened. Remove from heat; stir in oranges. Spoon chicken mixture over rice, and sprinkle with cashews. Serve immediately. **Yield:** 6 servings (serving size: ¾ cup chicken mixture and ½ cup rice).

Per Serving:

Calories 311	**Fiber** 1.3g
Fat 5.3g (sat 0.9g)	**Cholesterol** 44mg
Protein 22.4g	**Sodium** 275mg
Carbohydrate 42.8g	**Exchanges:** 2 Starch, 2 Vegetable, 2 Lean Meat

Apple-Sesame Chicken

1 tablespoon reduced-calorie margarine
2 (6-ounce) skinless, boneless chicken breast halves, cut into thin strips
3 cups fresh broccoli florets
1 cup cubed Red Delicious apple (about 1 medium)
¾ cup sliced mushrooms
¼ cup thinly sliced celery
1 tablespoon water
¼ teaspoon salt
¼ teaspoon curry powder
1½ cups hot cooked long-grain rice
½ teaspoon sesame seeds, toasted

Melt margarine in a large nonstick skillet over medium-high heat. Add chicken; stir-fry 3 minutes. Add broccoli and next 6 ingredients; cover, reduce heat, and simmer 5 minutes or until vegetables are crisp-tender, stirring often.

To serve, spoon ¾ cup rice onto each plate; top evenly with chicken mixture. Sprinkle with sesame seeds. **Yield:** 2 servings (serving size: ¾ cup rice, ½ of chicken mixture, ¼ teaspoon sesame seeds).

Per Serving:

Calories 450	Fiber 5.8g
Fat 9.1g (sat 2.1g)	Cholesterol 94mg
Protein 42.0g	Sodium 486mg
Carbohydrate 49.7g	Exchanges: 2 Starch, 1 Fruit, 1 Vegetable, 5 Very Lean Meat, 1 Fat

Cordon Bleu Casserole

6   (6-ounce) skinless, boneless chicken breast halves
Butter-flavored cooking spray
3   (1-ounce) slices reduced-fat, low-salt ham, cut in half
3   (1¼-ounce) slices reduced-fat Swiss cheese, cut in half
2   cups sliced mushrooms
1   (10¾-ounce) can condensed reduced-fat, reduced-sodium
        cream of mushroom soup, undiluted
3   tablespoons low-sodium chicken broth
1½ cups reduced-sodium chicken-flavored stuffing mix

Preheat oven to 350°.

Arrange chicken in a 13- x 9-inch baking dish coated with cooking spray. Top chicken with ham and cheese.

Coat a nonstick skillet with cooking spray; place over medium-high heat until hot. Add mushrooms; sauté 5 minutes or until tender. Combine mushrooms, soup, and broth. Spoon mixture over chicken. Top with stuffing mix; coat well with cooking spray. Bake at 350° for 45 minutes. **Yield:** 6 servings (serving size: 1 chicken breast half, ½ slice ham, ½ slice cheese, and ⅙ of stuffing mixture).

Per Serving:

Calories 340	**Fiber** 1.3g
Fat 8.6g (sat 3.3g)	**Cholesterol** 102mg
Protein 45.4g	**Sodium** 594mg
Carbohydrate 16.3g	**Exchanges:** 1 Starch, 6 Very Lean Meat, 1 Fat

This dish is a casserole version of classic chicken cordon bleu in which a thin piece of chicken is topped with a slice of prosciutto, a slice of Swiss cheese, and another slice of chicken. The stacked chicken is then breaded and sautéed until golden.

Crispy Cornmeal Chicken

4	(6-ounce) skinless, boneless chicken breast halves
1/3	cup yellow cornmeal
1	teaspoon chili powder
1/4	teaspoon garlic powder
1/4	teaspoon salt
1	tablespoon all-purpose flour
2	large egg whites, lightly beaten
2	teaspoons vegetable oil
1/2	cup salsa

Place chicken between 2 sheets of heavy-duty plastic wrap, and flatten to 1/2-inch thickness, using a meat mallet or rolling pin.

Combine cornmeal and next 3 ingredients in a small bowl. Sprinkle flour evenly over each chicken breast half; dip in egg whites, and dredge in cornmeal mixture.

Heat oil in a large nonstick skillet over medium heat. Add chicken, and cook 5 to 6 minutes on each side or until chicken is done. Serve with salsa. **Yield:** 4 servings (serving size: 1 chicken breast half and 2 tablespoons salsa).

Per Serving:

Calories 272	**Fiber** 1.4g
Fat 6.7g (sat 1.4g)	**Cholesterol** 94mg
Protein 37.9g	**Sodium** 464mg
Carbohydrate 13.7g	**Exchanges:** 1 Starch, 5 Very Lean Meat

Grilled Caribbean Chicken

4   (6-ounce) skinless, boneless chicken breast halves
2   teaspoons lime juice
1   teaspoon vegetable oil
2   teaspoons jerk seasoning
Cooking spray

Place chicken between 2 sheets of heavy-duty plastic wrap, and flatten to ¼-inch thickness, using a meat mallet or rolling pin.

Combine lime juice and oil; brush over both sides of chicken. Rub both sides of chicken with jerk seasoning.

Prepare grill.

Place chicken on grill rack coated with cooking spray; grill, covered, 5 to 6 minutes on each side or until done. **Yield:** 4 servings (serving size: 1 chicken breast half).

Per Serving:

Calories 198	**Fiber** 0.0g
Fat 3.3g (sat 1.0g)	**Cholesterol** 99mg
Protein 39.3g	**Sodium** 261mg
Carbohydrate 0.2g	**Exchanges:** 5 Very Lean Meat

Jerk seasoning is a Jamaican seasoning blend often used on grilled meats. The blend is generally a combination of chiles, thyme, cinnamon, allspice, garlic, and onions. Look for jerk seasoning in the spice section of the supermarket.

Mushroom Chicken

2½ cups sliced mushrooms
¾ cup dry white wine or low-sodium chicken broth
2 tablespoons chopped fresh parsley
1½ teaspoons chopped fresh tarragon or ½ teaspoon dried
    tarragon
½ teaspoon salt
¼ teaspoon pepper
4 (6-ounce) skinless, boneless chicken breast halves
1 tablespoon cornstarch
2 teaspoons water
4 cups cooked fettuccine
Fresh tarragon sprigs (optional)

Combine first 6 ingredients in a large nonstick skillet; bring to a boil over high heat. Arrange chicken in a single layer in pan; cover, reduce heat, and simmer 20 minutes or until chicken is tender. Remove chicken from wine mixture; set aside, and keep warm.

Combine cornstarch and water; add to pan. Bring to a boil; boil, stirring constantly, 1 minute. Return chicken to pan, coating chicken with mushroom mixture. To serve, place chicken over fettuccine and top with sauce. Garnish with fresh tarragon, if desired. **Yield:** 4 servings (serving size: 1 chicken breast half, 1 cup pasta, and about ¾ cup sauce).

Per Serving:

Calories 405	**Fiber** 3.2g
Fat 5.1g (sat 1.3g)	**Cholesterol** 94mg
Protein 43.0g	**Sodium** 385mg
Carbohydrate 44.3g	**Exchanges:** 3 Starch, 5 Very Lean Meat

Ham and Cheese Chicken

4   (6-ounce) skinless, boneless chicken breast halves
¼   teaspoon pepper
1   ounce very thinly sliced lean cooked ham
1   tablespoon plus 1 teaspoon reduced-fat garlic-flavored
      cream cheese
3   tablespoons dry breadcrumbs
1   teaspoon dried Italian seasoning
1   teaspoon grated Parmesan cheese
½   cup fat-free milk
Cooking spray
1   tablespoon plus 1 teaspoon reduced-calorie margarine, melted
2   teaspoons lemon juice
Dash of paprika

Preheat oven to 350°.

Place chicken between 2 sheets of heavy-duty plastic wrap; flatten
to ¼-inch thickness, using a rolling pin. Sprinkle with pepper.

Place one-fourth of ham on each chicken breast half. Spread cream
cheese evenly over ham. Roll up chicken, starting with short end and
tucking ends under. Secure with wooden picks.

Combine breadcrumbs, Italian seasoning, and Parmesan cheese.
Dip chicken rolls in milk, and dredge in breadcrumb mixture. Place,
seam sides down, in a baking dish coated with cooking spray.
Combine margarine and lemon juice; drizzle over chicken. Sprinkle
with paprika. Bake, uncovered, at 350° for 30 minutes or until tender.
To serve, remove wooden picks, and slice. **Yield:** 4 servings (serving
size: 1 chicken breast half).

Per Serving:

Calories 245	**Fiber** 0.3g
Fat 7.5g (sat 2.3g)	**Cholesterol** 101mg
Protein 37.7g	**Sodium** 259mg
Carbohydrate 4.5g	**Exchanges:** 5 Very Lean Meat, 1 Fat

Crispy Cheese-Filled Chicken

4 (8-ounce) skinless, bone-in chicken breast halves
3 ounces reduced-fat extra-sharp Cheddar cheese
1 tablespoon Dijon mustard
1 cup coarsely crushed cornflakes
2 teaspoons salt-free lemon-herb seasoning (such as Mrs. Dash)
½ cup nonfat buttermilk
Cooking spray

Preheat oven to 375°.

Cut a 2-inch-long slit in side of meaty portion of each breast without cutting all the way through the breast. Slice cheese into 4 portions; brush with mustard. Place 1 cheese slice in each slit; secure with wooden picks.

Combine cereal and seasoning. Dip chicken in buttermilk; dredge in cereal mixture. Place chicken in a 13- x 9-inch baking dish coated with cooking spray. Bake at 375° for 1 hour. Remove picks, and serve immediately. **Yield:** 4 servings (serving size: 1 chicken breast half).

Per Serving:

Calories 302	**Fiber** 0.3g
Fat 8.8g (sat 4.2g)	**Cholesterol** 117mg
Protein 44.0g	**Sodium** 416mg
Carbohydrate 7.8g	**Exchanges:** ½ Starch, 6 Very Lean Meat, 1 Fat

These stuffed bone-in chicken breasts are also tasty filled with Swiss cheese or provolone. Instead of the lemon-herb seasoning, you can use extra-spicy herb seasoning or Italian seasoning.

Grilled Lime Chicken

1   cup dry white wine or low-sodium chicken broth
¼   cup chopped fresh parsley
½   teaspoon grated lime rind
2   tablespoons fresh lime juice
½   teaspoon freshly ground black pepper
6   (6-ounce) skinless, boneless chicken breast halves
Cooking spray

Combine first 5 ingredients in a shallow baking dish. Add chicken, turning to coat. Cover and marinate in refrigerator 1 hour.

Prepare grill.

Remove chicken from marinade, reserving marinade. Place marinade in a small saucepan; bring to a boil, and remove from heat. Place chicken on grill rack coated with cooking spray; grill, covered, 5 minutes on each side or until done, basting with marinade. Remove from grill, and serve immediately. **Yield:** 6 servings (serving size: 1 chicken breast half).

Per Serving:

Calories 188	**Fiber** 0.2g
Fat 4.0g (sat 1.1g)	**Cholesterol** 94mg
Protein 34.5g	**Sodium** 86mg
Carbohydrate 1.3g	**Exchanges:** 5 Very Lean Meat

Chicken in Mustard Sauce

½ teaspoon paprika
¼ teaspoon salt
¼ teaspoon coarsely ground black pepper
4 (6-ounce) skinless, boneless chicken breast halves
Cooking spray
¼ cup dry white wine or low-sodium chicken broth
1½ tablespoons all-purpose flour
¾ cup 1% low-fat milk, divided
1 tablespoon prepared mustard

Combine first 3 ingredients; sprinkle over chicken. Coat a nonstick skillet with cooking spray; place over medium-high heat until hot. Add chicken; cook 3 to 5 minutes on each side or until browned. Remove chicken from pan, and set aside.

Add wine to pan; deglaze by scraping particles that cling to bottom. Combine flour and ¼ cup milk, stirring until smooth; add to pan. Stir in remaining ½ cup milk and mustard. Cook over medium heat, stirring constantly, until thickened. Return chicken to pan. Bring to a boil; cover, reduce heat, and simmer 5 minutes or until chicken is done. To serve, spoon sauce over chicken. **Yield:** 4 servings (serving size: 1 chicken breast half and about ¼ cup sauce).

Per Serving:

Calories 220	**Fiber** 0.3g
Fat 4.7g (sat 1.5g)	**Cholesterol** 96mg
Protein 36.6g	**Sodium** 300mg
Carbohydrate 5.5g	**Exchanges:** ½ Starch, 5 Very Lean Meat

Lemon-Roasted Chicken

1½ teaspoons salt
2 teaspoons freshly ground black pepper
2 to 3 teaspoons dried rosemary, crushed
1 (3-pound) broiler-fryer
1 medium lemon, cut in half
Cooking spray

Combine first 3 ingredients; set aside.

Loosen skin from chicken breast by running fingers between the two; rub 1 teaspoon seasoning mixture under skin. Rub remaining mixture over outside of chicken. Place chicken in a heavy-duty zip-top plastic bag; seal and refrigerate 8 hours.

Preheat oven to 450°.

Remove chicken from bag. Insert lemon halves in cavity; tie ends of legs together with string. Lift wing tips up and over back, and tuck under bird. Place chicken, breast side down, in a roasting pan coated with cooking spray.

Bake, uncovered, at 450° for 50 minutes or until a meat thermometer inserted in thigh registers 180°. Let stand 10 minutes before serving. **Yield:** 4 servings (serving size: about 5 ounces chicken).

Per Serving:

Calories 225	**Fiber** 0.5g
Fat 8.6g (sat 2.3g)	**Cholesterol** 101mg
Protein 33.3g	**Sodium** 978mg
Carbohydrate 3.9g	**Exchanges:** 5 Lean Meat

Roast the chicken with the skin on to keep it moist, but be sure to remove the skin before you eat it because most of the fat in chicken is in the skin.

Turkey French Bread Pizzas

Cooking spray
1½ pounds ground turkey breast
1½ cups sliced mushrooms
¾ cup chopped onion (about 1 medium)
1 garlic clove, crushed
1 (15-ounce) can pizza sauce
⅛ teaspoon salt
2 (8-ounce) loaves French bread
1½ cups (6 ounces) shredded part-skim mozzarella cheese

Preheat broiler.

Coat a large nonstick skillet with cooking spray; place over medium-high heat until hot. Add turkey and next 3 ingredients. Cook until turkey is browned, stirring until it crumbles. Stir in pizza sauce and salt; cook until thoroughly heated.

Cut each loaf in half horizontally; cut each horizontal piece in half crosswise. Place on an ungreased baking sheet, cut sides up. Broil 1 minute or until lightly toasted. Spoon turkey mixture over French bread pieces; sprinkle with cheese. Broil until cheese melts. **Yield:** 8 servings (serving size: 1 piece).

Per Serving:

Calories 355	**Fiber** 3.0g
Fat 8.4g (sat 3.3g)	**Cholesterol** 56mg
Protein 30.7g	**Sodium** 638mg
Carbohydrate 37.6g	**Exchanges:** 2 Starch, 1 Vegetable, 3 Lean Meat

Ground turkey breast is the leanest form of ground turkey (about 3 percent fat) and is white meat only with no skin. Regular ground turkey is made from white and dark meat with some skin and is about 10 percent fat. Frozen ground turkey is usually all dark meat with skin, and the fat content is similar to that of ground sirloin.

Turkey Enchiladas

1   pound ground turkey breast
2   cups salsa, divided
1   (10-ounce) package frozen chopped spinach, thawed and
        drained
1   (8-ounce) package fat-free cream cheese, cut into pieces
12 (6-inch) corn tortillas
Cooking spray
1   (14½-ounce) can no-salt-added diced tomatoes, undrained
1   teaspoon ground cumin
¾   cup (3 ounces) shredded reduced-fat Cheddar cheese
3   cups shredded iceberg lettuce
6   tablespoons fat-free sour cream

Cook turkey in a nonstick skillet over medium heat until browned,
stirring until it crumbles. Add 1 cup salsa, spinach, and cream cheese.
Cook until cheese melts. Remove mixture from pan. Wipe pan with
paper towels; place over medium heat until hot.

Preheat oven to 350°.

Coat both sides of tortillas with cooking spray. Place 1 tortilla in pan.
Cook 15 seconds on each side. Spoon ⅓ cup turkey mixture across
center of tortilla. Roll up; place, seam side down, in a 13- x 9-inch
baking dish coated with cooking spray. Repeat with remaining tortillas
and turkey.

Combine remaining salsa, tomato, and cumin; pour over tortillas.
Bake, uncovered, at 350° for 25 minutes. Sprinkle with shredded
Cheddar cheese; let stand 2 minutes. Place ½ cup lettuce on each
plate; place 2 enchiladas over lettuce. Top each serving with 1 tablespoon sour cream. **Yield:** 6 servings (serving size: 2 enchiladas).

Per Serving:

Calories 349	**Fiber** 5.1g
Fat 6.0g (sat 2.6g)	**Cholesterol** 63mg
Protein 34.2g	**Sodium** 883mg
Carbohydrate 39.7g	**Exchanges:** 2 Starch, 1 Vegetable, 3 Lean Meat

Turkey Stroganoff

8	ounces uncooked medium egg noodles
1	tablespoon chopped fresh parsley

Cooking spray

1	pound ground turkey
½	cup chopped onion (about 1 small)
1½	cups sliced mushrooms
⅓	cup dry white wine or low-sodium chicken broth
¼	teaspoon salt
⅛	teaspoon ground nutmeg
⅛	teaspoon freshly ground black pepper
1	cup 1% low-fat cottage cheese
½	cup fat-free sour cream
1	tablespoon lemon juice

Hungarian paprika

Cook noodles according to package directions, omitting salt and fat. Drain; toss with parsley.

Coat a nonstick skillet with cooking spray; place over medium heat until hot. Add turkey and onion; cook until turkey is browned. Add mushrooms and next 4 ingredients. Cook over low heat 10 minutes or until liquid evaporates, stirring occasionally. Remove from heat.

Combine cottage cheese, sour cream, and lemon juice in a blender; process until smooth. Add to turkey mixture; cook over low heat, stirring constantly, until thoroughly heated. Serve over noodles. Sprinkle with paprika. **Yield:** 4 servings (serving size: 1 cup noodles and about 1 cup turkey mixture).

Per Serving:

Calories 440	**Fiber** 2.0g
Fat 6.5g (sat 2.0g)	**Cholesterol** 130mg
Protein 42.4g	**Sodium** 491mg
Carbohydrate 47.0g	**Exchanges:** 3 Starch, 5 Very Lean Meat

Italian Turkey with Polenta

Cooking spray
½   pound ground turkey breast
1   garlic clove, minced
1   (15-ounce) can stewed tomatoes, undrained and chopped
1   teaspoon dried Italian seasoning
¼   teaspoon ground red pepper
1   (16-ounce) tube polenta
¼   cup shredded fresh Parmesan cheese

Coat a medium skillet with cooking spray. Place over medium-high heat until hot. Add turkey and garlic, and cook over medium heat until turkey is browned, stirring until turkey crumbles. Stir in tomatoes, Italian seasoning, and pepper. Bring to a boil; cover, reduce heat, and simmer 10 minutes. Set aside.

Preheat broiler.

Slice polenta into 12 rounds. Place on a baking sheet coated with cooking spray. Broil 10 minutes on each side or until lightly browned. To serve, top polenta with turkey mixture; sprinkle with cheese.
Yield: 4 servings (serving size: 3 rounds and ⅔ cup turkey mixture).

Per Serving:

Calories 209	**Fiber** 2.6g
Fat 3.1g (sat 1.5g)	**Cholesterol** 39mg
Protein 19.1g	**Sodium** 621mg
Carbohydrate 23.8g	**Exchanges:** 1 Starch, 1 Vegetable, 2 Very Lean Meat

Polenta is a cornmeal product similar to yellow grits. Precooked polenta comes in a package that looks like a tube of sausage and is usually found in the produce section of the grocery store.

Turkey Parmesan

1   large egg, lightly beaten
2   teaspoons vegetable oil
½   cup Italian-seasoned breadcrumbs
2   tablespoons grated Parmesan cheese
1½ pounds turkey breast cutlets
Cooking spray
½   cup marinara sauce or pasta sauce

Preheat oven to 350°.

Combine egg and oil in a shallow dish. Combine breadcrumbs and cheese in a shallow dish. Dip cutlets in egg mixture; dredge in breadcrumb mixture. Place cutlets on a baking sheet coated with cooking spray.

Coat cutlets lightly with cooking spray. Bake at 350° for 12 to 15 minutes or until done.

Place marinara sauce in a microwave-safe bowl. Cover with lid or wax paper, and microwave at MEDIUM-HIGH (70% power) 2 minutes or until thoroughly heated, stirring once. Spoon warm sauce over cutlets. Serve immediately. **Yield:** 4 servings (about 5 ounces turkey and 2 tablespoons sauce).

Per Serving:

Calories 310	**Fiber** 0.9g
Fat 6.6g (sat 1.3g)	**Cholesterol** 123mg
Protein 47.3g	**Sodium** 620mg
Carbohydrate 14.0g	**Exchanges:** 1 Starch, 6 Very Lean Meat

You'll have an Italian-inspired classic on the table in less than 30 minutes with this super-quick entrée.

Turkey Scaloppine with Tomatoes

½   cup dry breadcrumbs
1   tablespoon chopped fresh basil or 1 teaspoon dried basil
¼   teaspoon garlic powder
¼   teaspoon pepper
⅛   teaspoon salt
1½ pounds turkey breast slices
2   large egg whites, lightly beaten
1   teaspoon olive oil, divided
Olive oil-flavored cooking spray
¼   cup dry vermouth
¼   cup fat-free, less-sodium chicken broth
1   teaspoon cornstarch
1   cup chopped tomato (about 1 small)

Combine first 5 ingredients in a small bowl; stir well. Dip each turkey slice in egg whites; dredge in breadcrumb mixture.

Heat ½ teaspoon oil in a large nonstick skillet coated with cooking spray over medium-high heat. Add half of turkey slices; cook 2 to 3 minutes on each side or until turkey is done. Repeat procedure with remaining oil and turkey. Set aside, and keep warm.

Combine vermouth, broth, and cornstarch; stir. Add to pan; cook over medium heat, stirring constantly, 1 minute or until slightly thickened. Add tomato; cook until thoroughly heated. Spoon over turkey. Serve immediately. **Yield:** 4 servings (serving size: about 5 ounces turkey and ⅓ cup tomato mixture).

Per Serving:

Calories 243	**Fiber** 0.8g
Fat 2.6g (sat 0.5g)	**Cholesterol** 112mg
Protein 43.9g	**Sodium** 234mg
Carbohydrate 8.3g	**Exchanges:** ½ Starch, 6 Very Lean Meat

Turkey Piccata

2   tablespoons lemon juice, divided
¾   pound turkey breast cutlets
1½   tablespoons all-purpose flour
½   teaspoon paprika
¼   teaspoon ground white pepper
½   teaspoon olive oil
¼   cup dry white wine or low-sodium chicken broth
1   tablespoon drained capers
1½   teaspoons chopped fresh parsley

Drizzle 1 tablespoon lemon juice evenly over cutlets. Combine flour, paprika, and pepper; dredge cutlets in flour mixture.

Heat oil in a medium nonstick skillet over medium-high heat. Add turkey; cook 2 minutes on each side or until browned. Transfer turkey to a serving platter; set aside, and keep warm.

Combine wine and remaining 1 tablespoon lemon juice in pan; bring to a boil over medium heat, stirring constantly. Add capers, and cook 1 minute. To serve, pour caper mixture over cutlets; sprinkle with parsley. **Yield:** 2 servings (serving size: about 5 ounces turkey and 2 tablespoons caper mixture).

Per Serving:

Calories 221	**Fiber** 0.6g
Fat 2.0g (sat 0.2g)	**Cholesterol** 68mg
Protein 43.0g	**Sodium** 281mg
Carbohydrate 6.9g	**Exchanges:** ½ Starch, 6 Very Lean Meat

salads

ready in **15** minutes

Fresh Fruit Salad

1   (8-ounce) carton low-fat sour cream
2   tablespoons "measures-like-sugar" brown sugar calorie-free
        sweetener (such as Brown Sugar Twin)
½   teaspoon ground cinnamon
1¾   cups sliced banana (about 2 small)
1½   cups chopped apple (about 2 small)
1½   cups chopped pear (about 2 medium)
1¼   cups fresh orange sections (about 2 medium)

Combine first 3 ingredients, stirring well. Combine banana and
remaining 3 ingredients in a large bowl; toss well.

To serve, spoon fruit mixture evenly into each of 7 bowls; top evenly
with sour cream mixture. **Yield:** 7 servings (serving size: about 1 cup).

Per Serving:

Calories 145	**Fiber** 4.9g
Fat 4.4g (sat 2.5g)	**Cholesterol** 12mg
Protein 2.0g	**Sodium** 18mg
Carbohydrate 27.1g	**Exchanges:** 2 Fruit, 1 Fat

This is a good salad
to prepare in the
fall and early winter
because apples,
pears, and oranges
are at their peak.

Melon-Cucumber Salad

1   medium cucumber
3   cups cubed cantaloupe
2   tablespoons frozen pineapple juice concentrate
1   tablespoon water
1   teaspoon vegetable oil
½   teaspoon chili powder

Cut cucumber in half lengthwise; cut each half crosswise into ¼-inch-thick slices. Combine cucumber and cantaloupe in a medium bowl.

Combine pineapple juice concentrate and remaining 3 ingredients, stirring well. Pour mixture over cantaloupe mixture; toss lightly. Cover and chill at least 1 hour. Toss lightly before serving. **Yield:** 4 servings (serving size: 1 cup).

Per Serving:

Calories 77	**Fiber** 2.1g
Fat 1.6g (sat 0.4g)	**Cholesterol** 0mg
Protein 1.6g	**Sodium** 15mg
Carbohydrate 15.8g	**Exchange:** 1 Fruit

make-ahead

Holiday Cranberry Salad

2   cups fresh or frozen cranberries, thawed
¼   cup "measures-like-sugar" calorie-free sweetener
1   (0.3-ounce) package sugar-free lemon gelatin
1¼ cups boiling water
½   cup finely chopped celery (about 2 stalks)
1   cup finely chopped Granny Smith apple (about 1 medium)
Cooking spray
Green leaf lettuce (optional)

Place cranberries in a food processor; process 30 seconds or until chopped. Combine cranberries and sweetener in a large bowl; let stand 30 minutes or until sweetener dissolves. Combine gelatin and boiling water in a large bowl; stir 2 minutes or until gelatin dissolves. Chill until the consistency of unbeaten egg white.

Stir cranberry mixture, celery, and apple into gelatin mixture. Pour mixture into a 3-cup mold coated with cooking spray. Cover and chill until firm.

To serve, unmold salad onto a lettuce-lined serving plate, if desired. **Yield:** 5 servings (serving size: ½ cup).

Per Serving:

Calories 50	**Fiber** 1.2g
Fat 0.8g (sat 0.0g)	**Cholesterol** 0mg
Protein 1.4g	**Sodium** 17mg
Carbohydrate 9.8g	**Exchange:** ½ Fruit

ready in **10** minutes

Grapefruit and Greens

⅓   cup grapefruit juice
2   tablespoons white wine vinegar
½   teaspoon olive oil
¼   teaspoon salt
¼   teaspoon pepper
1   packet calorie-free sweetener with aspartame (such as Equal
      packets)
4   cups mixed salad greens
2   large pink grapefruit, peeled and sectioned
1   green onion, thinly sliced

Combine first 6 ingredients in a small bowl; set aside.

Place 1 cup salad greens on each of 4 plates. Arrange grapefruit
sections evenly over greens, and sprinkle evenly with green onions.
Stir juice mixture until well blended; spoon dressing over salads.
Yield: 4 servings (serving size: 1 cup greens, ½ cup grapefruit sections,
and 2 tablespoons dressing).

Per Serving:

Calories 119	**Fiber** 1.5g
Fat 1.1g (sat 0.1g)	**Cholesterol** 0mg
Protein 2.1g	**Sodium** 152mg
Carbohydrate 25.4g	**Exchanges:** 1 Fruit, 2 Vegetable

Section the grapefruit over a bowl, then use the juice to make the dressing for this salad.

Orange-Pecan Mixed Green Salad

¼   cup balsamic vinegar
¼   cup water
1   tablespoon minced onion
1   teaspoon olive oil
¾   teaspoon cornstarch
4   cups mixed salad greens
1   large navel orange, peeled and cut into 8 slices
2   tablespoons chopped pecans

Combine first 5 ingredients in a 2-cup glass measure; stir well. Microwave, uncovered, at HIGH 1 minute or until mixture boils and is slightly thickened. Stir until smooth. Let cool to room temperature.

Place 1 cup salad greens on each of 4 plates. Drizzle evenly with vinaigrette. Cut orange slices in half. Arrange slices over salad greens, and sprinkle with pecans. **Yield:** 4 servings (serving size: 1 cup greens, about 2 tablespoons vinaigrette, 4 orange slices, and ½ tablespoon pecans).

Per Serving:

Calories 61	**Fiber** 2.6g
Fat 3.8g (sat 0.4g)	**Cholesterol** 0mg
Protein 1.5g	**Sodium** 5mg
Carbohydrate 6.5g	**Exchanges:** 1 Vegetable, 1 Fat

For a richer, nuttier salad, toast the pecans in a skillet over medium heat for 5 minutes, stirring often.

Spinach Salad with the Blues

⅓ cup fat-free, less-sodium chicken broth
¼ cup white wine vinegar
1 tablespoon prepared mustard
1 teaspoon "measures-like-sugar" calorie-free sweetener
1 (10-ounce) package torn fresh spinach
5 heads Belgian endive (about 10 ounces), washed and trimmed
2 Red Delicious apples, cored and thinly sliced
1 (4-ounce) package crumbled blue cheese
¼ cup chopped walnuts, toasted

Combine first 4 ingredients in a jar. Cover tightly, and shake vigorously.

Combine spinach and dressing in a large bowl, tossing gently. Divide spinach mixture evenly among 6 salad plates. Arrange endive leaves and apple slices beside spinach mixture.

To serve, sprinkle evenly with blue cheese and walnuts. **Yield:** 6 servings (serving size: 1 cup spinach, about 1 cup endive, about 2 apple slices, 2½ tablespoons cheese, and 2 teaspoons walnuts).

Per Serving:

Calories 159	**Fiber** 4.1g
Fat 8.7g (sat 3.8g)	**Cholesterol** 14mg
Protein 7.0g	**Sodium** 331mg
Carbohydrate 15.4g	**Exchanges:** ½ Fruit, 1 Vegetable, 1 High-Fat Meat

If you're a true blue-cheese lover, this salad will become one of your favorites.

Corn Bread Salad

1   (7.5-ounce) package corn muffin mix
6   cups torn romaine lettuce
1   cup chopped seeded tomato (about 1 medium)
1   cup chopped green bell pepper (about 1 medium)
¾   cup chopped red onion (about 1 small)
3   turkey-bacon slices, cooked and crumbled
⅔   cup fat-free ranch dressing

Preheat oven to 400°.

Prepare muffin mix according to package directions in an 8-inch square pan, using water instead of milk. Cool in pan 10 minutes. Remove corn bread from pan; cut into cubes.

Place corn bread cubes on a baking sheet; bake at 400° for 10 minutes or until crisp and lightly browned. Place half of corn bread cubes in a large bowl; reserve remaining corn bread cubes for another use.

Combine toasted corn bread cubes, lettuce, and next 4 ingredients; toss well. Pour dressing over salad, and toss well.

Serve immediately. **Yield:** 6 servings (serving size: 2 cups).

Per Serving:

Calories 152	**Fiber** 1.8g
Fat 2.6g (sat 0.5g)	**Cholesterol** 5mg
Protein 4.1g	**Sodium** 501mg
Carbohydrate 27.7g	**Exchanges:** 1 Starch, 2 Vegetable

Use a corn muffin mix (such as Martha White) that is prepared with only milk or water.

make-ahead

Colorful Coleslaw

1   (8.5-ounce) package preshredded coleslaw mix (6 cups)
1   cup frozen whole-kernel corn, thawed
¾   cup chopped red onion
¾   cup chopped red bell pepper
⅓   cup white vinegar
2   tablespoons "measures-like-sugar" calorie-free sweetener
1   teaspoon celery seeds
½   teaspoon salt
½   teaspoon chicken-flavored bouillon granules
¼   teaspoon mustard seeds
1   tablespoon water
2   teaspoons vegetable oil
Dash of hot sauce

Remove dressing packet from coleslaw mix; reserve for another use. Combine coleslaw mix and next 3 ingredients in a large bowl; toss well.

Combine vinegar and remaining 8 ingredients in a small saucepan. Bring to a boil, stirring constantly until sweetener dissolves. Pour over coleslaw mixture; toss well. Cover and chill at least 2 hours.

Toss before serving. Serve with a slotted spoon. **Yield:** 5 servings (serving size: 1 cup).

Per Serving:

Calories 82	**Fiber** 2.9g
Fat 2.6g (sat 0.4g)	**Cholesterol** 0mg
Protein 2.2g	**Sodium** 340mg
Carbohydrate 14.9g	**Exchanges:** 1 Starch, ½ Fat

Cabbage-Pineapple Slaw

1   (8-ounce) can pineapple tidbits in juice, undrained
3   cups finely shredded cabbage
1½   cups chopped Red Delicious apple (about 2 medium)
½   cup chopped celery
¼   cup golden raisins
¼   cup light mayonnaise
Cabbage leaves (optional)
Apple slices (optional)

Drain pineapple, reserving 3 tablespoons juice. Combine drained pineapple, shredded cabbage, and next 3 ingredients in a large bowl.

Combine reserved pineapple juice and mayonnaise; add to cabbage mixture, tossing gently. Cover and chill.

To serve, spoon mixture into a cabbage leaf-lined bowl, and garnish with apple slices, if desired (cabbage leaves and apple slices not included in analysis). **Yield:** 5 servings (serving size: 1 cup).

Per Serving:

Calories 108	**Fiber** 2.9g
Fat 3.5g (sat 0.3g)	**Cholesterol** 4mg
Protein 1.2g	**Sodium** 109mg
Carbohydrate 20.2g	**Exchanges:** 1 Fruit, 1 Vegetable, 1 Fat

This tasty chilled salad is a cross between Waldorf salad and coleslaw.

Vinaigrette Coleslaw

3	cups finely shredded cabbage
¼	cup chopped red bell pepper
2	tablespoons thinly sliced green onions
2	tablespoons chopped fresh parsley
⅓	cup water
¼	cup white wine vinegar
1	tablespoon "measures-like-sugar" calorie-free sweetener
2	teaspoons olive oil
¼	teaspoon freshly ground black pepper
¼	teaspoon dried basil
⅛	teaspoon garlic powder

Combine first 4 ingredients in small bowl; toss well. Combine water and remaining 6 ingredients in a jar; cover tightly, and shake vigorously. Pour vinegar mixture over cabbage mixture. Cover and chill thoroughly.

Toss gently before serving. Serve with a slotted spoon. **Yield:** 5 servings (serving size: ½ cup).

Per Serving:

Calories 34	**Fiber** 1.3g
Fat 1.9g (sat 0.3g)	**Cholesterol** 0mg
Protein 0.7g	**Sodium** 13mg
Carbohydrate 3.6g	**Exchange:** 1 Vegetable

Apple Slaw

⅓ cup cider vinegar
2 teaspoons olive oil
1 teaspoon "measures-like-sugar" calorie-free sweetener
1 teaspoon Dijon mustard
½ teaspoon caraway seeds
¼ teaspoon salt
¼ teaspoon pepper
7 cups shredded red cabbage
1½ cups diced Golden Delicious apple (about 2 medium)

Combine first 7 ingredients in a large bowl, stirring with a whisk until blended. Add cabbage and apple; toss well.

Cover and chill thoroughly, tossing occasionally. **Yield:** 6 servings (serving size: 1 cup).

Per Serving:

Calories 55	**Fiber** 2.1g
Fat 1.9g (sat 0.2g)	**Cholesterol** 0mg
Protein 1.1g	**Sodium** 132mg
Carbohydrate 10.0g	**Exchanges:** ½ Fruit, 1 Vegetable

If you want to add a little more tartness to this salad, you can make it with Granny Smith apples.

Three-Bean Salad

1	(16-ounce) can no-salt-added green beans, drained
1	(16-ounce) can wax beans, drained
1	(15-ounce) can no-salt-added kidney beans, rinsed and drained
1	green bell pepper, chopped
4	green onions, chopped
⅔	cup apple juice
⅓	cup cider vinegar
½	teaspoon black pepper
¼	teaspoon dry mustard
¼	teaspoon paprika
⅛	teaspoon dried whole oregano

Combine first 5 ingredients in a large bowl, stirring gently.

Combine apple juice and remaining 5 ingredients in a jar; cover tightly, and shake vigorously. Pour over vegetables, stirring gently. Cover and chill at least 2 hours. Serve with a slotted spoon. **Yield:** 10 servings (serving size: ½ cup).

Per Serving:

Calories 54	**Fiber** 1.8g
Fat 0.3g (sat 0.0g)	**Cholesterol** 0mg
Protein 2.9g	**Sodium** 79mg
Carbohydrate 11.2g	**Exchange:** 1 Starch

make-ahead

Broccoli Salad

1   (1-pound) bag broccoli florets, chopped
1   cup seedless grapes, halved
½   cup raisins
3   green onions, thinly sliced
⅔   cup light mayonnaise
2   tablespoons tarragon vinegar
2   tablespoons slivered almonds, toasted
4   turkey-bacon slices, cooked and crumbled

Combine first 4 ingredients in a large bowl. Combine mayonnaise and vinegar; stir into broccoli mixture. Cover and chill.

Stir in almonds and bacon just before serving. **Yield:** 9 servings (serving size: ¾ cup).

Per Serving:

Calories 129	**Fiber** 2.1g
Fat 7.5g (sat 1.1g)	**Cholesterol** 10mg
Protein 3.1g	**Sodium** 222mg
Carbohydrate 14.7g	**Exchanges:** ½ Fruit, 1 Vegetable, 1½ Fat

Sweet and savory, creamy and crunchy— this all-purpose salad is one of our favorites.

Corn Salad

2   (11-ounce) cans white shoepeg corn, drained
1   green bell pepper, chopped
½   cup chopped red onion
½   cup fat-free sour cream
1   tablespoon white vinegar
¼   teaspoon celery salt
⅛   teaspoon black pepper

Combine all ingredients in a medium bowl, stirring well. Cover and chill at least 3 hours. Serve with a slotted spoon. **Yield:** 8 servings (serving size: ½ cup).

Per Serving:

Calories 71
Fat 0.4g (sat 0.1g)
Protein 2.9g
Carbohydrate 15.8g

Fiber 1.0g
Cholesterol 0mg
Sodium 257mg
Exchange: 1 Starch

This colorful salad is great for pot-luck dinners and covered-dish meals.

Mexican Corn Salad

1   (8¾-ounce) can no-salt-added whole-kernel corn, drained
¼   cup chopped cucumber
¼   cup chopped seeded tomato
1   tablespoon chopped green onions
¾   teaspoon minced seeded jalapeño pepper
2   teaspoons fresh lime juice
½   teaspoon vegetable oil
⅛   teaspoon ground cumin
Dash of salt
Dash of black pepper

Combine first 5 ingredients in a medium bowl; toss well.

Combine lime juice and remaining 4 ingredients, stirring with a wire whisk. Pour lime juice mixture over vegetable mixture, and toss well. Cover and chill at least 2 hours. Stir just before serving. **Yield:** 2 servings (serving size: ⅔ cup).

Per Serving:

Calories 73	**Fiber** 0.8g
Fat 1.9g (sat 0.2g)	**Cholesterol** 0mg
Protein 1.8g	**Sodium** 77mg
Carbohydrate 12.6g	**Exchanges:** 1 Starch, ½ Fat

This jalapeño-hot corn side dish is great served with Tex-Mex entrées like burritos and enchiladas.

make-ahead

Marinated Tomato Slices

4   large red or yellow tomatoes, each cut into 4 slices
¼   cup lemon juice
2   tablespoons minced red onion
2   tablespoons red wine vinegar
1   tablespoon chopped fresh basil or 1 teaspoon dried basil
¼   teaspoon freshly ground black pepper
1   garlic clove, minced
Green leaf lettuce leaves (optional)

Arrange tomato slices in a large shallow dish. Combine lemon juice and next 5 ingredients; pour over tomato slices, turning to coat. Cover and marinate in refrigerator at least 2 hours.

Arrange tomato slices evenly on 8 lettuce-lined salad plates, if desired. Spoon marinade evenly over tomato slices. **Yield:** 8 servings (serving size: 2 tomato slices and 1 tablespoon marinade).

Per Serving:

Calories 25	**Fiber** 1.4g
Fat 0.3g (sat 0.0g)	**Cholesterol** 0mg
Protein 1.0g	**Sodium** 9mg
Carbohydrate 5.9g	**Exchange:** 1 Vegetable

Confetti Rice Salad

1	(10½-ounce) can low-sodium chicken broth
1	cup water
1	cup long-grain rice, uncooked
½	cup chopped carrot
¼	cup lemon juice
1	tablespoon olive oil
¾	cup chopped seeded plum tomato (about 2 medium)
¾	cup chopped cooked reduced-fat, low-salt ham
⅓	cup grated fresh Parmesan cheese
⅓	cup sliced green onions
⅓	cup chopped fresh parsley

Combine broth and water in a large saucepan; bring to a boil. Add rice and carrot; stir well. Reduce heat to low; cover and simmer 20 minutes or until liquid is absorbed and rice is tender.

Add lemon juice and oil to rice mixture; stir well. Add tomato and remaining ingredients; toss well. Transfer to a serving bowl. Cover and chill at least 2 hours. Stir just before serving. **Yield:** 5 servings (serving size: 1 cup).

Per Serving:

Calories 244	**Fiber** 1.5g
Fat 6.6g (sat 2.5g)	**Cholesterol** 17mg
Protein 10.9g	**Sodium** 339mg
Carbohydrate 35.4g	**Exchanges:** 2 Starch, 1 Vegetable, 1 Fat

make-ahead

Hoppin' John Salad

2½ cups low-sodium chicken broth, divided
1 cup converted rice, uncooked
¼ cup cider vinegar
1½ teaspoons salt-free Cajun seasoning
2 teaspoons olive oil
½ teaspoon dried thyme
½ teaspoon minced garlic
¼ teaspoon hot sauce
1 (15.8-ounce) can black-eyed peas, drained
½ cup finely chopped celery
½ cup thinly sliced green onions
3 (1-ounce) slices lean ham, cut into thin strips
Fresh thyme (optional)

Place 2¼ cups broth in a medium saucepan; bring to a boil. Add rice, stirring well. Cover, reduce heat, and simmer 20 minutes. Remove from heat; let stand, covered, 5 minutes.

Combine remaining ¼ cup broth, vinegar, and next 5 ingredients in a small bowl.

Combine rice, peas, and next 3 ingredients in a large bowl. Add vinegar mixture, stirring gently to combine. Cover and chill at least 30 minutes. Garnish with fresh thyme, if desired. **Yield:** 6 servings (serving size: 1 cup).

Per Serving:

Calories 227	**Fiber** 3.6g
Fat 3.7g (sat 0.5g)	**Cholesterol** 6mg
Protein 10.2g	**Sodium** 540mg
Carbohydrate 37.9g	**Exchanges:** 2 Starch, 1 Vegetable, ½ High-Fat Meat

Tabbouleh

1	cup bulgur (or cracked wheat), uncooked
2	cups boiling water
1	large tomato, chopped
1	cup minced fresh parsley
1	green onion, chopped
2	tablespoons minced fresh mint leaves
¼	cup lemon juice
1	tablespoon olive oil
¼	teaspoon salt
¼	teaspoon pepper

Combine bulgur and water; let stand 1 hour. Drain bulgur. Add tomato and next 3 ingredients to bulgur; toss well.

Combine lemon juice and remaining 3 ingredients; pour over bulgur mixture, and toss well. Cover and chill 8 hours. Stir just before serving. **Yield:** 8 servings (serving size: ¾ cup).

Per Serving:

Calories 85	**Fiber** 3.8g
Fat 2.1g (sat 0.3g)	**Cholesterol** 0mg
Protein 2.7g	**Sodium** 82mg
Carbohydrate 15.6g	**Exchange:** 1 Starch

Tabbouleh (tuh-BOO-luh) is a traditional Middle Eastern bulgur salad. There are many variations, but the key ingredients are always bulgur, chopped tomato, onions, parsley or mint, lemon juice, and olive oil.

Pasta-Vegetable Salad

6	ounces tricolor rotini pasta, uncooked
1	(1-pound) bag broccoli florets
3	celery stalks, sliced
1	(8-ounce) can sliced water chestnuts, drained
1	(1.05-ounce) package fat-free Italian dressing mix
3	tablespoons chopped fresh oregano
¾	cup sliced radishes
⅓	cup crumbled reduced-fat feta cheese

Prepare pasta according to package directions, omitting salt and fat; drain. Rinse with cold water; drain.

Combine pasta, broccoli, celery, and water chestnuts in a bowl; set aside.

Prepare dressing mix according to package directions; stir in oregano. Pour over pasta mixture, stirring to coat. Cover and chill at least 6 hours, stirring occasionally. Just before serving, stir in radishes, and sprinkle with cheese. **Yield:** 11 servings (serving size: 1 cup).

Per Serving:

Calories 101	**Fiber** 0.7g
Fat 1.0g (sat 0.3g)	**Cholesterol** 2mg
Protein 3.5g	**Sodium** 281mg
Carbohydrate 19.6g	**Exchanges:** 1 Starch, 1 Vegetable

Add the radishes to the salad just before serving. Otherwise, their red color will bleed onto the pasta and vegetables.

Jalapeño Potato Salad

4	round red potatoes (about 1 pound)
2	tablespoons finely chopped green onions
2	tablespoons minced fresh cilantro
¼	cup low-fat sour cream
2	tablespoons fat-free mayonnaise
2	teaspoons Dijon mustard
2	teaspoons minced seeded jalapeño pepper
½	teaspoon black pepper
¼	teaspoon salt

Wash potatoes. Cook in boiling water to cover 20 to 25 minutes or until tender; drain and cool slightly. Coarsely chop potatoes, and place in a medium bowl.

Combine onions and remaining 7 ingredients in a small bowl, stirring well. Spoon mixture over potato, and toss gently. Cover and chill at least 3 hours. **Yield:** 6 servings (serving size: ½ cup).

Per Serving:

Calories 76	**Fiber** 1.6g
Fat 1.4g (sat 0.8g)	**Cholesterol** 4mg
Protein 2.1g	**Sodium** 222mg
Carbohydrate 14.1g	**Exchange:** 1 Starch

This potato salad will add punch to a meal featuring a mildly flavored meat or sandwich.

make-ahead

Garden Pasta Salad

6   ounces corkscrew pasta, uncooked
3   cups coarsely chopped seeded peeled tomato (about
      3 medium)
1   cup chopped seeded peeled cucumber (about 1 medium)
¼   cup chopped green bell pepper
¼   cup chopped fresh parsley
2   tablespoons sliced green onions
⅓   cup fat-free Italian dressing
Dash of hot sauce
¾   cup crumbled feta cheese
Chopped fresh parsley (optional)

Cook pasta according to package directions, omitting salt and fat. Drain; set aside.

Combine tomato and next 4 ingredients in a large bowl. Combine dressing and hot sauce, stirring well. Add pasta and dressing mixture to vegetable mixture, and toss. Cover and chill at least 30 minutes.

Sprinkle cheese evenly over salad just before serving. Garnish with chopped parsley, if desired. **Yield:** 6 servings (serving size: 1 cup).

Per Serving:

Calories 173	**Fiber** 2.1g
Fat 3.8g (sat 2.2g)	**Cholesterol** 13mg
Protein 6.7g	**Sodium** 313mg
Carbohydrate 28.5g	**Exchanges:** 2 Starch, 1 Fat

Grilled Salmon on Greens

1¼ pounds round red potatoes, quartered
¾ pound fresh green beans, trimmed
1 tablespoon lemon juice
2 teaspoons low-sodium Worcestershire sauce
1 teaspoon olive oil
1 pound salmon fillets
Cooking spray
½ cup reduced-fat olive oil vinaigrette
¼ cup sliced ripe olives
8 cups mixed salad greens

Cook potato in a saucepan in boiling water to cover 12 minutes or just until tender. Drain. Cook beans in saucepan in boiling water 5 minutes or until crisp-tender; drain. Cut beans in half crosswise.

Prepare grill.

Combine lemon juice, Worcestershire sauce, and oil; brush on fish. Place fish and potato on grill rack coated with cooking spray; grill, covered, 6 minutes on each side or until fish flakes easily when tested with a fork. Remove fish and potato from grill. Flake fish into chunks with a fork.

Combine fish, potato, beans, vinaigrette, and olives; spoon over greens. **Yield:** 4 servings (serving size: 2 cups greens and ¼ of fish mixture).

Per Serving:

Calories 415	**Fiber** 5.5g
Fat 18.3g (sat 2.1g)	**Cholesterol** 77mg
Protein 29.7g	**Sodium** 404mg
Carbohydrate 35.2g	**Exchanges:** 2 Starch, 1 Vegetable, 3 Medium-Fat Meat, 1 Fat

Shrimp and Spinach Salad

½   cup plain fat-free yogurt
½   cup fat-free salad dressing (such as fat-free Miracle Whip)
2   tablespoons grated orange rind
1   tablespoon crystallized ginger
2   tablespoons fresh orange juice
2   tablespoons lime juice
6   cups water
2   pounds medium shrimp, peeled and deveined
1   pound torn fresh spinach
1   cup very thinly sliced jícama
16 teardrop cherry tomatoes, halved
1   medium papaya, peeled, seeded, and sliced
Grated lime rind (optional)
Grated lemon rind (optional)

Combine first 6 ingredients in a blender; process until smooth, stopping once to scrape down sides. Cover and chill.

Bring 6 cups water to a boil in a medium saucepan; add shrimp. Cook 3 to 5 minutes or until shrimp are done. Drain well; rinse with cold water. Cover and chill.

Divide spinach evenly among 4 salad plates. Arrange shrimp, jícama, tomato, and papaya evenly over spinach. Top with yogurt mixture. If desired, garnish with lime and lemon rind. **Yield:** 4 servings (serving size: about 2½ cups spinach, 4 ounces shrimp, ¼ cup jícama, 8 tomato halves, 2 papaya slices, and about ⅓ cup yogurt mixture).

Per Serving:

Calories 216	**Fiber** 3.1g
Fat 1.7g (sat 0.4g)	**Cholesterol** 222mg
Protein 27.5g	**Sodium** 596mg
Carbohydrate 23.7g	**Exchanges:** ½ Fruit, 3 Vegetable, 3 Very Lean Meat

Fruited Chicken Salad

3   cups chopped cooked chicken breast
1   cup chopped celery
¼   cup minced onion
2   tablespoons lemon juice
¼   teaspoon salt
⅛   teaspoon pepper
1   (8-ounce) can pineapple chunks in juice, drained
1   cup seedless green grapes, halved
⅓   cup light mayonnaise
3   tablespoons slivered almonds, toasted
Lettuce leaves

Combine first 6 ingredients; cover and chill at least 3 hours.

To serve, add pineapple, grapes, mayonnaise, and almonds to chicken mixture; toss well. Serve on lettuce leaves. **Yield:** 5 servings (serving size: 1 cup).

Per Serving:

Calories 277	**Fiber** 2.0g
Fat 10.3g (sat 1.9g)	**Cholesterol** 84mg
Protein 30.7g	**Sodium** 331mg
Carbohydrate 15.0g	**Exchanges:** 1 Fruit, 4 Very Lean Meat, 1 Fat

Microwave 1½ pounds raw skinless, boneless chicken breast halves at HIGH for about 8 minutes to get 3 cups chopped chicken. Or look for cooked diced chicken in the freezer section of your grocery store.

Chicken Taco Salad

4   (4-ounce) skinless, boneless chicken breast halves
2   tablespoons salt-free Mexican seasoning, divided
4   (10-inch) flour tortillas
Cooking spray
½   cup chopped green bell pepper
½   cup chopped red bell pepper
½   cup chopped jícama
1   tablespoon chopped fresh cilantro
1   medium mango, peeled and chopped
2   tablespoons water
2   tablespoons lime juice
2   teaspoons vegetable oil
1   teaspoon "measures-like-sugar" calorie-free sweetener
6   cups shredded Bibb lettuce
Lime slices (optional)

Coat chicken with 1 tablespoon Mexican seasoning. Cover and refrigerate 8 hours.

Press each tortilla into a small microwave-safe bowl; microwave at HIGH 1½ minutes or until crisp.

Coat a nonstick skillet with cooking spray; place over medium heat. Add chicken; cook 5 minutes on each side or until done. Chop chicken.

Combine chicken, peppers, and next 3 ingredients. Combine remaining 1 tablespoon Mexican seasoning, water, and next 3 ingredients; drizzle over chicken mixture; toss well. Arrange lettuce evenly in tortilla bowls; top with chicken mixture. Serve with lime slices, if desired. **Yield:** 4 servings (serving size: 1 tortilla bowl, 1½ cups lettuce, and ¼ of chicken mixture).

Per Serving:

Calories 378	**Fiber** 4.2g
Fat 8.2g (sat 1.5g)	**Cholesterol** 66mg
Protein 32.4g	**Sodium** 341mg
Carbohydrate 43.5g	**Exchanges:** 3 Starch, 3 Lean Meat

Grilled Chicken Caesar Salad

4   (4-ounce) skinless, boneless chicken breast halves
½   cup reduced-fat Caesar dressing, divided
2   cups cubed French bread
Olive oil-flavored cooking spray
6   cups torn romaine lettuce
1   cup sliced cucumber
2   tomatoes, each cut into 8 wedges
2   tablespoons grated fresh Parmesan cheese
Freshly ground black pepper (optional)

Place chicken in a heavy-duty zip-top plastic bag; pour ¼ cup dressing over chicken. Seal bag, and shake until chicken is well coated. Marinate in refrigerator 1 hour, turning bag once.

Preheat oven to 350°.

Coat French bread cubes with cooking spray; place in a single layer on a baking sheet. Bake at 350° for 10 minutes or until lightly browned.

Prepare grill.

Remove chicken from marinade, discarding marinade. Place chicken on grill rack coated with cooking spray; grill, covered, 5 minutes on each side or until done. Cut chicken into slices.

Combine chicken, bread cubes, lettuce, and next 3 ingredients in a large serving bowl. Pour remaining ¼ cup dressing over lettuce mixture, and toss well. Sprinkle with pepper, if desired. **Yield:** 6 servings (serving size: 2 cups).

Per Serving:

Calories 206	**Fiber** 1.7g
Fat 7.2g (sat 1.3g)	**Cholesterol** 53mg
Protein 20.5g	**Sodium** 554mg
Carbohydrate 13.0g	**Exchanges:** 1 Starch, 2½ Lean Meat

Chicken and Fettuccine Salad

6 ounces uncooked fettuccine, broken in half
2½ cups broccoli florets
1 cup diagonally sliced carrot
¾ cup diagonally sliced celery
⅓ cup fat-free Italian dressing
⅓ cup low-fat mayonnaise
2½ tablespoons prepared horseradish
½ teaspoon freshly ground black pepper
2½ cups chopped cooked chicken breast
12 cherry tomatoes, halved

Cook fettuccine according to package directions, omitting salt and fat. Drain and rinse under cold water; drain again. Set aside.

Cook broccoli, carrot, and celery in a small amount of boiling water 6 minutes or until crisp-tender. Drain; plunge into ice water, and drain again.

Combine cooked fettuccine and broccoli mixture in a large bowl. Combine Italian dressing and next 3 ingredients; stir well. Add to fettuccine mixture; toss gently. Stir in chicken and tomato. **Yield:** 8 servings (serving size: 1 cup).

Per Serving:

Calories 196	**Fiber** 3.7g
Fat 4.7g (sat 0.9g)	**Cholesterol** 39mg
Protein 17.6g	**Sodium** 238mg
Carbohydrate 22.2g	**Exchanges:** 1 Starch, 1 Vegetable, 2 Lean Meat

Antipasto Platter

1   (10-ounce) package frozen artichoke hearts
1½   cups small mushrooms, halved
⅔   cup chopped red onion
1   (15-ounce) can chickpeas (garbanzo beans), rinsed and
       drained
1   (15-ounce) can no-salt-added kidney beans, rinsed and
       drained
¾   cup reduced-fat olive oil vinaigrette, divided
6   cups torn romaine lettuce
4   ounces thinly sliced fat-free turkey ham, cut into thin strips
4   ounces part-skim mozzarella cheese, thinly sliced
2   red bell peppers, seeded and thinly sliced
2   cucumbers, sliced

Cook artichoke hearts according to package directions, omitting salt and fat. Drain well.

Combine artichoke hearts, mushrooms, and next 3 ingredients in a large bowl; add ½ cup vinaigrette, and toss well. Cover and chill 2 hours, stirring occasionally.

Place romaine lettuce on a large serving platter; spoon artichoke mixture onto lettuce in center of platter. Arrange ham strips, cheese, red bell pepper, and cucumber around artichoke mixture. Drizzle remaining vinaigrette over salad. **Yield:** 4 servings (serving size: 1½ cups lettuce, ¼ of artichoke mixture, 1 ounce ham, 1 ounce cheese, ½ bell pepper, ½ cucumber, and 1 tablespoon vinaigrette).

Per Serving:

Calories 316	**Fiber** 6.1g
Fat 12.0g (sat 3.0g)	**Cholesterol** 22mg
Protein 19.6g	**Sodium** 596mg
Carbohydrate 37.0g	**Exchanges:** 2 Starch, 1 Vegetable, 2 Medium-Fat Meat

make-ahead

Ham and Potato Salad

1   pound small round red potatoes, cut into ½-inch slices
        (about 3 cups)
1   (16-ounce) package frozen mixed vegetables
⅓   cup light mayonnaise
⅓   cup fat-free sour cream
½   cup sliced green onions
½   teaspoon pepper
1½ cups diced lean cooked ham

Place potato in boiling water to cover; cover, reduce heat, and cook 10 minutes or until tender (do not overcook). Drain and set aside.

Cook frozen mixed vegetables according to package directions, omitting salt and fat; drain and set aside.

Combine mayonnaise and next 3 ingredients in a large bowl. Gently stir in potato, vegetables, and ham. Cover and chill at least 8 hours. **Yield:** 6 servings (serving size: 1½ cups).

Per Serving:

Calories 207	**Fiber** 4.4g
Fat 6.1g (sat 1.3g)	**Cholesterol** 30mg
Protein 13.1g	**Sodium** 729mg
Carbohydrate 25.2g	**Exchanges:** 1 Starch, 1 Vegetable, 1 Lean Meat, ½ Fat

Taco Salad Supreme

3   (6-inch) corn tortillas
Cooking spray
½   pound ground turkey
1   cup chopped onion
1   cup frozen whole-kernel corn, thawed
2   tablespoons minced jalapeño pepper
2   teaspoons chili powder
1   (15-ounce) can no-salt-added black beans, rinsed and drained
8   cups thinly sliced romaine lettuce leaves
¼   cup reduced-fat olive oil vinaigrette
1   cup (4 ounces) shredded reduced-fat Cheddar cheese
1   cup chopped seeded tomato (about 1 medium)
¼   cup minced fresh cilantro
2   tablespoons sliced ripe olives
½   cup fat-free sour cream

Preheat oven to 400°.

Coat tortillas with cooking spray; cut into strips. Place on a baking sheet; bake at 400° for 15 minutes.

Coat a nonstick skillet with cooking spray; place over medium heat until hot. Add turkey and next 3 ingredients; cook over medium heat until turkey is done, stirring until it crumbles. Stir in chili powder and beans; cook until thoroughly heated.

Combine lettuce and vinaigrette. Place 1⅓ cups lettuce mixture on each of 6 plates. Spoon turkey mixture over lettuce. Top evenly with cheese and remaining 4 ingredients; serve with tortilla strips. **Yield:** 6 servings (serving size: 1⅓ cups lettuce mixture, ⅙ of turkey mixture, about 2½ tablespoons cheese, 2 tablespoons tomato, 2 teaspoons cilantro, 1 teaspoon olives, about 1½ tablespoons sour cream, and about 6 tortilla strips).

Per Serving:

Calories 274	**Fiber** 5.5g
Fat 8.4g (sat 2.9g)	**Cholesterol** 37mg
Protein 22.1g	**Sodium** 337mg
Carbohydrate 29.5g	**Exchanges:** 2 Starch, 2 Medium-Fat Meat

sandwiches

Veggie Melts

⅔ cup thinly sliced cucumber
½ cup shredded carrot
2 tablespoons sliced green onions
2 tablespoons fat-free Italian dressing
½ cup (2 ounces) shredded part-skim mozzarella cheese
2 English muffins, split and toasted
¼ cup alfalfa sprouts

Preheat broiler.

Combine first 4 ingredients; set aside.

Sprinkle cheese evenly over muffin halves. Broil 1 minute or until cheese melts.

Top muffin halves evenly with cucumber mixture and sprouts. Serve immediately. **Yield:** 2 servings (serving size: 2 muffin halves).

Per Serving:

Calories 274	**Fiber** 3.0g
Fat 6.0g (sat 3.2g)	**Cholesterol** 16mg
Protein 13.1g	**Sodium** 639mg
Carbohydrate 41.9g	**Exchanges:** 2 Starch, 2 Vegetable, 1 Medium-Fat Meat

To add even more fiber to this veggie sandwich, use whole wheat English muffins.

Santa Fe Wraps

¾ cup canned chickpeas (garbanzo beans), rinsed and drained
¼ cup part-skim ricotta cheese
2 tablespoons tub-style light cream cheese, softened
1 tablespoon fresh lime juice
1 garlic clove
½ cup (2 ounces) crumbled feta cheese or queso fresco
¼ cup canned black beans, rinsed and drained
1 tablespoon minced fresh cilantro
½ teaspoon hot sauce
4 (10-inch) fat-free flour tortillas
1⅓ cups thinly sliced curly leaf lettuce
¾ cup shredded peeled jícama
6 tablespoons finely shredded Monterey Jack cheese
3 tablespoons finely diced red onion

Place first 5 ingredients in a food processor or blender; process until smooth. Add feta cheese, black beans, cilantro, and hot sauce; pulse 4 or 5 times or until combined.

Spread 1½ tablespoons bean mixture over each tortilla; top each with ⅓ cup lettuce. Divide jícama, cheese, and onion evenly among tortillas; roll up tortillas. **Yield:** 4 servings (serving size: 1 wrap).

Per Serving:

Calories 333	**Fiber** 6.5g
Fat 10.9g (sat 6.5g)	**Cholesterol** 35mg
Protein 16.0g	**Sodium** 826mg
Carbohydrate 41.9g	**Exchanges:** 2 Starch, 2 Vegetable, 1 High-Fat Meat

Grilled Cheese Sandwiches

⅓ cup light cream cheese, softened
½ teaspoon dried basil
8 (1-ounce) slices white or whole wheat bread
4 (¾-ounce) slices fat-free sharp Cheddar cheese
4 (¾-ounce) slices fat-free mozzarella cheese
1 tablespoon plus 1 teaspoon reduced-calorie margarine,
     softened
Cooking spray

Combine cream cheese and basil, stirring well. Spread cream cheese mixture evenly over 1 side of each of 4 bread slices. Place Cheddar and mozzarella cheese slices over cream cheese mixture; top with remaining bread slices.

Spread margarine evenly over both sides of sandwiches. Place in a sandwich press or hot skillet coated with cooking spray. Cook 1 minute on each side or until bread is lightly browned and cheese melts. Serve immediately. **Yield:** 4 servings (serving size: 1 sandwich).

Per Serving:

Calories 283	**Fiber** 1.1g
Fat 8.4g (sat 3.4g)	**Cholesterol** 22mg
Protein 17.7g	**Sodium** 898mg
Carbohydrate 33.7g	**Exchanges:** 2 Starch, 2 Very Lean Meat, 1 Fat

For a quick and easy supper, serve Grilled Cheese Sandwiches with Minestrone (page 297).

Garden Tuna Sandwiches

1   (6-ounce) can tuna in water, drained
¼   cup light mayonnaise
2   tablespoons finely chopped celery
2   tablespoons finely chopped onion
½   tablespoon chopped fresh dill
½   tablespoon Dijon mustard
¼   teaspoon grated lemon rind
⅛   teaspoon pepper
8   (1-ounce) slices whole wheat bread
2   (¾-ounce) slices fat-free Swiss cheese, halved diagonally
¼   cup shredded carrot
16   thin slices cucumber (about 1 cucumber)
4   green leaf lettuce leaves

Combine first 8 ingredients in a medium bowl, stirring well.

Spread ¼ cup tuna mixture on each of 4 slices of bread. Top evenly with cheese slices, carrot, cucumber, and lettuce. Top with remaining bread slices, and cut in half. **Yield:** 4 servings (serving size: 2 halves).

Per Serving:

Calories 269	**Fiber** 7.9g
Fat 9.5g (sat 1.3g)	**Cholesterol** 25mg
Protein 22.4g	**Sodium** 718mg
Carbohydrate 25.8g	**Exchanges:** 1 Starch, 2 Vegetable, 2 Very Lean Meat, 1 Fat

Eating tuna once or twice a week poses no health risk for healthy adults. However, avoid eating it more frequently because tuna—both canned and fresh—contains high levels of mercury that can cause chronic fatigue and memory loss in adults. Mercury can also harm an unborn child's developing nervous system. If you are pregnant, considering pregnancy, or nursing, it's best to avoid tuna.

ready in **10** minutes

Turkey-Avocado Sandwiches

¼ cup fat-free cream cheese
1 tablespoon shredded fresh basil
1½ tablespoons lemon juice
2 teaspoons chopped fresh oregano
½ teaspoon coarsely ground black pepper
½ teaspoon minced garlic
4 (¾-ounce) slices reduced-calorie whole wheat bread, toasted
6 ounces cooked turkey breast, sliced
½ medium avocado, thinly sliced
1 medium tomato, sliced
½ cup shredded lettuce
¼ cup alfalfa sprouts

Combine first 6 ingredients in a small bowl, stirring well. Spread cheese mixture evenly on 2 bread slices. Top evenly with sliced turkey and remaining 4 ingredients. Top with remaining 2 bread slices. **Yield:** 2 servings (serving size: 1 sandwich).

Per Serving:

Calories 310	**Fiber** 7.5g
Fat 9.9g (sat 1.1g)	**Cholesterol** 73mg
Protein 37.0g	**Sodium** 402mg
Carbohydrate 28.7g	**Exchanges:** 2 Starch, 4 Very Lean Meat, 1 Fat

Avocados are a great source of monounsaturated fat—a type of fat that appears to help prevent heart disease.

ready in **10** minutes

Club Sandwiches

¼ cup fat-free Thousand Island dressing
8 (1-ounce) slices whole wheat bread, toasted
4 green leaf lettuce leaves
8 slices tomato (about 2 medium)
4 ounces thinly sliced cooked turkey breast
4 (¾-ounce) slices fat-free sharp Cheddar cheese
4 turkey-bacon slices, cooked and cut in half

Spread 1 tablespoon dressing over 1 side of each of 4 bread slices. Arrange lettuce and remaining 4 ingredients evenly on slices; top with remaining bread slices.

To serve, cut each sandwich into 4 triangles. Secure triangles with wooden picks. **Yield:** 4 servings (serving size: 4 triangles).

Per Serving:

Calories 282	**Fiber** 3.3g
Fat 4.8g (sat 1.1g)	**Cholesterol** 34mg
Protein 21.9g	**Sodium** 982mg
Carbohydrate 38.2g	**Exchanges:** 2 Starch, 1 Vegetable, 2 Lean Meat

Asian Chicken Pitas

2   (4-ounce) skinless, boneless chicken breast halves
½   cup bean sprouts
¼   cup diced water chestnuts
¼   cup sliced green onions
1   tablespoon rice vinegar
1   tablespoon low-sodium soy sauce
1   teaspoon sesame oil
1   (7-inch) whole wheat pita bread round, cut in half crosswise
2   lettuce leaves

Place chicken in a medium saucepan; add water to cover. Bring to a boil. Reduce heat to medium, and cook, uncovered, 15 minutes or until chicken is done. Drain. Let chicken cool to touch. Chop chicken into bite-size pieces.

Combine chicken, bean sprouts, water chestnuts, and green onions. Combine vinegar, soy sauce, and oil; pour over chicken mixture, tossing gently.

Line each pita half with a lettuce leaf; spoon chicken mixture evenly into pita halves. **Yield:** 2 servings (serving size: 1 pita half).

Per Serving:

Calories 271	**Fiber** 3.4g
Fat 5.9g (sat 1.2g)	**Cholesterol** 70mg
Protein 28.2g	**Sodium** 264mg
Carbohydrate 22.4g	**Exchanges:** 1½ Starch, 3½ Very Lean Meat

Turkey-Roasted Pepper Sandwiches

2	tablespoons fat-free cream cheese, softened
1	tablespoon light mayonnaise
1	tablespoon spicy brown mustard
⅛	teaspoon black pepper
¼	cup chopped bottled roasted red bell peppers
2	tablespoons sliced green onions
8	(1-ounce) slices pumpernickel bread
¾	pound thinly sliced smoked turkey breast
¼	cup alfalfa sprouts
4	leaf lettuce leaves

Combine first 4 ingredients, stirring until smooth. Stir in red bell peppers and green onions.

Spread 1 side of bread slices evenly with cream cheese mixture. Top 4 bread slices evenly with turkey, alfalfa sprouts, and lettuce leaves. Top with remaining bread slices. **Yield:** 4 servings (serving size: 1 sandwich).

Per Serving:

Calories 296	**Fiber** 4.1g
Fat 3.0g (sat 0.6g)	**Cholesterol** 74mg
Protein 32.9g	**Sodium** 596mg
Carbohydrate 34.9g	**Exchanges:** 2 Starch, 1 Vegetable, 3 Very Lean Meat

Turkey Reubens

1½ cups finely shredded cabbage
1½ tablespoons fat-free Thousand Island dressing
1 tablespoon light mayonnaise
1 tablespoon Dijon mustard
12 (1-ounce) slices rye bread
6 ounces thinly sliced cooked turkey breast
6 (¾-ounce) slices reduced-fat Swiss cheese
Butter-flavored cooking spray

Combine first 3 ingredients in a medium bowl; toss well, and set aside.

Spread mustard evenly over 6 bread slices, and top with turkey. Top each with 1 cheese slice and ¼ cup cabbage mixture. Top with remaining bread slices.

Spray both sides of each sandwich with cooking spray; place on a hot griddle or skillet coated with cooking spray. Cook 2 minutes on each side or until bread is lightly browned and cheese melts. Serve immediately. **Yield:** 6 servings (serving size: 1 sandwich).

Per Serving:

Calories 274	**Fiber** 3.9g
Fat 7.1g (sat 2.7g)	**Cholesterol** 34mg
Protein 21.0g	**Sodium** 497mg
Carbohydrate 32.4g	**Exchanges:** 2 Starch, 1 Vegetable, 2 Lean Meat

make-ahead

Mexican Turkey Salad Pockets

1¾ cups shredded iceberg lettuce
⅔ cup chopped tomato
½ cup no-salt-added canned whole-kernel corn, drained
½ cup low-sodium canned kidney beans, drained
¼ cup chopped red onion
¾ pound thinly sliced reduced-fat smoked turkey breast,
    cut into strips
⅓ cup reduced-fat sour cream
1 tablespoon chopped fresh cilantro
1½ tablespoons fat-free milk
2 teaspoons 40%-less-salt taco seasoning
4 (6½-inch) whole wheat pita bread rounds, halved

Combine first 6 ingredients in a medium bowl. Combine sour cream and next 3 ingredients, stirring well. Spoon sour cream mixture over turkey mixture; toss gently. Cover and chill.

Divide mixture evenly among pita halves. **Yield:** 4 servings (serving size: 2 pita halves).

Per Serving:

Calories 338	**Fiber** 8.2g
Fat 5.5g (sat 1.9g)	**Cholesterol** 35mg
Protein 23.9g	**Sodium** 1,343mg
Carbohydrate 53.2g	**Exchanges:** 3 Starch, 2 Vegetable, 1 Medium-Fat Meat

The sodium is high for this sandwich because of the smoked turkey. If you are on a low-sodium diet, use fresh cooked turkey breast instead of smoked.

Roast Beef Wraps

⅓   cup light cream cheese
1½ tablespoons horseradish mustard
2   tablespoons finely chopped green onions
4   (8-inch) flour tortillas
1   (7-ounce) bottle roasted red bell peppers, drained
      and chopped
½   pound lean roast beef, very thinly sliced
4   romaine lettuce leaves

Combine first 3 ingredients; spread evenly over tortillas. Sprinkle red bell pepper over cheese mixture. Top evenly with roast beef and lettuce.

Roll up tightly, cut each roll in half, and wrap in parchment paper or plastic wrap. Refrigerate. **Yield:** 4 servings (serving size: 2 halves).

Per Serving:

Calories 259	**Fiber** 1.6g
Fat 8.2g (sat 4.5g)	**Cholesterol** 50mg
Protein 18.0g	**Sodium** 778mg
Carbohydrate 28.2g	**Exchanges:** 2 Starch, 2 Medium-Fat Meat

Ham, Spinach, and Pear Sandwiches

3 tablespoons coarse-grained mustard
1 tablespoon sugar-free maple syrup
12 (1-ounce) slices pumpernickel bread
¾ pound thinly sliced reduced-fat, low-salt ham
1 medium pear, cored and thinly sliced
2 ounces fresh spinach leaves

Combine mustard and syrup; spread evenly on 1 side of each slice of bread. Arrange ham, pear, and spinach evenly over 6 slices of bread. Top with remaining bread slices. Cut each sandwich in half. **Yield:** 6 servings (serving size: 2 halves).

Per Serving:

Calories 243	**Fiber** 4.9g
Fat 5.2g (sat 1.2g)	**Cholesterol** 28mg
Protein 16.0g	**Sodium** 903mg
Carbohydrate 34.5g	**Exchanges:** 2 Starch, 1 Vegetable, 1 Medium-Fat Meat

Spinach, like other dark, leafy greens, is abundant in disease-fighting beta carotene and folic acid. And while it's also high in iron, the form of iron is not as well absorbed as that found in meats.

Tangy Grouper Sandwiches

2	tablespoons lemon juice
1	teaspoon low-sodium Worcestershire sauce
1	teaspoon olive oil
½	teaspoon pepper
⅛	teaspoon paprika
3	tablespoons fat-free mayonnaise
1	tablespoon minced onion
2	teaspoons dill pickle relish
½	teaspoon prepared mustard
1	(1-pound) grouper fillet, cut into 4 pieces

Cooking spray

4	green leaf lettuce leaves
12	(¼-inch-thick) slices plum tomato
4	hamburger buns, split and toasted

Prepare grill.

Combine first 5 ingredients; set aside. Combine mayonnaise and next 3 ingredients; set aside.

Place fish on a grill rack coated with cooking spray; grill, covered, 5 minutes on each side or until fish flakes easily when tested with a fork, basting with lemon juice mixture.

Layer 1 lettuce leaf, 3 slices tomato, and 1 piece fish on bottom half of each bun. Spoon mayonnaise mixture evenly onto fish, and cover with top halves of buns. Serve immediately. **Yield:** 4 servings (serving size: 1 sandwich).

Per Serving:

Calories 243	**Fiber** 1.0g
Fat 5.3g (sat 0.8g)	**Cholesterol** 52mg
Protein 25.0g	**Sodium** 338mg
Carbohydrate 22.6g	**Exchanges:** 1½ Starch, 3 Very Lean Meat

Sausage-Pepper Buns

Cooking spray
1   (14-ounce) package fat-free smoked turkey sausage, sliced
1   teaspoon reduced-calorie margarine
2   medium-size green bell peppers, seeded and sliced
1   large onion, sliced
1   teaspoon salt-free Greek seasoning
6   whole wheat hot dog buns

Coat a large nonstick skillet with cooking spray, and place over medium-high heat until hot. Add sausage, and cook 5 minutes or until browned, stirring often. Remove from pan, and set aside. Wipe pan dry with a paper towel.

Coat pan with cooking spray, and add margarine. Place over medium-high heat until margarine melts. Add green bell pepper and onion; sauté 8 minutes or until vegetables are tender. Return sausage to pan; sprinkle Greek seasoning over sausage. Cook 1 minute or until thoroughly heated, stirring occasionally.

Spoon sausage mixture evenly into buns, and serve warm. **Yield:** 6 servings (serving size: 1 bun).

Per Serving:

Calories 249	**Fiber** 1.8g
Fat 4.5g (sat 0.7g)	**Cholesterol** 44mg
Protein 14.8g	**Sodium** 931mg
Carbohydrate 37.0g	**Exchanges:** 2 Starch, 1 Vegetable, 1 Medium-Fat Meat

Sloppy Joes

1½ pounds ground round
1   cup chopped onion
½   cup chopped green bell pepper
1   cup ketchup
1   (8-ounce) can no-salt-added tomato sauce
1½ tablespoons low-sodium Worcestershire sauce
1½ tablespoons lemon juice
1½ tablespoons prepared mustard
2   teaspoons "measures-like-sugar" calorie-free sweetener
¼   teaspoon garlic powder
¼   teaspoon black pepper
8   hamburger buns

Cook meat, onion, and green bell pepper in a large nonstick skillet over medium-high heat until meat is browned, stirring until it crumbles. Drain, if necessary.

Add ketchup and next 7 ingredients; stir well. Cook, uncovered, over medium heat 10 minutes or until thoroughly heated and slightly thickened, stirring frequently.

Spoon meat mixture evenly over bottom halves of buns. Top with remaining bun halves. **Yield:** 8 servings (serving size: 1 sandwich).

Per Serving:

Calories 306	**Fiber** 2.0g
Fat 7.8g (sat 2.5g)	**Cholesterol** 54mg
Protein 23.5g	**Sodium** 694mg
Carbohydrate 35.3g	**Exchanges:** 2 Starch, 1 Vegetable, 2 Medium-Fat Meat

Fiesta Burgers

1⅓ cups chopped seeded tomato
¼   cup finely chopped onion
¼   cup taco sauce
1   (4.5-ounce) can chopped green chiles, drained
2   pounds ground round
2   tablespoons low-sodium Worcestershire sauce
½   teaspoon ground cumin
¼   teaspoon onion powder
¼   teaspoon garlic powder
8   green leaf lettuce leaves
8   reduced-calorie hamburger buns, split and toasted

Combine first 4 ingredients; cover and chill 30 minutes.

Preheat broiler.

Combine meat and next 4 ingredients; divide mixture into 8 equal portions, shaping each into a 4-inch patty. Broil 4 minutes on each side or until done.

Place a lettuce leaf on bottom half of each bun; top each with a patty. Top evenly with tomato mixture, and cover with bun tops. **Yield:** 8 servings (serving size: 1 sandwich).

Per Serving:

Calories 266	**Fiber** 2.6g
Fat 8.0g (sat 2.5g)	**Cholesterol** 70mg
Protein 26.8g	**Sodium** 423mg
Carbohydrate 19.7g	**Exchanges:** 1 Starch, 1 Vegetable, 3 Lean Meat

Taco Burgers

¾   pound ground round
½   cup salsa, divided
Cooking spray
½   cup canned fat-free refried beans
4   reduced-calorie whole wheat hamburger buns
1   cup shredded lettuce
½   cup chopped tomato
½   cup (2 ounces) shredded reduced-fat sharp Cheddar cheese

Combine meat and ¼ cup salsa. Shape meat mixture into 4 (½-inch-thick) patties. Coat a nonstick skillet with cooking spray. Place over medium heat until hot. Add patties, and cook 4 to 5 minutes on each side or until done. Remove from pan; drain on paper towels.

Spread 2 tablespoons refried beans on bottom half of each bun. Top each with ¼ cup shredded lettuce, 2 tablespoons chopped tomato, and 2 tablespoons shredded cheese. Top each with a meat patty. Spoon remaining ¼ cup salsa evenly over patties. Top with remaining bun halves. **Yield:** 4 servings (serving size: 1 sandwich).

Per Serving:

Calories 296	**Fiber** 3.4g
Fat 9.6g (sat 3.4g)	**Cholesterol** 62mg
Protein 26.2g	**Sodium** 567mg
Carbohydrate 24.1g	**Exchanges:** 1½ Starch, 3 Lean Meat

This sandwich tastes like a taco but looks like a hamburger. And you can have it on the table in less time than it takes to go to a fast-food drive-through.

Italian Meatball Sandwich

6   (2-ounce) whole wheat submarine loaves
1   pound ground round
¼   cup finely chopped onion
3   tablespoons Italian-seasoned breadcrumbs
2   tablespoons water
¼   teaspoon pepper
1   large egg white, lightly beaten
1½ cups low-fat, reduced-sodium pasta sauce
¾   cup (3 ounces) shredded part-skim mozzarella cheese

Cut an oval piece out of top of each loaf. Reserve oval pieces for another use.

Combine meat and next 5 ingredients. Shape into 36 (1-inch) balls. Cook meatballs in a large nonstick skillet over medium heat 8 to 10 minutes or until browned on all sides. Remove from heat, and pat dry.

Preheat oven to 400°.

Return meatballs to pan; add pasta sauce. Cook over medium-low heat 10 minutes or until thoroughly heated.

Place loaves on a baking sheet; top each with 6 meatballs. Spoon sauce evenly over meatballs. Sprinkle evenly with cheese. Bake at 400° for 5 minutes or until cheese melts. **Yield:** 6 servings (serving size: 1 sandwich).

Per Serving:

Calories 269	**Fiber** 1.2g
Fat 7.6g (sat 2.4g)	**Cholesterol** 60mg
Protein 25.8g	**Sodium** 621mg
Carbohydrate 23.4g	**Exchanges:** 1½ Starch, 3 Lean Meat

Stromboli

Cooking spray
½   cup chopped onion
1   (13.8-ounce) can refrigerated pizza crust dough
2   tablespoons coarse-grained mustard
1   cup (4 ounces) shredded part-skim mozzarella cheese
6   ounces thinly sliced reduced-fat, low-salt ham
1   teaspoon dried Italian seasoning

Preheat oven to 425°.

Coat a small nonstick skillet with cooking spray; place over medium-high heat until hot. Add onion; sauté 5 minutes or until tender.

Unroll dough on a baking sheet coated with cooking spray; press into a 12- x 8-inch rectangle. Spread mustard over dough to within ½ inch of edges. Arrange cheese, onion, and ham lengthwise down the center of dough, leaving a ½-inch border at both ends. Sprinkle seasoning over ham. At 1-inch intervals on long sides of rectangle, cut slits from edge of ham to edge of dough. Alternating sides, fold strips at an angle across filling. Coat top of dough with cooking spray. Bake at 425° for 12 minutes or until browned. To serve, cut rectangle crosswise into 5 equal pieces. **Yield:** 5 servings (serving size: 1 piece).

Per Serving:

Calories 326	**Fiber** 1.6g
Fat 8.7g (sat 3.2g)	**Cholesterol** 27mg
Protein 19.3g	**Sodium** 1,005mg
Carbohydrate 41.9g	**Exchanges:** 3 Starch, 1½ Medium-Fat Meat

Lamb Pockets
with Cucumber Topping

1	cup grated cucumber
½	cup plain low-fat yogurt
¼	teaspoon seasoned salt
¼	teaspoon dried dillweed
1	pound ground lamb or ground round
¼	cup chopped onion
1	garlic clove, minced
¼	teaspoon salt
¼	teaspoon pepper
¾	cup chopped tomato
¼	cup sliced green onions
4	(6-inch) whole wheat pita bread rounds, cut in half crosswise
8	green leaf lettuce leaves

Press cucumber between layers of paper towels to remove excess moisture. Combine cucumber, yogurt, seasoned salt, and dillweed; cover and chill.

Cook meat, chopped onion, and garlic in a large nonstick skillet over medium-high heat until meat is browned, stirring until it crumbles. Drain, if necessary. Stir in ¼ teaspoon salt and pepper.

Combine tomato and green onions. Line each pita half with a lettuce leaf; top evenly with meat mixture, cucumber mixture, and tomato mixture. **Yield:** 8 servings (serving size: 1 pita half).

Per Serving:

Calories 195	**Fiber** 1.3g
Fat 4.9g (sat 1.7g)	**Cholesterol** 41mg
Protein 16.8g	**Sodium** 346mg
Carbohydrate 20.0g	**Exchanges:** 1 Starch, 1 Vegetable, 2 Lean Meat

Barbecue Pork Sandwiches

2   (½-pound) pork tenderloins
1   teaspoon vegetable oil
½   cup no-salt-added tomato sauce
1½ tablespoons "measures-like-sugar" calorie-free sweetener
2   tablespoons water
2   tablespoons cider vinegar
2   tablespoons low-sodium Worcestershire sauce
¼   teaspoon garlic powder
¼   teaspoon dry mustard
Dash of hot sauce
4   reduced-calorie whole wheat hamburger buns

Cut pork into slices; flatten, using a meat mallet or rolling pin.

Heat oil in a large nonstick skillet over medium-high heat. Add pork, and cook 3 minutes on each side or until browned. Drain and coarsely chop. Wipe drippings from pan; add tomato sauce and next 7 ingredients. Bring to a boil; add pork. Cover, reduce heat, and simmer 20 minutes, stirring often.

Spoon ¾ cup pork mixture onto each bun. **Yield:** 4 servings (serving size: 1 sandwich).

Per Serving:

Calories 230	Fiber 4.5g
Fat 6.1g (sat 1.4g)	Cholesterol 63mg
Protein 27.0g	Sodium 229mg
Carbohydrate 23.9g	Exchanges: 1½ Starch, 3 Lean Meat

Double this recipe if you use it in the Fourth of July menu on page 39. You'll need to brown the pork in two batches.

side dishes

Asparagus with Garlic Cream

1   (8-ounce) carton reduced-fat sour cream
3   tablespoons fat-free milk
1   tablespoon white wine vinegar
⅛   teaspoon salt
⅛   teaspoon freshly ground black pepper
2   garlic cloves, minced
2   pounds fresh asparagus
2   teaspoons chopped fresh chives

Combine first 6 ingredients, stirring well. Cover and chill at least 2 hours.

Snap off tough ends of asparagus; remove scales from stalks with a vegetable peeler, if desired.

Place asparagus in a small amount of boiling water. Cover, reduce heat, and cook 4 minutes or until crisp-tender; drain. Plunge into ice water to stop the cooking process; drain. Cover and chill.

To serve, place asparagus on a serving platter. Top with sauce, and sprinkle with chives. **Yield:** 8 servings (serving size: about 3 ounces asparagus and 2 tablespoons sauce).

Per Serving:

Calories 58	**Fiber** 1.5g
Fat 3.6g (sat 2.2g)	**Cholesterol** 11mg
Protein 2.7g	**Sodium** 51mg
Carbohydrate 5.0g	**Exchanges:** 1 Vegetable, 1 Fat

Drizzle crisp-tender asparagus spears with a garlicky cream sauce and top with a sprinkling of fragrant snipped chives.

Asparagus with Mock Hollandaise Sauce

2   pounds fresh asparagus
2   egg yolks
1   cup water
2   tablespoons cornstarch
½   teaspoon salt
2   tablespoons lemon juice
1   tablespoon margarine
Grated lemon rind (optional)

Snap off tough ends of asparagus; remove scales from stalks with a vegetable peeler, if desired.

Cook asparagus, covered, in a small amount of boiling water 8 to 10 minutes or until tender; drain. Set aside, and keep warm.

Place egg yolks in a small bowl; stir well with a wire whisk.

Combine water, cornstarch, and salt in a small, heavy saucepan. Cook over low heat, stirring constantly, until mixture comes to a boil and begins to thicken. Remove from heat; add 2 tablespoons cornstarch mixture to egg yolks, stirring constantly with a wire whisk. Add egg yolk mixture to remaining cornstarch mixture; cook, stirring constantly, 2 minutes or until temperature reaches 160°. Remove from heat; stir in lemon juice and margarine.

To serve, spoon sauce over asparagus, and sprinkle with lemon rind, if desired. **Yield:** 8 servings (serving size: about 3 ounces asparagus and 2 tablespoons sauce).

Per Serving:

Calories 57	**Fiber** 2.4g
Fat 2.7g (sat 0.7g)	**Cholesterol** 51mg
Protein 3.2g	**Sodium** 169mg
Carbohydrate 6.7g	**Exchanges:** 1 Vegetable, ½ Fat

Oriental Broccoli

1½ pounds broccoli, trimmed and coarsely chopped
3   tablespoons low-sodium soy sauce
2   teaspoons dark sesame oil
1   teaspoon honey
½   teaspoon grated peeled fresh ginger
¼   teaspoon dry mustard
8   small cherry tomatoes, halved
½   cup sliced water chestnuts
2   green onions, diagonally sliced

Arrange broccoli in a vegetable steamer over boiling water. Cover and steam 5 to 8 minutes or until crisp-tender. Drain; transfer to a serving bowl, and keep warm.

Combine soy sauce and next 4 ingredients in a small saucepan; stir well. Bring to a boil over medium heat. Pour over broccoli. Add tomato, water chestnuts, and green onions; toss gently. **Yield:** 6 servings (serving size: 1 cup).

Per Serving:

Calories 56	**Fiber** 3.2g
Fat 1.9g (sat 0.3g)	**Cholesterol** 0mg
Protein 3.1g	**Sodium** 223mg
Carbohydrate 8.2g	**Exchanges:** 2 Vegetable

Broccoli-Cheese Casserole

2   (10-ounce) packages frozen broccoli spears
Butter-flavored cooking spray
1   cup (4 ounces) shredded reduced-fat sharp Cheddar cheese
½   cup egg substitute
½   cup fat-free mayonnaise
½   cup finely chopped onion
1   (10¾-ounce) can condensed reduced-fat, reduced-sodium
       cream of mushroom soup, undiluted
1   (6-ounce) box reduced-sodium chicken-flavored stuffing mix

Preheat oven to 350°.

Cook broccoli according to package directions; drain. Arrange broccoli in an 11- x 7-inch baking dish coated with cooking spray. Sprinkle with cheese. Combine egg substitute and next 3 ingredients; spread over cheese.

Combine ¾ cup stuffing mix and 2½ teaspoons of the mix's seasoning packet, tossing well. Sprinkle over casserole; coat with cooking spray. (Reserve remaining stuffing mix and seasoning packet for another use.)

Bake at 350° for 30 minutes or until thoroughly heated. Serve warm.
Yield: 8 servings (serving size: about 1 cup).

Per Serving:

Calories 134	**Fiber** 1.7g
Fat 4.1g (sat 1.9g)	**Cholesterol** 13mg
Protein 8.9g	**Sodium** 537mg
Carbohydrate 16.1g	**Exchanges:** 1 Starch, 1 Fat

The seasoned stuffing mix makes a crunchy topping for the creamy broccoli mixture.

ready in **30** minutes

French-Style Green Beans

¾   pound fresh green beans, ends trimmed and strings removed
1   tablespoon fat-free margarine
¾   cup low-sodium chicken broth
¼   teaspoon freshly ground black pepper
⅛   teaspoon salt
1½ teaspoons cornstarch
1   tablespoon water
2   teaspoons lemon juice
2   tablespoons sliced almonds, toasted

Slice beans in half lengthwise. Melt margarine in a large skillet. Add beans, and sauté 5 minutes. Add chicken broth, pepper, and salt. Bring to a boil. Cover, reduce heat, and simmer 15 minutes.

Combine cornstarch and water; pour over beans. Cook, tossing gently, 1 minute. Stir in lemon juice. Just before serving, sprinkle with toasted almonds. **Yield:** 4 servings (serving size: ½ cup).

Per Serving:

Calories 49	**Fiber** 2.0g
Fat 1.3g (sat 0.2g)	**Cholesterol** 0mg
Protein 2.4g	**Sodium** 113mg
Carbohydrate 8.1g	**Exchange:** 1 Vegetable

Seasoned Green Beans

1	pound fresh green beans
1¾	cups coarsely chopped seeded peeled tomato (about 2 tomatoes)
⅓	cup less-sodium beef broth
1	teaspoon minced garlic
2	ounces reduced-fat, low-salt ham, diced
2	tablespoons chopped fresh parsley
1	teaspoon dried thyme
¼	teaspoon pepper

Trim stem end from beans. Arrange beans in a steamer basket over boiling water; cover and steam 10 minutes.

Combine tomato and next 3 ingredients in a large saucepan. Cook, uncovered, over medium heat 3 minutes, stirring often. Stir in beans, parsley, thyme, and pepper. Cover and cook over low heat 10 minutes or until beans are tender. **Yield:** 4 servings (serving size: about ⅔ cup).

Per Serving:

Calories 74	Fiber 3.4g
Fat 1.1g (sat 0.3g)	Cholesterol 7mg
Protein 5.4g	Sodium 126mg
Carbohydrate 12.8g	Exchanges: 2 Vegetable

When you season fresh beans with lean ham instead of ham hock, you get all of the flavor but none of the fat.

Lemon-Dill Carrots

8	medium carrots, scraped and diagonally sliced
1	teaspoon cornstarch
1	tablespoon lemon juice
⅓	cup water
1	teaspoon margarine
½	teaspoon dried dillweed
¼	teaspoon grated lemon rind
⅛	teaspoon salt

Arrange carrot in a vegetable steamer over boiling water. Cover; steam 2 to 3 minutes or until crisp-tender. Transfer carrot to a serving bowl, and keep warm.

Combine cornstarch and lemon juice in a small saucepan, stirring until smooth. Add water, and cook over medium heat, stirring constantly, until thickened.

Stir in margarine and next 3 ingredients. Cook, stirring constantly, until margarine melts. Pour lemon juice mixture over carrot, and toss gently. **Yield:** 8 servings (serving size: ½ cup).

Per Serving:

Calories 41	**Fiber** 2.6g
Fat 0.6g (sat 0.1g)	**Cholesterol** 0mg
Protein 0.9g	**Sodium** 71mg
Carbohydrate 8.8g	**Exchange:** 1 Vegetable

Orange-Glazed Carrots

1   pound carrots, scraped and cut into ¼-inch-thick slices
¾   cup fat-free, less-sodium chicken broth
2   tablespoons frozen orange juice concentrate
2   teaspoons "measures-like-sugar" calorie-free sweetener
¼   teaspoon ground ginger

Combine carrot and broth in a medium saucepan; bring to a boil. Cover, reduce heat, and simmer 10 minutes.

Add orange juice concentrate, sweetener, and ginger to carrot mixture, stirring well. Cook, uncovered, over medium heat 8 minutes or until carrot is tender and liquid is reduced, stirring occasionally.

Serve immediately. **Yield:** 4 servings (serving size: ½ cup).

Per Serving:

Calories 69	**Fiber** 3.3g
Fat 0.2g (sat 0.0g)	**Cholesterol** 0mg
Protein 1.3g	**Sodium** 36mg
Carbohydrate 16.0g	**Exchanges:** ½ Fruit, 2 Vegetable

If your carrots have gone limp, soak them in ice water for 20 to 30 minutes until they are crisp again.

Corn Pudding

¼ cup "measures-like-sugar" calorie-free sweetener
¼ cup all-purpose flour
2 teaspoons baking powder
½ teaspoon salt
2 cups fat-free evaporated milk
1½ cups egg substitute
2 tablespoons margarine, melted
6 cups fresh corn kernels (about 12 ears)
Cooking spray

Preheat oven to 350°.

Combine first 4 ingredients; set aside.

Combine milk, egg substitute, and margarine in a large bowl. Gradually add flour mixture, stirring until smooth. Stir in corn. Pour mixture into a 13- x 9-inch baking dish coated with cooking spray.

Bake, uncovered, at 350° for 40 to 45 minutes or until deep golden and set. Let stand 5 minutes before serving. **Yield:** 16 servings (serving size: ½ cup).

Per Serving:

Calories 122	**Fiber** 2.0g
Fat 2.3g (sat 0.5g)	**Cholesterol** 2mg
Protein 6.9g	**Sodium** 243mg
Carbohydrate 20.4g	**Exchanges:** 1½ Starch, ½ Medium-Fat Meat

If fresh corn is out of season, you can use thawed and drained frozen whole-kernel corn.

Crispy Oven-Fried Okra

1¾ pounds fresh okra
1½ cups yellow cornmeal
½   teaspoon salt
⅛   teaspoon pepper
½   cup nonfat buttermilk
1   large egg, lightly beaten
Cooking spray

Preheat oven to 450°.

Wash okra; trim ends, and cut into ½-inch pieces. Combine cornmeal, salt, and pepper in a medium bowl; stir well, and set aside.

Combine buttermilk and egg in a large bowl; stir in okra. Let stand 10 minutes.

Remove okra with a slotted spoon; discard remaining buttermilk mixture. Combine okra and cornmeal mixture, tossing to coat okra well. Place okra on a baking sheet coated with cooking spray. Bake at 450° for 40 minutes or until crisp, stirring occasionally. **Yield:** 12 servings (serving size: ½ cup).

Per Serving:

Calories 84	**Fiber** 2.1g
Fat 1.1g (sat 0.3g)	**Cholesterol** 19mg
Protein 3.1g	**Sodium** 123mg
Carbohydrate 15.9g	**Exchange:** 1 Starch

Okra-Tomato-Zucchini Medley

1   small zucchini
Cooking spray
1½ cups sliced fresh okra
2   tablespoons chopped onion
1   cup chopped tomato
⅛   teaspoon dried basil
⅛   teaspoon dried thyme
Dash of freshly ground black pepper

Cut zucchini in half lengthwise; cut into ¼-inch-thick slices.

Heat a nonstick skillet coated with cooking spray over medium-high heat. Add zucchini, okra, and onion; sauté 4 minutes. Stir in tomato and remaining ingredients. Cover and cook over low heat 5 minutes or until thoroughly heated, stirring frequently. **Yield:** 4 servings (serving size: ½ cup).

Per Serving:

Calories 31	**Fiber** 1.3g
Fat 0.4g (sat 0.0g)	**Cholesterol** 0mg
Protein 1.5g	**Sodium** 8mg
Carbohydrate 6.3g	**Exchange:** 1 Vegetable

Crispy Onion Rings

2   large sweet onions (about 1¼ pounds)
6   cups whole wheat flake cereal, finely crushed
1   tablespoon chili powder
2   teaspoons "measures-like-sugar" calorie-free sweetener
1   teaspoon ground cumin
¼   teaspoon ground red pepper
1   cup egg substitute
Cooking spray

Preheat oven to 375°.

Cut each onion into 4 thick slices; separate into rings. Reserve small rings for another use. Set large rings aside.

Combine cereal and next 4 ingredients in a shallow bowl. Dip onion rings in egg substitute; dredge in crumb mixture.

Place onion rings in a single layer on baking sheets coated with cooking spray. Bake at 375° for 10 to 15 minutes or until crisp. Serve warm. **Yield:** 6 servings (serving size: about 4 onion rings).

Per Serving:

Calories 159	**Fiber** 3.9g
Fat 1.4g (sat 0.2g)	**Cholesterol** 0mg
Protein 7.8g	**Sodium** 432mg
Carbohydrate 30.9g	**Exchanges:** 2 Starch

Spring Peas

2	(10-ounce) packages frozen English peas
2	teaspoons reduced-calorie margarine
2	teaspoons lemon juice
1½	teaspoons finely chopped fresh thyme or ½ teaspoon dried thyme
¼	teaspoon salt
⅛	teaspoon coarsely ground black pepper

Cook peas according to package directions, omitting salt; drain and transfer to a large bowl.

Add margarine and remaining 4 ingredients, stirring until margarine melts. Serve warm. **Yield:** 6 servings (serving size: ¾ cup).

Per Serving:

Calories 80	**Fiber** 4.3g
Fat 1.2g (sat 0.2g)	**Cholesterol** 0mg
Protein 4.9g	**Sodium** 216mg
Carbohydrate 13.1g	**Exchanges:** 2 Vegetable

These tasty, tender peas are wonderful with Grilled Leg of Lamb (page 161) and Roasted New Potatoes (page 278).

Pretty Pepper Kebabs

1   small yellow bell pepper, seeded and cut into 1-inch pieces
1   small red bell pepper, seeded and cut into 1-inch pieces
1   small green bell pepper, seeded and cut into 1-inch pieces
1   small onion, cut into wedges
Garlic- or olive oil-flavored cooking spray

Soak 8 (6-inch) wooden skewers in water 30 minutes.

Prepare grill.

Alternately thread vegetables onto skewers. Coat each kebab with cooking spray.

Place kebabs on grill rack coated with cooking spray; grill, covered, 10 minutes or until done, turning occasionally. Remove from grill, and serve immediately. **Yield:** 4 servings (serving size: 2 kebabs).

Per Serving:

Calories 52	**Fiber** 2.3g
Fat 1.9g (sat 0.3g)	**Cholesterol** 0mg
Protein 1.3g	**Sodium** 5mg
Carbohydrate 8.6g	**Exchanges:** 2 Vegetable

These colorful vegetable kebabs are great for cookouts. Serve them with chicken, beef, or pork, or over rice for a meatless dish.

Cheesy Squash Casserole

2   pounds yellow squash, sliced
¾   cup chopped onion
1   tablespoon reduced-calorie margarine
2   tablespoons all-purpose flour
1   cup fat-free milk
¾   cup (3 ounces) shredded reduced-fat Cheddar cheese
½   teaspoon salt
¼   teaspoon pepper
Cooking spray
½   cup soft breadcrumbs, toasted

Cook squash and onion in a small amount of boiling water 10 to 12 minutes or until vegetables are tender. Drain; set aside.

Preheat oven to 350°.

Melt margarine in a medium, heavy saucepan over medium heat. Add flour; cook, stirring constantly, 1 minute. Gradually add milk; cook, stirring constantly, until mixture is thickened and bubbly. Remove from heat; add cheese, salt, and pepper, stirring until cheese melts. Add squash mixture; stir well.

Spoon squash mixture into a shallow 1½-quart baking dish coated with cooking spray. Sprinkle squash mixture evenly with breadcrumbs. Bake at 350° for 20 to 25 minutes or until mixture is thoroughly heated. **Yield:** 8 servings (serving size: about ¾ cup).

Per Serving:

Calories 95	**Fiber** 2.2g
Fat 3.4g (sat 1.4g)	**Cholesterol** 8mg
Protein 6.2g	**Sodium** 277mg
Carbohydrate 11.0g	**Exchanges:** 2 Vegetable, ½ Fat

ready in **10** minutes

Simple Sesame Spinach

1   pound fresh spinach
Cooking spray
1   tablespoon sesame seeds, toasted
1   teaspoon lemon juice
¼   teaspoon salt

Wash spinach thoroughly; remove and discard stems from spinach. Tear into bite-size pieces.

Coat a Dutch oven with cooking spray; place over medium heat until hot. Add spinach; cover and cook 3 minutes or until spinach wilts, stirring occasionally. Remove from heat, and stir in sesame seeds, lemon juice, and salt, tossing gently. **Yield:** 4 servings (serving size: ½ cup).

Per Serving:

Calories 46	**Fiber** 4.2g
Fat 2.5g (sat 0.3g)	**Cholesterol** 0mg
Protein 3.9g	**Sodium** 229mg
Carbohydrate 4.0g	**Exchanges:** 1 Vegetable, ½ Fat

To toast sesame seeds, place them in a hot nonstick skillet over medium-high heat (no oil), and cook for 3 to 4 minutes, stirring constantly. Don't cook them much longer, or they'll burn.

Chili-Fried Potatoes

3   cups cubed unpeeled baking potato (about 1 pound)
½   teaspoon olive oil
Olive oil-flavored cooking spray
1   small onion, halved, thinly sliced, and separated into rings
1   teaspoon chili powder
¼   teaspoon salt
½   cup (2 ounces) shredded reduced-fat sharp Cheddar cheese

Arrange potato in a steamer basket over boiling water. Cover and steam 10 minutes or until tender. Remove from heat.

Heat oil in a large nonstick skillet coated with cooking spray over medium-high heat. Add onion; sauté 3 minutes or until tender. Add potato, chili powder, and salt. Cook 5 minutes or until potato is lightly browned, stirring often. Sprinkle cheese over potato. Cover, remove from heat, and let stand 1 minute or until cheese melts.
Yield: 4 servings (serving size: ¾ cup).

Per Serving:

Calories 152	**Fiber** 2.6g
Fat 3.7g (sat 1.7g)	**Cholesterol** 10mg
Protein 6.9g	**Sodium** 263mg
Carbohydrate 23.8g	**Exchanges:** 1½ Starch, 1 Fat

Roasted-Garlic Mashed Potatoes

2   garlic heads
1   teaspoon olive oil
2   pounds baking potatoes, peeled and cut into 1-inch pieces
⅓   cup fat-free milk
1½   tablespoons reduced-calorie margarine
½   teaspoon salt
¼   teaspoon pepper

Preheat oven to 425°.

Remove papery husks from garlic. Place garlic on a square of aluminum foil; drizzle with oil, and wrap in foil. Bake at 425° for 30 minutes; set aside.

Place potato in a medium saucepan; add water to cover. Bring to a boil; reduce heat. Cook, uncovered, 15 to 20 minutes or until tender; drain. Mash potato with a potato masher. Add milk and remaining 3 ingredients; mash until fluffy.

Cut off ends of garlic; squeeze pulp from cloves into potato mixture, and stir. **Yield:** 8 servings (serving size: ½ cup).

Per Serving:

Calories 120	**Fiber** 1.6g
Fat 2.1g (sat 0.3g)	**Cholesterol** 0mg
Protein 2.9g	**Sodium** 180mg
Carbohydrate 23.5g	**Exchanges:** 1½ Starch

Roasted New Potatoes

24 small round red potatoes (about 2⅓ pounds)
Olive oil-flavored cooking spray
¼ cup Italian-seasoned breadcrumbs
¼ cup grated fresh Parmesan cheese
¾ teaspoon paprika

Place potatoes in a Dutch oven; add water to cover. Bring to a boil; reduce heat, and cook, uncovered, 15 minutes or until tender; drain and cool slightly.

Preheat oven to 450°.

Quarter potatoes; coat with cooking spray. Combine breadcrumbs, cheese, and paprika; sprinkle over potatoes, tossing to coat well. Arrange in a single layer on a baking sheet coated with cooking spray. Bake at 450° for 20 to 25 minutes or until coating is crispy. **Yield:** 8 servings (serving size: 12 potato quarters).

Per Serving:

Calories 117	**Fiber** 2.4g
Fat 1.3g (sat 0.7g)	**Cholesterol** 2mg
Protein 4.3g	**Sodium** 91mg
Carbohydrate 22.8g	**Exchanges:** 1½ Starch

Enjoy these crispy Parmesan cheese-coated potatoes instead of high-fat French fries.

New Potatoes with Chives

1   pound round red potatoes, quartered
1   teaspoon olive oil
1   tablespoon chopped fresh chives or 1 teaspoon freeze-dried
      chives
¼   teaspoon salt
⅛   teaspoon pepper

Arrange potato in a steamer basket over boiling water. Cover and steam 17 minutes or until tender.

Place potato in a large bowl. Drizzle with olive oil, and sprinkle with chives, salt, and pepper. Toss well, and serve immediately. **Yield:** 4 servings (serving size: about 10 potato quarters).

Per Serving:

Calories 94	**Fiber** 2.1g
Fat 1.2g (sat 0.2g)	**Cholesterol** 0mg
Protein 2.5g	**Sodium** 154mg
Carbohydrate 18.9g	**Exchange:** 1 Starch

Double this recipe for the Springtime Celebration menu on page 39.

Orange Sweet Potatoes

3   medium sweet potatoes (about 2 pounds)
⅔   cup orange juice
1   tablespoon reduced-calorie margarine, melted
¼   teaspoon ground cinnamon

Preheat oven to 400°.

Peel sweet potatoes, and cut lengthwise into ¼-inch-thick slices. Arrange potato slices in a single layer in a 13- x 9-inch baking dish.

Combine orange juice, margarine, and cinnamon in a small bowl, stirring well. Pour over sweet potato slices. Bake, uncovered, at 400° for 30 minutes or until tender, turning once. **Yield:** 8 servings (serving size: about 4 slices).

Per Serving:

Calories 129	**Fiber** 3.3g
Fat 1.2g (sat 0.2g)	**Cholesterol** 0mg
Protein 1.9g	**Sodium** 28mg
Carbohydrate 28.3g	**Exchanges:** 1 Starch, 1 Fruit

Sweet potatoes are rich in beta carotene, vitamin C, and vitamin E—nutrients that can help prevent heart disease and certain cancers.

Sausage-Corn Bread Dressing

2   (7.5-ounce) packages corn muffin mix
1   cup fat-free milk
Cooking spray
1   pound turkey breakfast sausage
2   cups chopped onion (about 2 medium)
1¾ cups chopped celery (about 5 stalks)
3   cups white bread cubes, toasted
2   teaspoons rubbed sage
1   teaspoon pepper
4   cups fat-free, less-sodium chicken broth
½   cup egg substitute

Preheat oven to 400°.

Prepare muffin mix according to package directions for corn bread, using fat-free milk. Let cool; crumble and set aside.

Coat a large nonstick skillet with cooking spray. Place over medium heat until hot. Add sausage, onion, and celery; cook until sausage is browned and vegetables are tender, stirring until sausage crumbles. Drain and pat dry with paper towels.

Combine corn bread, bread cubes, sage, and pepper in a large bowl; stir in sausage mixture. Add chicken broth and egg substitute, stirring well. Spoon mixture into a 13- x 9-inch baking dish coated with cooking spray. Reduce oven temperature to 350°, and bake, uncovered, for 1 hour or until browned. Serve warm. **Yield:** 12 servings (serving size: ¾ cup).

Per Serving:

Calories 143	**Fiber** 1.2g
Fat 5.3g (sat 3.0g)	**Cholesterol** 24mg
Protein 9.6g	**Sodium** 501mg
Carbohydrate 13.8g	**Exchanges:** 1 Starch, 1 Medium-Fat Meat

Look for packages of corn muffin mix (such as Martha White) that are prepared with only milk or water.

ready in **20** minutes

Zippy Garlic-Cheese Grits

4   cups water
½   cup fat-free milk
1   cup uncooked quick-cooking grits
2   teaspoons low-sodium Worcestershire sauce
1   teaspoon minced garlic
¼   teaspoon salt
¼   teaspoon hot sauce
1½   cups (6 ounces) shredded reduced-fat Cheddar cheese

Combine water and milk in a medium saucepan; bring to a boil.
Stir in grits and next 4 ingredients. Cover, reduce heat, and simmer
5 to 7 minutes or until creamy, stirring occasionally.

Stir in cheese. Cook, uncovered, over medium heat until cheese
melts and grits are thickened, stirring often. **Yield:** 10 servings
(serving size: ½ cup).

Per Serving:

Calories 111	**Fiber** 0.8g
Fat 3.3g (sat 1.9g)	**Cholesterol** 11mg
Protein 6.9g	**Sodium** 196mg
Carbohydrate 13.4g	**Exchanges:** 1 Starch, ½ Medium-Fat Meat

Brown Rice Pilaf

2   cups fat-free, less-sodium chicken broth
1   cup uncooked brown rice
½   cup shredded carrot
½   cup finely chopped celery
½   teaspoon salt
¼   teaspoon ground red pepper
1   garlic clove, minced
¼   cup thinly sliced green onions
3   tablespoons slivered almonds, toasted

Bring broth to a boil in a heavy saucepan; stir in rice and next 5 ingredients.

Cover, reduce heat, and simmer 50 to 55 minutes or until rice is tender and liquid is absorbed. Stir in green onions and almonds.
Yield: 8 servings (serving size: ½ cup).

Per Serving:

Calories 117	**Fiber** 1.6g
Fat 2.6g (sat 0.3g)	**Cholesterol** 0mg
Protein 2.8g	**Sodium** 159mg
Carbohydrate 20.2g	**Exchanges:** 1 Starch, 1 Vegetable, ½ Fat

Brown rice has twice the fiber of white rice. Increasing the fiber in your diet may help control blood sugar.

Southwestern Rice

2   cups fat-free, less-sodium chicken broth
1   cup uncooked long-grain rice
1¼   teaspoons ground cumin
¼   cup thinly sliced green onions

Bring broth to a boil in a large saucepan; add rice and cumin. Return to a boil; cover, reduce heat, and simmer 25 minutes or until rice is tender and liquid is absorbed.

Add green onions; toss gently. **Yield:** 6 servings (serving size: ½ cup).

Per Serving:

Calories 122	**Fiber** 0.5g
Fat 0.3g (sat 0.1g)	**Cholesterol** 0mg
Protein 2.5g	**Sodium** 244mg
Carbohydrate 25.7g	**Exchanges:** 1½ Starch

Serve this spiced rice dish with Chicken Enchiladas (page 174).

Spicy Mexican Rice

1½ teaspoons vegetable oil
Cooking spray
1   cup uncooked long-grain rice
1   cup chopped onion
2   cups water
2   cups chopped tomato
⅔   cup chopped green bell pepper
2   teaspoons beef-flavored bouillon granules
1   teaspoon chili powder
½   teaspoon garlic powder
½   teaspoon ground red pepper
Fresh cilantro sprigs (optional)

Heat oil in a large saucepan coated with cooking spray over medium heat. Add rice and onion; cook 3 minutes, stirring occasionally. Add water and next 6 ingredients; bring to a boil. Cover, reduce heat, and simmer 25 minutes or until liquid is absorbed and rice is tender.

Transfer to a bowl; garnish with cilantro sprigs, if desired. **Yield:** 10 servings (serving size: ½ cup).

Per Serving:

Calories 93	**Fiber** 1.2g
Fat 1.3g (sat 0.3g)	**Cholesterol** 0mg
Protein 2.0g	**Sodium** 197mg
Carbohydrate 18.6g	**Exchange:** 1 Starch

Macaroni and Cheese

1   (8-ounce) package elbow macaroni
2   tablespoons reduced-calorie margarine
2   tablespoons all-purpose flour
2   cups fat-free milk
1½ cups (6 ounces) shredded reduced-fat sharp Cheddar cheese
½   teaspoon salt
3   tablespoons egg substitute
Cooking spray
¼   teaspoon paprika

Preheat oven to 350°.

Cook pasta according to package directions, omitting salt and fat.

Melt margarine in a heavy saucepan over low heat; add flour, stirring until smooth. Cook, stirring constantly, 1 minute. Gradually add milk; cook over medium heat, stirring constantly, until thickened and bubbly. Add cheese and salt, stirring until cheese melts. Gradually stir about one-fourth cheese mixture into egg substitute. Add egg substitute mixture to remaining cheese mixture, stirring constantly.

Combine cheese sauce and pasta; pour into a 2-quart baking dish coated with cooking spray. Sprinkle with paprika. Bake at 350° for 25 to 30 minutes or until thoroughly heated. **Yield:** 11 servings (serving size: ½ cup).

Per Serving:

Calories 111	**Fiber** 0.4g
Fat 4.6g (sat 2.0g)	**Cholesterol** 11mg
Protein 7.6g	**Sodium** 268mg
Carbohydrate 9.8g	**Exchanges:** 1 Starch, 1 Fat

Linguine with Red Pepper Sauce

1   teaspoon olive oil
Cooking spray
1½ cups chopped red bell pepper
1   garlic clove, crushed
2   tablespoons chopped fresh basil
2   tablespoons balsamic vinegar
⅛   teaspoon salt
⅛   teaspoon black pepper
6   ounces uncooked linguine
Fresh basil sprigs (optional)

Heat oil in a nonstick skillet coated with cooking spray over medium heat. Add red bell pepper and garlic; cook, uncovered, 30 minutes, stirring occasionally. Set aside, and cool slightly.

Place pepper mixture in a blender; add chopped basil and next 3 ingredients. Process until smooth, stopping once to scrape down sides.

Cook pasta according to package directions, omitting salt and fat.

To serve, top pasta with pepper sauce. Garnish with basil sprigs, if desired. **Yield:** 6 servings (serving size: ½ cup).

Per Serving:

Calories 117	**Fiber** 1.7g
Fat 1.5g (sat 0.2g)	**Cholesterol** 0mg
Protein 3.7g	**Sodium** 51mg
Carbohydrate 22.2g	**Exchanges:** 1 Starch, 1 Vegetable

Garlic-Lemon Pasta

5   ounces uncooked angel hair pasta
1½ tablespoons reduced-calorie margarine
¼   cup grated Parmesan cheese
2   tablespoons lemon juice
½   teaspoon pepper
2   garlic cloves, crushed

Cook pasta according to package directions, omitting salt and fat.

Melt margarine in a small saucepan over medium heat; stir in Parmesan cheese and remaining 3 ingredients. Pour over pasta; toss gently. **Yield:** 5 servings (serving size: ½ cup).

Per Serving:

Calories 80	**Fiber** 0.5g
Fat 3.6g (sat 1.1g)	**Cholesterol** 3mg
Protein 3.1g	**Sodium** 108mg
Carbohydrate 9.2g	**Exchanges:** 1 Starch, 1 Fat

Pair this lemony pasta side dish with Turkey Parmesan (page 202) and a mixed green salad, or try it with the Valentine's Day Dinner menu on page 38.

Vermicelli with Tomato Basil

8   ounces uncooked vermicelli
Cooking spray
2   garlic cloves, minced
1   onion, thinly sliced
5   cups chopped seeded peeled tomato (about 5 tomatoes)
1   (8-ounce) can no-salt-added tomato sauce
¼   cup minced fresh basil
¼   teaspoon salt
⅛   teaspoon pepper
¼   cup grated fresh Parmesan cheese

Cook pasta according to package directions, omitting salt and fat. Drain.

Coat a Dutch oven with cooking spray; place over medium heat until hot. Add garlic and onion; sauté 5 minutes or until onion is tender. Stir in chopped tomato and next 4 ingredients; bring to a boil. Reduce heat, and simmer, uncovered, 15 minutes, stirring occasionally.

Add cooked pasta to tomato mixture; cook, uncovered, until mixture is thoroughly heated, stirring occasionally. Sprinkle with cheese, and serve immediately. **Yield:** 8 servings (serving size: 1 cup).

Per Serving:

Calories 163	**Fiber** 2.9g
Fat 1.9g (sat 0.6g)	**Cholesterol** 2mg
Protein 6.3g	**Sodium** 147mg
Carbohydrate 29.9g	**Exchanges:** 2 Starch

Tangy Dijon Pasta

4	ounces uncooked angel hair pasta
2	cups fresh snow pea pods
Cooking spray	
½	cup diced red onion
1	(2-ounce) jar sliced pimiento, drained
⅓	cup low-fat sour cream
3	tablespoons dry white wine or low-sodium chicken broth
2	tablespoons Dijon mustard

Cook pasta according to package directions, omitting salt and fat. Drain and set aside.

Wash peas; trim ends, and remove strings. Cook, uncovered, in a small amount of boiling water 3 minutes. Drain; set aside.

Coat a large skillet with cooking spray; place over medium-high heat until hot. Add onion, and sauté 2 to 3 minutes or until tender. Add pasta, snow peas, and pimiento. Combine sour cream, wine, and mustard in a small bowl; stir well using a wire whisk. Add sour cream mixture to pan. Cook, stirring constantly, 2 to 3 minutes or until thoroughly heated. Serve immediately. **Yield:** 7 servings (serving size: ½ cup).

Per Serving:

Calories 102	**Fiber** 1.3g
Fat 2.3g (sat 1.0g)	**Cholesterol** 5mg
Protein 3.4g	**Sodium** 137mg
Carbohydrate 16.5g	**Exchanges:** 1 Starch, ½ Fat

soups

Spicy Pepper Soup

2   cups chopped red bell pepper
2   cups cubed peeled potato
¾   cup chopped red onion
2   cups water
1   (16-ounce) can tomato sauce
½   cup low-sodium chicken broth
¼   cup chopped fresh cilantro
½   teaspoon ground cumin
½   teaspoon ground red pepper
⅛   teaspoon ground cinnamon
7   tablespoons fat-free sour cream

Combine first 4 ingredients in a Dutch oven; bring to a boil. Cover, reduce heat, and simmer 20 minutes or until vegetables are tender.

Add tomato sauce and next 5 ingredients to pan; bring to a boil, stirring occasionally. Reduce heat, and simmer, uncovered, 10 minutes.

Place mixture, in batches, in a blender, and process until smooth. Ladle soup into individual bowls; top each serving with 1 tablespoon sour cream. **Yield:** 7 servings (serving size: 1 cup).

Per Serving:

Calories 106	**Fiber** 2.9g
Fat 0.5g (sat 0.1g)	**Cholesterol** 0mg
Protein 3.5g	**Sodium** 411mg
Carbohydrate 19.1g	**Exchanges:** 1 Starch, 1 Vegetable

Cheddar Potato Soup

1 (32-ounce) carton fat-free, less-sodium chicken broth
5 cups frozen shredded potato
1 cup frozen chopped onion
½ teaspoon salt
½ teaspoon pepper
2 tablespoons all-purpose flour
1 (12-ounce) can fat-free evaporated milk
1 cup (4 ounces) shredded reduced-fat sharp Cheddar cheese
⅓ cup chopped green onions

Combine first 5 ingredients in a Dutch oven; bring to a boil. Reduce heat, and simmer, uncovered, 20 minutes.

Combine flour and milk, stirring until smooth. Add to potato mixture. Cook over medium heat, stirring constantly, 5 minutes or until mixture is thickened.

Pour half of potato mixture into a blender; process until smooth. Pour into a large bowl. Repeat procedure with remaining potato mixture.

Return mixture to pan. Add cheese; cook over medium heat, stirring until cheese melts. Ladle soup into individual bowls; sprinkle evenly with green onions. **Yield:** 7 servings (serving size: 1 cup).

Per Serving:

Calories 158	**Fiber** 1.2g
Fat 3.2g (sat 1.9g)	**Cholesterol** 13mg
Protein 10.6g	**Sodium** 623mg
Carbohydrate 17.3g	**Exchanges:** 1 Starch, 1 Lean Meat

Potato-Corn Chowder

Cooking spray
¾   cup chopped green bell pepper
⅓   cup chopped onion
2¾   cups fat-free, less-sodium chicken broth
2   cups chopped red potato
½   teaspoon salt
¼   teaspoon black pepper
¼   cup cornstarch
2¼   cups fat-free milk
2¼   cups frozen whole-kernel corn
1   (2-ounce) jar diced pimiento, drained

Coat a medium saucepan with cooking spray; place over medium-high heat until hot. Add chopped green bell pepper and onion; sauté 5 minutes or until tender. Stir in broth and next 3 ingredients. Bring to a boil; reduce heat, and simmer, uncovered, 6 to 8 minutes or until potato is tender.

Combine cornstarch and milk, stirring until smooth; gradually add to potato mixture, stirring constantly. Stir in corn and diced pimiento; bring to a boil over medium heat, stirring constantly. Cook, stirring constantly, 1 minute or until mixture is thickened. Serve immediately. **Yield:** 5 servings (serving size: 1½ cups).

Per Serving:

Calories 167
Fat 0.9g (sat 0.2g)
Protein 8.4g
Carbohydrate 33.5g

Fiber 2.6g
Cholesterol 2mg
Sodium 606mg
Exchanges: 2 Starch, 1 Vegetable

French Onion Soup

2   tablespoons reduced-calorie margarine
Cooking spray
6   large onions (about 3 pounds), cut into ¼-inch-thick slices
2   (10½-ounce) cans beef consommé
1   (14-ounce) can less-sodium beef broth
1⅓ cups water
¼   teaspoon pepper
¼   cup dry white wine
8   (1-inch) slices French bread
¼   cup grated Parmesan cheese

Melt margarine in a large Dutch oven coated with cooking spray over medium-high heat. Add onion; sauté 5 minutes. Stir in consommé, broth, water, and pepper; bring to a boil. Reduce heat, and simmer, uncovered, 35 minutes. Add wine, and simmer, uncovered, 5 minutes.

Preheat broiler.

Place bread on a baking sheet; sprinkle with cheese. Broil 2 to 3 minutes or until cheese is golden. Ladle soup evenly into bowls; top each serving with a bread slice. **Yield:** 8 servings (serving size: 1½ cups soup and 1 bread slice).

Per Serving:

Calories 177	**Fiber** 2.8g
Fat 3.6g (sat 0.9g)	**Cholesterol** 17mg
Protein 8.0g	**Sodium** 710mg
Carbohydrate 27.1g	**Exchanges:** 2 Starch, ½ Fat

Italian Pasta and Bean Soup

1   tablespoon olive oil
Cooking spray
1   cup chopped onion
1   cup sliced carrot
½   cup chopped green bell pepper
2   garlic cloves, crushed
2   (14-ounce) cans less-sodium beef broth
1   (28-ounce) can crushed tomatoes
1   (15-ounce) can cannellini beans, rinsed and drained
1   (15-ounce) can red kidney beans, rinsed and drained
1½ teaspoons dried Italian seasoning
½   teaspoon salt
¼   teaspoon black pepper
6   ounces uncooked ditalini pasta
½   cup grated fresh Parmesan cheese

Heat oil in a large Dutch oven coated with cooking spray over medium-high heat. Add onion and next 3 ingredients; sauté until vegetables are crisp-tender.

Add beef broth and next 6 ingredients; bring to a boil. Cover, reduce heat, and simmer 20 minutes, stirring occasionally.

Add pasta to vegetable mixture. Cover and cook 10 to 15 minutes or until pasta is tender. Ladle soup into individual bowls; top each serving with 1 tablespoon cheese. **Yield:** 8 servings (serving size: 1¼ cups soup and 1 tablespoon cheese).

Per Serving:

Calories 232	**Fiber** 4.2g
Fat 4.5g (sat 1.5g)	**Cholesterol** 5mg
Protein 10.8g	**Sodium** 497mg
Carbohydrate 36.2g	**Exchanges:** 2 Starch, 1 Vegetable, ½ High-Fat Meat

Minestrone

Cooking spray
1   (10-ounce) package frozen chopped onion, celery, and
        pepper blend, thawed
4   (14-ounce) cans less-sodium beef broth
1   (16-ounce) package frozen vegetables with zucchini, cauliflower,
        carrots, and beans, thawed
1   (14½-ounce) can Italian-style tomatoes, undrained and
        chopped
½   teaspoon dried basil
¼   teaspoon salt
¼   teaspoon pepper
1   cup uncooked small pasta shells
7   tablespoons grated fresh Parmesan cheese

Coat a Dutch oven with cooking spray; place over medium-high heat until hot. Add chopped onion blend; sauté 5 minutes. Add broth and next 5 ingredients. Bring to a boil; cover, reduce heat, and simmer 30 minutes.

Add pasta to vegetable mixture; simmer 15 minutes or until pasta is tender.

Spoon evenly into 7 bowls; sprinkle each serving with 1 tablespoon cheese, and serve immediately. **Yield:** 7 servings (serving size: 1½ cups soup and 1 tablespoon cheese).

Per Serving:

Calories 136	**Fiber** 3.0g
Fat 1.5g (sat 0.8g)	**Cholesterol** 3mg
Protein 6.7g	**Sodium** 477mg
Carbohydrate 21.5g	**Exchanges:** 1 Starch, 1 Vegetable

Chunky Chicken Noodle Soup

1	(3-pound) broiler-fryer, cut up and skinned
4	cups water
¾	teaspoon poultry seasoning
¼	teaspoon dried thyme
3	celery tops
2	cups water
2	ounces uncooked medium egg noodles
½	cup sliced celery
½	cup sliced carrot
⅓	cup sliced green onions
2	tablespoons minced fresh parsley
2	teaspoons chicken-flavored bouillon granules
¼	teaspoon coarsely ground black pepper
1	bay leaf

Additional coarsely ground black pepper (optional)

Combine first 5 ingredients in a Dutch oven; bring to a boil. Cover, reduce heat, and simmer 45 minutes or until chicken is tender. Remove chicken from broth, discarding celery and reserving broth.

Skim fat from broth. Add 2 cups water and next 8 ingredients to broth; bring to a boil. Cover, reduce heat, and simmer 20 minutes.

Bone and chop chicken; add to broth mixture. Cook 5 minutes or until thoroughly heated. Discard bay leaf. Ladle soup into bowls, and sprinkle with additional pepper, if desired. **Yield:** 6 servings (serving size: 1 cup).

Per Serving:

Calories 204	**Fiber** 1.0g
Fat 6.9g (sat 1.9g)	**Cholesterol** 82mg
Protein 25.4g	**Sodium** 358mg
Carbohydrate 9.1g	**Exchanges:** 1 Starch, 3 Lean Meat

ready in **30** minutes

Chicken Divan Soup

Cooking spray
1¼ pounds skinless, boneless chicken breasts, cut into bite-size
        pieces
¾   cup chopped onion
2   garlic cloves, minced
1   cup cooked long-grain rice
½   teaspoon pepper
¼   teaspoon salt
2   (4-ounce) cans sliced mushrooms, drained
1   (16-ounce) package frozen chopped broccoli, thawed
1   (14-ounce) can fat-free, less-sodium chicken broth
1   (12-ounce) can evaporated fat-free milk
1   (10¾-ounce) can condensed reduced-fat, reduced-sodium
        cream of chicken soup, undiluted

Coat a Dutch oven with cooking spray; place over medium-high heat until hot. Add chicken, onion, and garlic; sauté until onion is tender. Add rice and remaining ingredients, stirring well. Bring to a boil; cover, reduce heat, and simmer 15 minutes. **Yield:** 6 servings (serving size: 1½ cups).

Per Serving:

Calories 264	**Fiber** 2.4g
Fat 2.8g (sat 0.8g)	**Cholesterol** 61mg
Protein 31.2g	**Sodium** 591mg
Carbohydrate 26.7g	**Exchanges:** 1½ Starch, 1 Vegetable, 3 Very Lean Meat

Spinach-Chicken Noodle Soup

4   (14-ounce) cans fat-free, less-sodium chicken broth
1   cup chopped onion (about 1 medium)
1   cup sliced carrot
2   (10¾-ounce) cans condensed reduced-fat, reduced-sodium
     cream of chicken soup, undiluted
1   (10-ounce) package frozen chopped spinach, thawed
4   cups chopped cooked chicken
4   ounces uncooked medium egg noodles
½   teaspoon salt
½   teaspoon pepper

Combine first 3 ingredients in a Dutch oven. Bring to a boil; cover, reduce heat, and simmer 15 minutes. Add soup and remaining ingredients. Bring to a boil; reduce heat, and simmer, uncovered, 15 minutes. **Yield:** 8 servings (serving size: 1½ cups).

Per Serving:

Calories 227	**Fiber** 2.3g
Fat 5.9g (sat 1.7g)	**Cholesterol** 71mg
Protein 22.0g	**Sodium** 388mg
Carbohydrate 18.9g	**Exchanges:** 1 Starch, 1 Vegetable, 2 Lean Meat

During the holidays, use your leftover turkey instead of chicken in this soup.

Nacho Chicken Soup

2   (15-ounce) cans no-salt-added pinto beans, undrained
4   cups frozen cooked diced chicken breast, thawed
2   cups low-sodium chicken broth
1   (14½-ounce) can diced tomatoes, undrained
1   (11-ounce) jar salsa (about 1¼ cups)
1   (10-ounce) can diced tomatoes and green chiles, undrained
1½ cups (6 ounces) shredded reduced-fat Cheddar cheese
Low-fat tortilla chips (optional)

Place pinto beans in a food processor; process until smooth.

Spoon bean puree into a large Dutch oven. Add chicken and next
4 ingredients; stir well. Cook over medium heat 15 minutes or until
thoroughly heated.

Ladle soup into bowls; top each with about 3 tablespoons cheese.
Serve with low-fat tortilla chips, if desired (chips not included in
analysis). **Yield:** 7 servings (serving size: 1½ cups soup and about
3 tablespoons cheese).

Per Serving:

Calories 362	**Fiber** 7.8g
Fat 8.8g (sat 4.4g)	**Cholesterol** 91mg
Protein 42.0g	**Sodium** 797mg
Carbohydrate 26.9g	**Exchanges:** 2 Starch, 5 Very Lean Meat

If you need to reduce
the amount of sodium
in this recipe, use
1 (14½-ounce) can
no-salt-added tomatoes.

Wagon Wheel Beef Soup

2¼ cups (6 ounces) uncooked wagon wheel pasta
Cooking spray
¾ pound ground round
1 cup chopped onion (about 1 medium)
3 cups low-fat spaghetti sauce
½ teaspoon ground oregano
2 (14-ounce) cans less-sodium beef broth
1 (15-ounce) can no-salt-added kidney beans, undrained

Cook pasta according to package directions, omitting salt and fat. Drain.

Coat a Dutch oven with cooking spray; place over medium-high heat until hot. Add meat and onion; cook over medium heat until meat is browned, stirring until it crumbles. Drain.

Return meat mixture to pan; add cooked pasta and remaining ingredients. Cook 10 minutes or until thoroughly heated. **Yield:** 10 servings (serving size: 1 cup).

Per Serving:

Calories 223	**Fiber** 2.4g
Fat 4.2g (sat 1.1g)	**Cholesterol** 29mg
Protein 17.1g	**Sodium** 261mg
Carbohydrate 29.2g	**Exchanges:** 2 Starch, 1½ Lean Meat

Vegetable-Beef Soup

1   pound ground round
½   medium cabbage, coarsely chopped
2   large carrots, sliced
2   celery stalks, sliced
1   onion, coarsely chopped
1   green bell pepper, chopped
1   (14½-ounce) can no-salt-added French-style green beans,
          drained
1   beef bouillon cube
1   (46-ounce) can vegetable juice
2   cups water
¼   teaspoon black pepper

Cook meat in a large Dutch oven over medium heat until browned, stirring until it crumbles. Drain, if necessary.

Return meat to pan. Add cabbage and remaining ingredients; stir. Bring to a boil over medium-high heat; cover, reduce heat, and simmer 2 hours, stirring occasionally. **Yield:** 6 servings (serving size: 1½ cups).

Per Serving:

Calories 222	**Fiber** 5.6g
Fat 5.2g (sat 1.8g)	**Cholesterol** 46mg
Protein 20.2g	**Sodium** 981mg
Carbohydrate 25.9g	**Exchanges:** 1 Starch, 2 Vegetable, 2 Lean Meat

This soup is high in sodium because of the vegetable juice and bouillon cube. Substitute low-sodium tomato juice if you're on a low-sodium diet.

Black Bean Soup

3   (15-ounce) cans no-salt-added black beans, drained
2   (14-ounce) cans fat-free, less-sodium chicken broth
1   cup chopped onion (about 1 medium)
1   cup chopped red bell pepper (about 1 medium)
2   garlic cloves, minced
½   pound extra-lean cooked ham, diced
¾   teaspoon dried oregano
½   teaspoon black pepper
¼   teaspoon salt

Combine first 5 ingredients in a Dutch oven; bring to a boil. Cover, reduce heat, and simmer 30 minutes.

Transfer 2 cups bean mixture to a blender or food processor; process until smooth, stopping once to scrape down sides. Return pureed bean mixture to pan. Add ham and remaining ingredients. Bring to a boil; reduce heat, and simmer, uncovered, 20 minutes or until thickened. **Yield:** 8 servings (serving size: 1 cup).

Per Serving:

Calories 164	**Fiber** 3.9g
Fat 2.1g (sat 0.6g)	**Cholesterol** 15mg
Protein 13.4g	**Sodium** 418mg
Carbohydrate 22.2g	**Exchanges:** 1½ Starch, 1 Lean Meat

Spicy Ham and Bean Soup

1   pound dried Great Northern beans
4   quarts water
1   pound reduced-salt lean ham, cubed
2¾ cups chopped red potato (about 4 medium)
1¾ cups chopped onion (about 2 medium)
1   cup chopped carrot (about 1 large)
¾   cup chopped celery (about 2 stalks)
1   (5.5-ounce) can spicy vegetable juice
1   (4.5-ounce) can chopped green chiles, undrained
1   tablespoon chopped pickled jalapeño pepper
1   tablespoon pickled jalapeño pepper juice
1   tablespoon low-sodium Worcestershire sauce
½   teaspoon garlic powder
½   teaspoon chili powder

Sort and wash beans; place in a large Dutch oven. Add 4 quarts water; cover and let stand 2 hours.

Bring beans to a boil; reduce heat, and simmer, uncovered, 1 hour. Add ham and next 4 ingredients; bring to a boil. Reduce heat, and simmer, uncovered, 1 hour.

Add vegetable juice and remaining ingredients; bring to a boil. Reduce heat, and simmer, uncovered, 1 hour or until beans are tender and soup is thickened. **Yield:** 10 servings (serving size: 1½ cups).

Per Serving:

Calories 255	**Fiber** 20.1g
Fat 3.0g (sat 1.0g)	**Cholesterol** 19mg
Protein 16.9g	**Sodium** 427mg
Carbohydrate 41.4g	**Exchanges:** 2 Starch, 2 Vegetable, 1 Lean Meat

Jambalaya Stew

4 cups water
2½ cups chopped tomato (about 2 large)
1½ cups chopped green bell pepper (about 2 small)
1 cup chopped onion (about 1 medium)
1 teaspoon dried Italian seasoning
1 teaspoon chili powder
1 teaspoon hot sauce
¾ teaspoon salt
3 garlic cloves, minced
1 bay leaf
2 cups uncooked instant rice
3 (8-ounce) cans no-salt-added tomato sauce
2 (15-ounce) cans no-salt-added red kidney beans, undrained
1 (16-ounce) package frozen sliced okra, thawed

Combine first 10 ingredients in a large Dutch oven. Bring to a boil; reduce heat, and cook, uncovered, 5 minutes.

Add rice and remaining ingredients. Bring to a boil; reduce heat, and cook, uncovered, 5 minutes or until okra is tender. Remove and discard bay leaf. **Yield:** 16 servings (serving size: 1 cup).

Per Serving:

Calories 151	**Fiber** 3.2g
Fat 0.6g (sat 0.1g)	**Cholesterol** 0mg
Protein 7.0g	**Sodium** 129mg
Carbohydrate 30.7g	**Exchanges:** 2 Starch

Creole Shrimp Stew

1   teaspoon vegetable oil
Cooking spray
½   cup chopped onion (about 1 small)
½   cup chopped celery
½   teaspoon salt
1½ teaspoons minced fresh thyme or ½ teaspoon dried thyme
¼   teaspoon pepper
2   tablespoons dry red wine
1   (14½-ounce) can no-salt-added diced tomatoes, undrained
6   ounces peeled and deveined shrimp
6   ounces halibut fillets, cut into bite-size pieces

Heat oil in a Dutch oven coated with cooking spray over medium-high heat. Add onion and next 4 ingredients; sauté 5 minutes. Add wine and tomato. Bring to a boil; reduce heat, and simmer, uncovered, 5 minutes.

Add shrimp and halibut to pan. Cover and simmer 5 additional minutes or until shrimp are done and fish flakes easily when tested with a fork. **Yield:** 4 servings (serving size: 1 cup).

Per Serving:

Calories 132	**Fiber** 1.4g
Fat 3.0g (sat 0.5g)	**Cholesterol** 85mg
Protein 18.7g	**Sodium** 406mg
Carbohydrate 7.3g	**Exchanges:** 1 Vegetable, 2 Very Lean Meat

If you're buying unpeeled shrimp, you'll need to buy ½ pound to get 6 ounces of peeled and deveined.

Chicken-Chili Stew

2   cups fat-free, less-sodium chicken broth
1   (15-ounce) can chunky chili tomato sauce, undrained
1   (4.5-ounce) can chopped green chiles
1½ cups frozen chopped onion
1   cup frozen whole-kernel corn
2   tablespoons chili powder
1   (15-ounce) can kidney beans, rinsed and drained
¾   pound skinless, boneless chicken breast halves, cut into 1-inch
      pieces
¼   cup chopped fresh cilantro or parsley

Combine first 6 ingredients in a Dutch oven. Bring to a boil; cover, reduce heat, and simmer 10 minutes.

Add beans and chicken; cover and simmer 10 additional minutes. Remove from heat; add cilantro. **Yield:** 8 servings (serving size: 2 cups).

Per Serving:

Calories 147	**Fiber** 3.9g
Fat 1.0g (sat 0.2g)	**Cholesterol** 25mg
Protein 14.0g	**Sodium** 523mg
Carbohydrate 19.9g	**Exchanges:** 1 Starch, 1 Vegetable, 1 Very Lean Meat

Harvest Stew

Cooking spray
1   pound ground round
¾   cup chopped onion
½   teaspoon pepper
2   garlic cloves, minced
3½   cups water
1   (14½-ounce) can no-salt-added diced tomatoes, undrained
2¼   cups chopped peeled sweet potato
1   cup coarsely chopped unpeeled round red potato
1   cup chopped peeled acorn squash
2   teaspoons vegetable-flavored bouillon granules
½   teaspoon chili powder
¼   teaspoon ground allspice
¼   teaspoon ground cloves
2   bay leaves

Coat a Dutch oven with cooking spray; place over medium-high heat until hot. Add meat and next 3 ingredients. Cook until meat is browned, stirring until it crumbles. Drain, if necessary.

Combine meat mixture, water, and remaining ingredients in pan; bring to a boil. Cover, reduce heat, and simmer 30 minutes or until vegetables are tender. Remove and discard bay leaves before serving. **Yield:** 8 servings (serving size: 1¼ cups).

Per Serving:

Calories 156	**Fiber** 2.3g
Fat 3.9g (sat 1.4g)	**Cholesterol** 36mg
Protein 12.4g	**Sodium** 163mg
Carbohydrate 19.6g	**Exchanges:** 1 Starch, 1 Vegetable, 1 Lean Meat

Hamburger Stew

¾ pound ground round
1 onion, chopped
6 large carrots, peeled and sliced into 1-inch pieces
3 (10-ounce) baking potatoes, unpeeled and cut into 1-inch
    pieces
1 (10¾-ounce) can condensed tomato soup, undiluted
2 cups water
½ teaspoon pepper
¼ teaspoon salt

Cook meat and onion in a Dutch oven over medium heat until meat is browned, stirring until meat crumbles.

Add carrot and remaining ingredients. Bring to a boil over medium-high heat; cover, reduce heat, and simmer 45 minutes or until vegetables are tender. **Yield:** 8 servings (serving size: 1 cup).

Per Serving:

Calories 203
Fat 3.5g (sat 1.1g)
Protein 13.2g
Carbohydrate 30.9g

Fiber 3.3g
Cholesterol 24mg
Sodium 350mg
Exchanges: 2 Starch, 1 Lean Meat

Hearty Pork Stew

Cooking spray
1   pound lean boneless pork loin, cut into cubes
1   cup chopped onion (about 1 medium)
1   (14½-ounce) can no-salt-added diced tomatoes, undrained
2   cups low-sodium chicken broth
1   (10-ounce) package frozen baby lima beans
1   (10-ounce) package frozen whole-kernel corn
1   (4.5-ounce) can chopped green chiles
½   teaspoon salt
½   teaspoon hot sauce
¼   teaspoon garlic powder
¼   teaspoon onion powder
¼   teaspoon freshly ground black pepper
2   tablespoons all-purpose flour
2   tablespoons water

Coat a Dutch oven with cooking spray; place over medium-high heat until hot. Add pork and onion; cook 5 minutes or until pork is browned, stirring frequently.

Add tomato and next 9 ingredients to pan. Bring to a boil; cover, reduce heat, and simmer 40 minutes.

Combine flour and water; stir until smooth; add to stew. Cook, stirring constantly, until thickened. **Yield:** 8 servings (serving size: 1 cup).

Per Serving:

Calories 211
Fat 6.6g (sat 2.2g)
Protein 16.5g
Carbohydrate 22.7g

Fiber 2.4g
Cholesterol 37mg
Sodium 258mg
Exchanges: 1 Starch, 2 Vegetable, 1 Medium-Fat Meat

White Bean Chili

Cooking spray
1   cup chopped onion (about 1 medium)
1   garlic clove, minced
2   (15-ounce) cans cannellini beans, rinsed, drained, and divided
1   (4.5-ounce) can chopped green chiles
2¼ cups fat-free, less-sodium chicken broth
1½ cups chopped cooked chicken
1   teaspoon chili powder
⅛   teaspoon salt

Coat a large saucepan with cooking spray; place over medium-high heat until hot. Add onion and garlic; sauté until tender. Add 1 can beans and next 5 ingredients.

Mash remaining 1 can beans with a fork; add to chicken mixture in pan. Bring to a boil; cover, reduce heat, and simmer 20 minutes. **Yield:** 4 servings (serving size: 1½ cups).

Per Serving:

Calories 207

Fat 4.3g (sat 1.0g)

Protein 19.4g

Carbohydrate 19.6g

Fiber 3.3g

Cholesterol 43mg

Sodium 554mg

Exchanges: 1 Starch, 1 Vegetable, 2 Lean Meat

Turkey Chili

Cooking spray
2   pounds ground turkey
2   (15-ounce) cans kidney beans, undrained
2   (14½-ounce) cans no-salt-added whole tomatoes, undrained
        and chopped
2   (8-ounce) cans no-salt-added tomato sauce
½   cup chopped onion (about 1 small)
¼   cup dry red wine
2   tablespoons chili powder
1   teaspoon dried parsley flakes
¾   teaspoon dried basil
¾   teaspoon dried oregano
½   teaspoon salt
½   teaspoon black pepper
½   teaspoon ground cinnamon
½   teaspoon ground red pepper
2   garlic cloves, minced
1   bay leaf
Shredded reduced-fat Cheddar cheese (optional)

Coat a Dutch oven with cooking spray; place over medium heat until hot. Add turkey, and cook until browned, stirring until it crumbles.

Add beans and next 14 ingredients; bring to a boil. Cover, reduce heat, and simmer 2 hours, stirring occasionally. Discard bay leaf. Top with cheese, if desired (cheese not included in analysis). **Yield:** 8 servings (serving size: 1½ cups).

Per Serving:

Calories 310	**Fiber** 9.5g
Fat 9.1g (sat 2.1g)	**Cholesterol** 96mg
Protein 29.1g	**Sodium** 693mg
Carbohydrate 28.4g	**Exchanges:** 2 Starch, 3 Lean Meat

Hearty Sausage-Bean Chili

1   pound turkey breakfast sausage
¾   pound ground round
1½   cups frozen chopped onion, celery, and pepper blend, thawed
2   (15-ounce) cans no-salt-added dark red kidney beans,
          undrained
2   (14½-ounce) cans no-salt-added stewed tomatoes, undrained
1   (15-ounce) can no-salt-added pinto beans, undrained
1   (15-ounce) can chunky chili tomato sauce

Combine first 3 ingredients in a large Dutch oven. Place over medium-high heat, and cook until meat is browned, stirring until it crumbles. Drain.

Return meat mixture to pan; add kidney beans and remaining ingredients. Bring to a boil; reduce heat, and simmer, uncovered, 20 minutes or until thickened, stirring occasionally.

Remove from heat, and serve immediately. **Yield:** 7 servings (serving size: 1½ cups).

Per Serving:

Calories 298	**Fiber** 6.5g
Fat 8.5g (sat 1.9g)	**Cholesterol** 61mg
Protein 26.1g	**Sodium** 740mg
Carbohydrate 28.6g	**Exchanges:** 2 Starch, 3 Lean Meat

Look for turkey breakfast sausage in the refrigerator section with the other tubes of breakfast sausage or in the freezer section of the grocery store.

Five-Ingredient Chili

1½ pounds ground round
1   onion, chopped
4   (16-ounce) cans chili-hot beans, undrained
1   (1¾-ounce) package chili seasoning mix
1   (46-ounce) can no-salt-added tomato juice

Cook meat and onion in a Dutch oven over medium-high heat until meat is browned, stirring until it crumbles; drain, if necessary. Stir in beans and remaining ingredients.

Bring to a boil; reduce heat, and simmer, uncovered, 30 minutes or until thickened to desired consistency, stirring occasionally. **Yield:** 14 servings (serving size: 1 cup).

Per Serving:

Calories 220	**Fiber** 6.2g
Fat 3.9g (sat 1.6g)	**Cholesterol** 30mg
Protein 17.8g	**Sodium** 803mg
Carbohydrate 26.1g	**Exchanges:** 1 Starch, 2 Vegetable, 2 Lean Meat

With only five ingredients and a 10-minute prep time, this hot-and-spicy chili is one of our favorites.

Easy Weeknight Chili

Cooking spray
1   pound ground round
1¼ cups chopped onion (about 1 large)
1¼ cups chopped green bell pepper (about 2 small)
6   garlic cloves, minced
2   (14½-ounce) cans no-salt-added stewed tomatoes, undrained
        and chopped
1   (15-ounce) can no-salt-added kidney beans, rinsed and
        drained
1   (8-ounce) can no-salt-added tomato sauce
1   (1-ounce) envelope onion soup mix
1   cup water
3   tablespoons chili powder
1   tablespoon paprika
1¼ teaspoons hot sauce
6   tablespoons (1½ ounces) shredded reduced-fat sharp
        Cheddar cheese

Coat a Dutch oven with cooking spray; place over medium-high heat until hot. Add meat and next 3 ingredients; cook until meat is browned, stirring until it crumbles. Drain.

Return mixture to pan; add tomatoes and next 7 ingredients. Bring to a boil; cover, reduce heat, and simmer 20 minutes, stirring occasionally. To serve, ladle chili into bowls; top each with 1 tablespoon cheese. **Yield:** 6 servings (serving size: 1½ cups and 1 tablespoon cheese).

Per Serving:

Calories 302	**Fiber** 9.5g
Fat 6.6g (sat 2.2g)	**Cholesterol** 52mg
Protein 29.0g	**Sodium** 277mg
Carbohydrate 34.7g	**Exchanges:** 2 Starch, 1 Vegetable, 3 Lean Meat

desserts

Fresh Berries with Creamy Peach Topping

1   cup sliced fresh or frozen peaches, thawed
¼   cup low-fat sour cream
1   tablespoon "measures-like-sugar" brown sugar calorie-free
       sweetener (such as Brown Sugar Twin)
½   teaspoon lemon juice
3   cups fresh strawberry halves
1   cup fresh blackberries

Combine first 4 ingredients in a blender; process until smooth.

Spoon ⅔ cup berries into each of 6 dessert dishes. Spoon peach mixture evenly over berries. **Yield:** 6 servings (serving size: ⅔ cup berries and about 3 tablespoons topping).

Per Serving:

Calories 61	**Fiber** 3.6g
Fat 1.6g (sat 0.8g)	**Cholesterol** 4mg
Protein 1.1g	**Sodium** 7mg
Carbohydrate 11.9g	**Exchange:** 1 Fruit

Bananas Foster

3   firm ripe bananas, peeled
¾   cup apple juice
⅛   teaspoon apple pie spice
2   teaspoons cornstarch
2   tablespoons rum
⅛   teaspoon maple flavoring
⅛   teaspoon butter flavoring
3   cups vanilla no-sugar-added, fat-free ice cream

Cut bananas in half lengthwise; cut each half crosswise to make 12 pieces. Combine apple juice and apple pie spice in a large skillet. Add banana pieces to juice mixture; cook over medium heat just until banana is heated, basting often with juice mixture.

Combine cornstarch, rum, and flavorings, stirring until smooth; add to banana mixture. Bring to a boil; cook, stirring constantly, 1 minute.

To serve, spoon ½ cup ice cream into each of 6 dishes. Spoon banana mixture evenly over ice cream, and serve immediately. **Yield:** 6 servings (serving size: ½ cup ice cream and 2 banana pieces).

Per Serving:

Calories 164	**Fiber** 2.5g
Fat 0.3g (sat 0.1g)	**Cholesterol** 0mg
Protein 4.6g	**Sodium** 77mg
Carbohydrate 39.5g	**Exchanges:** 1½ Starch, 1 Fruit

If you don't want to use rum, add an extra 2 tablespoons of apple juice.

Cantaloupe Sherbet

1 large ripe cantaloupe, peeled and finely chopped (about 5 cups)
⅓ cup "measures-like-sugar" calorie-free sweetener
2 tablespoons lemon juice
2 teaspoons unflavored gelatin
¼ cup cold water
1 (8-ounce) carton vanilla fat-free yogurt sweetened with aspartame
Cantaloupe wedge (optional)

Combine cantaloupe, sweetener, and lemon juice in a blender or food processor; process until smooth. Transfer mixture to a medium bowl.

Sprinkle gelatin over cold water in a small saucepan; let stand 1 minute. Cook over low heat, stirring until gelatin dissolves, about 4 minutes. Add to cantaloupe mixture, stirring well. Add yogurt, stirring until smooth.

Pour mixture into an 8-inch square pan; freeze until almost firm.

Transfer mixture to a large bowl; beat with a mixer at high speed until fluffy. Spoon mixture back into pan; freeze until firm.

Scoop into 5 individual serving dishes to serve. Garnish each serving with a cantaloupe wedge, if desired (cantaloupe wedge not included in analysis). **Yield:** 5 servings (serving size: 1 cup).

Per Serving:

Calories 93	**Fiber** 1.3g
Fat 0.5g (sat 0.2g)	**Cholesterol** 1mg
Protein 5.1g	**Sodium** 50mg
Carbohydrate 18.9g	**Exchanges:** 1 Fruit, ½ Skim Milk

make-ahead

Chocolate Chip Ice Cream

⅔ cup "measures-like-sugar" calorie-free sweetener
2 cups fat-free evaporated milk
1 cup fat-free milk
½ cup egg substitute
1½ teaspoons vanilla extract
2 (2.8-ounce) sugar-free milk chocolate bars, chopped

Combine first 5 ingredients in a large bowl; beat with a mixer at medium speed until well blended. Stir in chocolate.

Pour mixture into freezer can of a 2-quart hand-turned or electric freezer. Freeze according to manufacturer's instructions. Pack freezer with additional ice and rock salt, and let stand at least 1 hour before serving. **Yield:** 12 servings (serving size: ½ cup).

Per Serving:

Calories 119	**Fiber** 0.0g
Fat 4.8g (sat 0.1g)	**Cholesterol** 5mg
Protein 6.0g	**Sodium** 88mg
Carbohydrate 14.3g	**Exchanges:** 1 Starch, 1 Fat

Egg substitute is pasteurized to kill any harmful bacteria. It can safely be used in recipes that traditionally call for raw eggs, such as no-cook ice creams.

make-ahead

Chocolate Ice Cream

2   envelopes unflavored gelatin
4   cups evaporated fat-free milk, divided
¾   cup egg substitute
1   tablespoon vanilla extract
⅓   cup unsweetened cocoa
7¼   teaspoons or 24 packets calorie-free sweetener with
        aspartame (such as Equal for Recipes or Equal packets)
1   (2.8-ounce) sugar-free milk chocolate bar, chopped

Sprinkle gelatin over 2 cups evaporated milk in a medium saucepan;
let stand 5 minutes. Cook over medium heat until gelatin dissolves
and mixture just comes to a boil. Gradually stir about 1 cup of hot
milk mixture into egg substitute; add to remaining hot milk mixture,
stirring constantly. Cook, stirring constantly, 2 additional minutes
(do not boil). Remove from heat. Stir in remaining 2 cups milk and
vanilla.

Combine cocoa and sweetener in a large bowl. Gradually add hot
milk mixture, stirring until smooth. Stir in chopped candy. Chill
approximately 30 minutes just until cold, stirring occasionally (do not
overchill).

Pour chocolate mixture into freezer container of a 4-quart hand-turned
or electric freezer. Freeze according to manufacturer's instructions.
Pack freezer with additional ice and rock salt; let stand at least 1 hour
before serving. **Yield:** 8 servings (serving size: ½ cup).

Per Serving:

Calories 168	**Fiber** 0.1g
Fat 4.0g (sat 2.3g)	**Cholesterol** 3mg
Protein 7.6g	**Sodium** 168mg
Carbohydrate 21.4g	**Exchanges:** 1 Starch, ½ Skim Milk, 1 Fat

Fudgy Peanut Butter Ice Cream

1   (1.4-ounce) package chocolate sugar-free, fat-free instant
      pudding mix
1   (12-ounce) can evaporated fat-free milk
1½ cups fat-free milk
1   (3.5-ounce) package mini sugar-free chocolate peanut butter
      cups, chopped (such as Russell Stover)

Combine first 3 ingredients in a large bowl, stirring with a wire whisk
until smooth. Stir in chopped candy.

Pour chocolate mixture into freezer container of a 2-quart hand-turned
or electric freezer. Freeze according to manufacturer's instructions.
Pack freezer with additional ice and rock salt, and let stand at least
1 hour before serving. **Yield:** 8 servings (serving size: ½ cup).

Per Serving:

Calories 130	**Fiber** 0.7g
Fat 4.7g (sat 2.2g)	**Cholesterol** 1mg
Protein 6.2g	**Sodium** 157mg
Carbohydrate 17.5g	**Exchanges:** 1 Starch, 1 Fat

We tested this recipe with a package of mini sugar-free chocolate peanut butter cups. If you want to use the larger ones, you'll need 2½ (1.5-ounce) packages (5 pieces).

Homemade Peach Ice Cream

2   cups evaporated fat-free milk
1   cup fat-free milk
⅔   cup "measures-like-sugar" calorie-free sweetener
½   cup egg substitute
¼   teaspoon almond extract
1   cup chopped fresh or frozen peaches (about 2 medium peaches)

Combine first 5 ingredients in a large bowl; beat with a mixer at medium speed until blended. Stir in peaches.

Pour mixture into freezer container of a 2-quart hand-turned or electric freezer. Freeze according to manufacturer's instructions. Pack freezer with additional ice and rock salt, and let stand at least 1 hour before serving. **Yield:** 12 servings (serving size: ½ cup).

Per Serving:

Calories 58	**Fiber** 0.5g
Fat 0.1g (sat 0.1g)	**Cholesterol** 2mg
Protein 5.1g	**Sodium** 75mg
Carbohydrate 10.5g	**Exchanges:** ½ Fruit, ½ Skim Milk

If you don't have almond extract, use ½ teaspoon vanilla extract.

Peanut Butter Ice Cream Sandwiches

3   tablespoons no-sugar-added creamy peanut butter
2   cups vanilla no-sugar-added, fat-free ice cream, softened
16 (2-inch-diameter) gingersnaps

Swirl peanut butter into ice cream. Place in freezer 30 minutes or until firm enough to spread.

Spread ¼ cup ice cream mixture onto each of 8 gingersnaps. Top with remaining 8 gingersnaps. Place sandwiches on a 15- x 10-inch jelly-roll pan; freeze until firm. Wrap sandwiches in plastic wrap, and store in freezer. **Yield:** 8 sandwiches (serving size: 1 sandwich).

Per Serving:

Calories 124	**Fiber** 0.9g
Fat 4.7g (sat 0.9g)	**Cholesterol** 4mg
Protein 4.3g	**Sodium** 52mg
Carbohydrate 18.1g	**Exchanges:** 1 Starch, 1 Fat

Ice Cream Sandwich Dessert

1½ teaspoons instant coffee granules
1 packet calorie-free sweetener with aspartame (such as Equal packets)
2 tablespoons hot water
1 (8-ounce) container fat-free frozen whipped topping, thawed
6 no-sugar-added, reduced-fat ice cream sandwiches
1 (2.75-ounce) package sugar-free chocolate wafer bars, coarsely chopped (such as Sweet 'N Low)

Dissolve coffee and sweetener in hot water, stirring well; let cool slightly. Fold coffee mixture into whipped topping. Set aside.

Arrange 6 ice cream sandwiches in bottom of an 11- x 7-inch baking dish. Spread whipped topping mixture evenly over ice cream sandwiches. Sprinkle with chopped wafer bars. Cover and freeze 2 hours or until firm. To serve, cut into squares. **Yield:** 12 servings (serving size: 1 square).

Per Serving:

Calories 135   **Fiber** 0.5g
Fat 3.0g (sat 1.8g)   **Cholesterol** 5mg
Protein 2.5g   **Sodium** 86mg
Carbohydrate 24.3g   **Exchanges:** 1½ Starch, ½ Fat

No one will know that this scrumptious dessert is low in sugar. And if they do figure it out, they won't care because it's so good!

Cookies 'n' Cream Crunch

1   (6½-ounce) package sugar-free chocolate sandwich
      cookies, crushed
⅓   cup chopped pecans
3   tablespoons reduced-calorie margarine, melted
1   quart vanilla no-sugar-added, fat-free ice cream, softened

Combine first 3 ingredients; reserve 1 cup mixture. Press remaining crumb mixture firmly in bottom of a 9-inch square pan. Freeze 10 minutes.

Spread ice cream over crumb mixture in pan. Sprinkle reserved crumb mixture over ice cream; gently press mixture into ice cream. Cover and freeze at least 8 hours.

To serve, let stand at room temperature 5 minutes; cut into 9 squares. **Yield:** 9 servings (serving size: 1 square).

Per Serving:

Calories 232	**Fiber** 0.7g
Fat 10.1g (sat 1.7g)	**Cholesterol** 0mg
Protein 6.3g	**Sodium** 182mg
Carbohydrate 34.2g	**Exchanges:** 2 Starch, 2 Fat

Strawberry Shortcakes

1   tablespoon "measures-like-sugar" calorie-free sweetener
1   tablespoon cornstarch
1   cup orange juice
¼   teaspoon vanilla or almond extract
1½   cups sliced fresh strawberries (about 1 pint)
6   spongecake dessert shells (5-ounce package)

Combine sweetener and cornstarch in a small saucepan. Stir in orange juice. Bring to a boil; cook, stirring constantly, 1 minute or until mixture is thickened and bubbly. Remove from heat, and stir in extract. Cool completely.

Combine orange juice mixture and strawberries in a bowl; stir gently. Cover and chill 30 minutes.

To serve, spoon sauce over dessert shells. **Yield:** 6 servings (serving size: 1 cake and ⅓ cup sauce).

Per Serving:

Calories 113	**Fiber** 0.2g
Fat 0.9g (sat 0.3g)	**Cholesterol** 33mg
Protein 2.0g	**Sodium** 169mg
Carbohydrate 24.3g	**Exchanges:** 1 Starch, ½ Fruit

This luscious sauce is also good spooned over no-sugar-added ice cream, angel food cake, or fat-free pound cake.

Banana Spice Cake

4   large ripe bananas, peeled and mashed (about 2 cups)
1½   cups vanilla fat-free yogurt sweetened with aspartame
¼   cup margarine, softened
2   large eggs
2   teaspoons vanilla extract
3   cups all-purpose flour
1   tablespoon plus 1 teaspoon baking powder
2   teaspoons baking soda
½   teaspoon salt
1   teaspoon ground cinnamon
½   teaspoon ground cloves
1   cup "measures-like-sugar" calorie-free sweetener
Cooking spray
2   (8-ounce) packages ⅓-less-fat cream cheese
¾   cup "measures-like-sugar" calorie-free sweetener
⅓   cup vanilla fat-free yogurt sweetened with aspartame
2   large ripe bananas, thinly sliced

Preheat oven to 375°.

Combine first 5 ingredients; beat with a mixer at medium speed until blended. Combine flour and next 6 ingredients; add to banana mixture, beating well.

Pour batter into 2 (9-inch) round cakepans coated with cooking spray and sprinkled with flour. Bake at 375° for 25 minutes or until a wooden pick inserted in center comes out clean. Cool in pans on wire racks 10 minutes. Remove from pans; cool completely on wire racks.

Beat cream cheese, ¾ cup sweetener, and ⅓ cup yogurt just until smooth. Spread ½ cup frosting on 1 cake layer. Top with banana slices. Add second cake layer. Spread remaining frosting on top and sides of cake. **Yield:** 16 servings (serving size: 1 slice).

Per Serving:

Calories 235	**Fiber** 1.6g
Fat 9.4g (sat 4.5g)	**Cholesterol** 44mg
Protein 6.6g	**Sodium** 465mg
Carbohydrate 31.4g	**Exchanges:** 2 Starch, 2 Fat

Blueberry Pound Cake

2   cups plus 6 tablespoons "measures-like-sugar" calorie-free
       sweetener, divided
⅓   cup margarine, softened
½   cup (4 ounces) ⅓-less-fat cream cheese, softened
3   large eggs
1   large egg white
2   teaspoons vanilla extract
3   cups all-purpose flour, divided
2   cups fresh or frozen blueberries
1   teaspoon baking powder
½   teaspoon baking soda
½   teaspoon salt
1   (8-ounce) carton lemon low-fat yogurt
Cooking spray
1½   tablespoons lemon juice

Preheat oven to 350°.

Beat 2 cups sweetener, margarine, and cream cheese with a mixer at medium speed until blended. Add eggs and egg white, 1 at a time, beating after each addition. Beat in vanilla. Combine 2 tablespoons flour and blueberries; toss. Combine remaining flour, baking powder, soda, and salt. Add flour mixture to cheese mixture alternately with yogurt. Fold in blueberries.

Pour batter into a 10-inch tube pan coated with cooking spray. Bake at 350° for 1 hour and 5 minutes or until a wooden pick inserted in center comes out clean. Cool in pan 10 minutes on a wire rack. Remove cake from pan, and cool completely on a wire rack.

Combine 6 tablespoons sweetener and lemon juice; drizzle over cake. **Yield:** 18 servings (serving size: 1 slice).

Per Serving:

Calories 220	**Fiber** 1.0g
Fat 6.5g (sat 2.1g)	**Cholesterol** 47mg
Protein 4.8g	**Sodium** 215mg
Carbohydrate 49.0g	**Exchanges:** 2 Starch, 1 Fruit, 1 Fat

Triple-Chocolate Bundt Cake

½ cup applesauce
1 (18.25-ounce) package devil's food cake mix with pudding
1 (1.4-ounce) package chocolate sugar-free, fat-free
 pudding mix
1 cup fat-free sour cream
⅓ cup fat-free milk
3 large egg whites
1 large egg
1 teaspoon almond extract
Cooking spray
3 tablespoons or 31 packets calorie-free sweetener with
 aspartame (such as Equal for Recipes or Equal packets)
2½ teaspoons fat-free milk
1 ounce sugar-free milk chocolate
1 tablespoon fat-free milk

Preheat oven to 350°.

Spread applesauce onto several layers of paper towels. Cover with additional paper towels; let stand 5 minutes. Scrape into a bowl. Combine cake mix and next 6 ingredients in a large bowl; add applesauce. Beat with a mixer at medium speed for 2 minutes.

Pour batter into a 12-cup Bundt pan coated with cooking spray. Bake at 350° for 53 minutes or until a wooden pick inserted in center comes out clean. Cool in pan on a wire rack 10 minutes; remove from pan. Cool completely on wire rack.

Combine sweetener and 2½ teaspoons milk; drizzle over cake. Place chocolate in a microwave-safe dish; microwave at HIGH 1½ minutes, stirring after 1 minute. Add 1 tablespoon milk; stir. Drizzle over cake. **Yield:** 18 servings (serving size: 1 slice).

Per Serving:

Calories 156	**Fiber** 0.7g
Fat 2.5g (sat 0.4g)	**Cholesterol** 13mg
Protein 3.5g	**Sodium** 310mg
Carbohydrate 29.3g	**Exchanges:** 2 Starch

Raspberry-Mocha Cake

2   (8-ounce) packages chocolate sugar-free, low-fat cake mix (such as Sweet 'N Low)
1½ cups strongly brewed chocolate-almond flavored coffee
¼   cup raspberry spreadable fruit, melted
2   (0.53-ounce) packages sugar-free instant cocoa mix
1   (1.3-ounce) envelope sugar-free, reduced-calorie whipped topping mix (such as Dream Whip)
½   cup fat-free cold milk
½   teaspoon vanilla extract

Preheat oven to 375°.

Prepare cake mix according to package directions, substituting coffee for water.

Pour batter into 2 (8-inch) round cake pans. Bake at 375° for 20 to 25 minutes or until a wooden pick inserted into center comes out clean. Cool cakes in pans 10 minutes on a wire rack.

Remove cakes from pans. Poke several holes in each cake layer with a wooden pick. Brush warm cake layers with melted raspberry spread. Let cool completely on wire racks.

Combine cocoa mix and whipped topping mix in a large bowl. Add milk and vanilla; beat with a mixer at low speed until blended. Beat at high speed for 4 minutes or until soft peaks form.

Place 1 cake layer on a serving plate; top with half of frosting. Top first layer with second cake layer; spread remaining frosting on sides and top of cake. Chill frosted cake until ready to serve. **Yield:** 16 servings (serving size: 1 slice).

Per Serving:

Calories 133	**Fiber** 0.7g
Fat 2.5g (sat 0.5g)	**Cholesterol** 0mg
Protein 2.4g	**Sodium** 47mg
Carbohydrate 28.1g	**Exchanges:** 2 Starch, ½ Fat

Mocha Angel Food Cake

1¼ cups sifted cake flour
1   cup sugar, divided
⅓   cup unsweetened cocoa
1   teaspoon ground cinnamon
12   large egg whites
1   teaspoon cream of tartar
1   tablespoon instant coffee granules
2   tablespoons warm water
1   teaspoon vanilla extract

Preheat oven to 300°.

Sift flour, ¾ cup sugar, cocoa, and cinnamon together 3 times.

Beat egg whites and cream of tartar in an extra-large bowl with a mixer at high speed until foamy. Gradually add remaining ¼ cup sugar, beating until soft peaks form. Sift flour mixture over egg white mixture, 1 tablespoon at a time; fold in gently after each addition. Combine coffee granules and water. Fold coffee mixture and vanilla into batter.

Spoon batter into an ungreased 10-inch tube pan; spread evenly with a spatula. Break large air pockets by cutting through batter with knife.

Bake at 300° for 50 minutes or until cake springs back when lightly touched. Remove cake from oven; invert pan, and cool completely. Loosen cake from sides of pan, using a narrow metal spatula; remove from pan. **Yield:** 12 servings (serving size: 1 slice).

Per Serving:

Calories 135	**Fiber** 0.3g
Fat 0.4g (sat 0.2g)	**Cholesterol** 0mg
Protein 5.1g	**Sodium** 54mg
Carbohydrate 27.5g	**Exchanges:** 2 Starch

Orange Chiffon Cake

2½ cups sifted all-purpose flour
1 tablespoon plus 1 teaspoon baking powder
1 teaspoon salt
1½ cups "measures-like-sugar" calorie-free sweetener
⅓ cup vegetable oil
1½ teaspoons vanilla extract
1 cup orange juice
10 large eggs, separated
½ teaspoon cream of tartar
Fresh orange slices (optional)

Preheat oven to 325°.

Combine first 4 ingredients; make a well in center of mixture. Add oil, vanilla, orange juice, and egg yolks; beat with a mixer at medium speed until smooth.

Beat egg whites and ½ teaspoon cream of tartar until stiff peaks form. Gently stir one-fourth of egg white mixture into batter. Gently fold in remaining egg white mixture.

Pour batter into an ungreased 10-inch tube pan. Bake at 325° for 55 minutes or until a wooden pick inserted in center comes out clean. Invert pan; cool completely on a wire rack. Garnish with orange slices, if desired. **Yield:** 16 servings (serving size: 1 slice).

Per Serving:

Calories 177	**Fiber** 0.6g
Protein 6.3g	**Cholesterol** 138mg
Fat 8.0g (sat 1.3g)	**Sodium** 310mg
Carbohydrate 19.6g	**Exchanges:** 1½ Starch, 1½ Fat

We recommend using canola oil in recipes that call for vegetable oil. Made from rapeseeds, canola oil has the lowest saturated fat of all common cooking oils.

Lemon Cheesecake

1½ cups graham cracker crumbs
¼ cup reduced-calorie margarine, melted
2 cups 1% low-fat cottage cheese
¾ cup egg substitute
½ cup fat-free evaporated milk
⅓ cup fresh lemon juice
¼ cup all-purpose flour
¼ cup sugar
5 packets calorie-free sweetener with aspartame
    (such as Equal packets)
Lemon slices (optional)

Combine cracker crumbs and margarine; stir well. Press into bottom of a 9-inch springform pan. Freeze 30 minutes.

Preheat oven to 300°.

Place cottage cheese in a food processor or blender; process 1 minute or until very smooth, stopping once to scrape down sides. Add egg substitute and next 5 ingredients; process until smooth.

Pour mixture into prepared crust. Bake at 300° for 50 minutes or until almost set (center will be soft but will become firm when chilled). Remove from oven; cool on a wire rack. Cover and chill at least 8 hours. To serve, cut into wedges. Garnish with lemon slices, if desired. **Yield:** 12 servings (serving size: 1 wedge).

Per Serving:

Calories 136	**Fiber** 0.4g
Fat 3.8g (sat 0.9g)	**Cholesterol** 2mg
Protein 7.9g	**Sodium** 305mg
Carbohydrate 17.8g	**Exchanges:** 1 Starch, ½ High-Fat Meat

Chocolate Peppermint Cookies

½ cup margarine, softened
⅓ cup sugar
½ cup "measures-like-sugar" brown sugar calorie-free sweetener
  (such as Brown Sugar Twin)
½ cup egg substitute
1 teaspoon vanilla extract
2¼ cups all-purpose flour
1 teaspoon baking powder
¾ teaspoon baking soda
¼ teaspoon salt
⅓ cup unsweetened cocoa
⅔ cup finely crushed sugar-free peppermint candies
  (about 30 candies)
Cooking spray

Preheat oven to 350°.

Beat margarine with a mixer at medium speed until creamy; gradually add sugar and sweetener, beating well. Add egg substitute and vanilla; beat well.

Combine flour and next 4 ingredients. Add to margarine mixture, stirring just until blended. Stir in crushed candy. Drop dough by level tablespoonfuls onto wax paper. Roll into balls; place balls, 2 inches apart, on baking sheets coated with cooking spray. Flatten balls with a fork. Bake at 350° for 10 to 12 minutes. Remove from pans, and let cool on wire racks. **Yield:** 38 servings (serving size: 1 cookie).

Per Serving:

Calories 70	**Fiber** 0.2g
Fat 2.7g (sat 0.5g)	**Cholesterol** 0mg
Protein 1.2g	**Sodium** 90mg
Carbohydrate 12.0g	**Exchanges:** 1 Starch, ½ Fat

Peanut Butter-and-Jelly Sandwich Cookies

¼   cup margarine, softened
¼   cup no-sugar-added creamy peanut butter
½   cup "measures-like-sugar" calorie-free sweetener
¼   cup sugar
2   large egg whites
1   teaspoon vanilla extract
1¾ cups all-purpose flour
1   teaspoon baking soda
⅛   teaspoon salt
Cooking spray
¾   cup low-sugar strawberry spread

Preheat oven to 350°.

Beat margarine and peanut butter with a mixer at medium speed until creamy. Gradually add sweetener and sugar, beating well. Add egg whites and vanilla; beat well. Combine flour, soda, and salt in a small bowl, stirring well. Gradually add flour mixture to creamed mixture, beating well.

Shape dough into 40 (1-inch) balls. Place balls 2 inches apart on baking sheets coated with cooking spray. Flatten cookies into 2-inch circles using a flat-bottomed glass. Bake at 350° for 8 minutes or until lightly browned. Cool slightly on pans; remove, and let cool completely on wire racks.

Spread about 1½ teaspoons strawberry spread on the bottom of each of 20 cookies; top with remaining cookies. **Yield:** 20 servings (serving size: 1 sandwich cookie).

Per Serving:

Calories 97	**Fiber** 0.5g
Fat 4.3g (sat 0.8g)	**Cholesterol** 0mg
Protein 2.5g	**Sodium** 112mg
Carbohydrate 13.3g	**Exchanges:** 1 Starch, 1 Fat

make-ahead

Chocolate Cereal Bars

3   tablespoons margarine
¼   cup "measures-like-sugar" brown sugar calorie-free
      sweetener (such as Brown Sugar Twin)
2   cups miniature marshmallows
4   cups crispy rice cereal
2   cups whole wheat flake cereal
Cooking spray
1   (5¼-ounce) package sugar-free chocolate whipped frosting
      mix (such as Sweet 'N Low)

Melt margarine in a large saucepan over medium heat. Add sweetener; stir well. Add marshmallows; cook, stirring constantly, until marshmallows melt. Remove from heat; stir in cereals.

Press cereal mixture evenly into bottom of a 13- x 9-inch pan coated with cooking spray. Let cool at least 1 hour.

Prepare chocolate frosting mix according to package directions. Spread frosting over cereal mixture. Cover and chill 8 hours or until frosting is slightly firm. Cut into 3- x 2-inch bars. **Yield:** 18 servings (serving size: 1 bar).

Per Serving:

Calories 109	**Fiber** 0.3g
Fat 4.7g (sat 1.4g)	**Cholesterol** 0mg
Protein 1.5g	**Sodium** 123mg
Carbohydrate 16.9g	**Exchanges:** 1 Starch, 1 Fat

Fudgy Cream Cheese Brownies

¾   cup sugar
¼   cup plus 2 tablespoons reduced-calorie stick margarine,
       softened
1   large egg
1   large egg white
1   tablespoon vanilla extract
½   cup all-purpose flour
¼   cup unsweetened cocoa
Cooking spray
1   (8-ounce) block ⅓-less-fat cream cheese, softened
¼   cup "measures-like-sugar" calorie-free sweetener
3   tablespoons 1% low-fat milk

Preheat oven to 350°.

Beat sugar and margarine with a mixer at medium speed until light and fluffy. Add egg, egg white, and vanilla; beat well. Gradually add flour and cocoa, beating well. Pour into an 8-inch square pan coated with cooking spray.

Beat cream cheese and sweetener with a mixer at high speed until smooth. Add milk; beat well. Pour cream cheese mixture over chocolate mixture; swirl together using the tip of a knife to create a marbled effect.

Bake at 350° for 30 minutes. Cool completely in pan on a wire rack. Cut into squares. **Yield:** 16 servings (serving size: 1 square).

Per Serving:

Calories 127	**Fiber** 0.1g
Fat 6.7g (sat 2.8g)	**Cholesterol** 25mg
Protein 2.9g	**Sodium** 107mg
Carbohydrate 14.1g	**Exchanges:** 1 Starch, 1 Fat

Don't use reduced-calorie or fat-free tub margarine in this recipe because those products contain water, which will make the brownies gummy.

Apple Crisp

4   medium apples, peeled and sliced
¼   cup apple juice
2   tablespoons "measures-like-sugar" brown sugar calorie-free
     sweetener (such as Brown Sugar Twin), divided
2   teaspoons lemon juice
½   teaspoon ground cinnamon
¼   teaspoon ground nutmeg
½   cup regular oats, uncooked
2   tablespoons chopped walnuts
2   tablespoons margarine
Vanilla no-sugar-added ice cream (optional)

Preheat oven to 375°.

Combine apple, apple juice, 1 tablespoon sweetener, lemon juice, cinnamon, and nutmeg; toss lightly to coat apple. Place in an 8-inch square baking dish.

Combine oats, nuts, remaining 1 tablespoon sweetener, and margarine; sprinkle over apple mixture. Bake at 375° for 30 minutes or until apple is tender and topping is lightly browned. Serve warm. Top with ice cream, if desired (ice cream not included in analysis). **Yield:** 4 servings (serving size: about 1 cup).

Per Serving:

Calories 184
Fat 8.9g (sat 1.2g)
Protein 2.9g
Carbohydrate 26.4g

Fiber 3.0g
Cholesterol 0mg
Sodium 81mg
Exchanges: 1 Starch, 1 Fruit, 1½ Fat

Apple Pie

1   cup all-purpose flour
½   teaspoon salt
¼   cup vegetable shortening
4   to 5 tablespoons cold water
½   cup "measures-like-sugar" calorie-free sweetener
1   tablespoon cornstarch
1   teaspoon ground cinnamon
¼   teaspoon ground nutmeg
4   medium Granny Smith apples, peeled and sliced
1   teaspoon fresh lemon juice
Butter-flavored cooking spray
½   cup vanilla no-sugar-added ice cream (optional)

Preheat oven to 425°.

Combine flour and salt; cut in shortening with pastry blender until mixture is crumbly. Sprinkle water, 1 tablespoon at a time, over surface of mixture. Stir with a fork until dry ingredients are moistened.

Shape dough into a ball. Roll into a 10-inch circle on a floured surface. Combine sweetener and next 3 ingredients; sprinkle over apple, and toss.

Spoon mixture into a 9-inch pieplate; sprinkle with lemon juice. Place pastry over apple mixture; fold edges under, and crimp. Coat with cooking spray.

Bake at 425° for 25 minutes. Serve warm. Top with ice cream, if desired (ice cream not included in analysis). **Yield:** 8 servings (serving size: 1 wedge).

Per Serving:

Calories 243	**Fiber** 1.4g
Fat 16.4g (sat 3.4g)	**Cholesterol** 0mg
Protein 1.8g	**Sodium** 148mg
Carbohydrate 22.8g	**Exchanges:** ½ Starch, 1 Fruit, 3 Fat

Banana Cream Pie

1   (0.9-ounce) package banana sugar-free, fat-free instant
      pudding mix
1   cup 1% low-fat milk
1¾ cups frozen reduced-calorie whipped topping, thawed and
      divided
1¼ cups sliced peeled banana (about 2 medium)
1   tablespoon lemon juice
1   (6-ounce) chocolate graham cracker crust

Combine pudding mix and milk in a medium bowl, stirring with a
wire whisk until smooth. Gently fold 1 cup whipped topping into
pudding mixture.

Toss banana slices with lemon juice. Arrange banana slices over crust.
Spoon pudding mixture over banana. Cover and chill 1½ hours or
until set. Pipe or spoon remaining ¾ cup whipped topping around
edge of pie just before serving. **Yield:** 8 servings (serving size:
1 wedge).

Per Serving:

Calories 182	**Fiber** 0.6g
Fat 6.8g (sat 2.1g)	**Cholesterol** 1mg
Protein 3.0g	**Sodium** 310mg
Carbohydrate 28.0g	**Exchanges:** 1 Starch, 1 Fruit, 1 Fat

If you can't find a chocolate
graham cracker crust, you
can use a regular one. The
amount of carbohydrate will
be about the same.

Buttermilk Pie

½   cup baking mix (such as Bisquick)
¼   cup sugar
5   packets calorie-free sweetener with aspartame
      (such as Equal packets)
1   cup egg substitute
1   cup low-fat buttermilk
3   tablespoons margarine, melted
1   teaspoon vanilla extract
Cooking spray
2   cups assorted fresh berries (strawberries, blackberries,
      raspberries)

Preheat oven to 325°.

Combine first 7 ingredients in a blender; process until smooth. Pour mixture into a 9-inch pieplate coated with cooking spray. Bake at 325° for 28 to 30 minutes or until set. Serve warm or chilled. Top each serving with ⅓ cup mixed berries. **Yield:** 6 servings (serving size: 1 wedge and ⅓ cup berries).

Per Serving:

Calories 186	**Fiber** 2.7g
Fat 7.8g (sat 1.6g)	**Cholesterol** 2mg
Protein 6.7g	**Sodium** 319mg
Carbohydrate 22.7g	**Exchanges:** 1 Fruit, 1 Milk, 1 Fat

Top this quick-and-easy version of an old-fashioned buttermilk pie with the fresh fruit of your choice.

Deep-Dish Cherry Pie

1½ cups all-purpose flour
1½ tablespoons "measures-like-sugar" calorie-free sweetener
¼ teaspoon salt
6 tablespoons vegetable shortening
6 tablespoons ice water
¾ teaspoon cider vinegar
4 (16-ounce) cans tart cherries in water
½ cup "measures-like-sugar" calorie-free sweetener
⅓ cup cornstarch
1 teaspoon ground cinnamon
½ teaspoon almond extract

Preheat oven to 400°.

Combine flour, 1½ tablespoons sweetener, and salt. Cut in shortening until mixture resembles coarse meal. Add ice water and vinegar; toss with a fork until moist. Shape into a ball. Roll into a 14-inch circle on a lightly floured surface. Place dough in a 10-inch pieplate; press against bottom and sides of plate. Flute edges.

Drain cherries, reserving 1¼ cups liquid. Set cherries aside. Combine reserved cherry liquid, ½ cup sweetener, and cornstarch in a saucepan; stir well. Cook over medium heat until very thick, stirring constantly. Stir in cherries, cinnamon, and almond extract.

Pour mixture into pastry shell. Shield pastry with foil, and bake at 400° for 20 minutes. Reduce heat to 375°; bake, unshielded, 25 to 30 minutes or until hot and bubbly. Serve warm or at room temperature. **Yield:** 10 servings (serving size: 1 wedge).

Per Serving:

Calories 220
Fat 8.0g (sat 2.0g)
Protein 2.7g
Carbohydrate 35.5g

Fiber 0.5g
Cholesterol 0mg
Sodium 87mg
Exchanges: 1 Starch, 1½ Fruit, 1½ Fat

make-ahead

Chocolate-Macadamia Nut Pie

1²⁄₃ cups crushed sugar-free chocolate sandwich cookies
3 tablespoons butter
Cooking spray
2 cups chocolate no-sugar-added ice cream, softened
1 (3½-ounce) jar macadamia nuts, coarsely chopped
2 (8-ounce) containers fat-free frozen whipped topping, thawed
Shaved sugar-free chocolate bars (optional)
Toasted macadamia nuts (optional)
Whipped topping (optional)

Combine crushed cookies and butter. Press mixture firmly in bottom of a 9-inch springform pan coated with cooking spray.

Combine softened ice cream and nuts, stirring well. Fold in whipped topping. Pour mixture into prepared crust.

Cover and freeze until firm.

To serve, remove sides of springform pan, let stand 10 minutes before serving. Garnish with chocolate shavings, toasted nuts, and whipped topping, if desired (chocolate, nuts, and whipped topping not included in analysis). **Yield:** 10 servings (serving size: 1 wedge).

Per Serving:

Calories 276	**Fiber** 1.1g
Fat 15.6g (sat 4.2g)	**Cholesterol** 9mg
Protein 2.9g	**Sodium** 134mg
Carbohydrate 32.7g	**Exchanges:** 2 Starch, 3 Fat

(pictured on cover)

Double Chocolate Pudding Pie

1   (1.4-ounce) package chocolate sugar-free, fat-free instant
       pudding mix
2   cups fat-free milk, divided
1   (8-ounce) container frozen reduced-calorie whipped topping,
       thawed
2   (6-ounce) reduced-fat graham cracker crusts
1   (1-ounce) package white chocolate sugar-free, fat-free
       instant pudding mix

Beat chocolate pudding mix and 1 cup milk with a mixer at medium-high speed for 3 minutes or until thickened. Gently fold in half of whipped topping.

Divide chocolate pudding mixture in half, and pour evenly into 2 graham cracker crusts. Repeat procedure with white chocolate pudding mix, remaining 1 cup milk, and remaining half of whipped topping. Divide mixture in half; pour over chocolate pudding mixture in both crusts. Cover and chill 3 hours or until set. **Yield:** 2 pies, 8 servings each (serving size: 1 wedge).

Per Serving:

Calories 145	**Fiber** 0.0g
Fat 5.4g (sat 2.1g)	**Cholesterol** 1mg
Protein 2.5g	**Sodium** 276mg
Carbohydrate 21.8g	**Exchanges:** 1½ Starch, 1 Fat

This recipe makes two pies, so you can freeze one for later. It's good frozen, or you can thaw it in the refrigerator overnight.

Lemon Meringue Pie

½   (15-ounce) package refrigerated piecrusts
1   (0.3-ounce) package lemon sugar-free gelatin
1   cup boiling water
½   cup cold water
3   egg yolks, lightly beaten
3   tablespoons cornstarch
3   tablespoons fresh lemon juice
6   packets calorie-free sweetener with aspartame
      (such as Equal packets)
3   egg whites
¼   teaspoon cream of tartar
3   tablespoons granulated fructose

Preheat oven to 450°.

Bake 1 piecrust in a 9-inch pie-plate according to package directions. Set aside. Reduce oven temperature to 350°.

Combine gelatin and boiling water in a saucepan, stirring until gelatin dissolves. Stir in cold water; let stand 10 minutes.

Add egg yolks, cornstarch, and lemon juice; stir. Place over medium heat; cook, stirring constantly, until mixture comes to a boil. Boil 1 minute. Remove from heat; stir in sweetener. Pour into crust.

Beat egg whites and cream of tartar with a mixer at high speed until foamy. Add fructose; beat until stiff peaks form. Spoon meringue smoothly over filling. Bake at 350° on lower rack in oven for 12 minutes. Cool on a wire rack; chill. **Yield:** 8 servings (serving size: 1 wedge).

Per Serving:

Calories 186	**Fiber** 0.0g
Fat 9.0g (sat 3.6g)	**Cholesterol** 87mg
Protein 3.7g	**Sodium** 124mg
Carbohydrate 22.0g	**Exchanges:** 1½ Starch, 2 Fat

We used fructose in the meringue because it browns better than other sugar replacements.

Oven-Fried Peach Pies

1   cup drained canned peaches in light syrup, chopped
3   tablespoons "measures-like-sugar" calorie-free sweetener,
      divided
¾   teaspoon ground cinnamon, divided
1   tablespoon all-purpose flour
1   (10-ounce) can refrigerated buttermilk biscuits
Butter-flavored cooking spray

Preheat oven to 375°.

Combine peaches, 2 tablespoons sweetener, and ½ teaspoon cinnamon. Sprinkle flour over work surface. Separate biscuits; place on floured surface. Roll each biscuit to a 4½-inch circle. Place 1 heaping tablespoon peach mixture over half of each circle. Brush edges of circles with water; fold in half. Seal edges by pressing with a fork.

Place pies on a large ungreased baking sheet; coat with cooking spray. Combine remaining 1 tablespoon sweetener and ¼ teaspoon cinnamon; sprinkle over pies. Bake at 375° for 10 minutes. Serve warm. **Yield:** 10 pies (serving size: 1 pie).

Per Serving:

Calories 116	**Fiber** 0.8g
Fat 4.3g (sat 1.0g)	**Cholesterol** 0mg
Protein 2.0g	**Sodium** 331mg
Carbohydrate 18.0g	**Exchanges:** 1 Starch, 1 Fat

Orange-Pumpkin Tarts

1   cup crumbled sugar-free oatmeal cookies (about 5 cookies)
2   tablespoons reduced-calorie margarine, melted
Cooking spray
1   teaspoon all-purpose flour
½   cup canned pumpkin
½   cup evaporated fat-free milk
¼   cup "measures-like-sugar" calorie-free sweetener
¼   cup egg substitute
2   tablespoons orange juice
½   teaspoon pumpkin pie spice
¼   cup frozen reduced-calorie whipped topping, thawed

Preheat oven to 375°.

Combine cookie crumbs and margarine, stirring well. Coat 4 (4-inch) tartlet pans with cooking spray. Sprinkle flour evenly over bottoms of pans. Press crumb mixture into bottoms and three-fourths way up sides of pans. Bake at 375° for 5 minutes.

Combine pumpkin and next 5 ingredients, stirring well with a wire whisk. Pour evenly into prepared crusts. Bake at 375° for 25 minutes or until set. Let cool completely on a wire rack.

To serve, top each tart with 1 tablespoon whipped topping. **Yield:** 4 servings (serving size: 1 tart).

Per Serving:

Calories 234	**Fiber** 1.3g
Fat 10.9g (sat 2.2g)	**Cholesterol** 1mg
Protein 5.8g	**Sodium** 213mg
Carbohydrate 30.0g	**Exchanges:** 2 Starch, 2 Fat

make-ahead

Strawberry Tarts

⅓ cup vanilla low-fat yogurt sweetened with aspartame
1 cup graham cracker crumbs
⅛ teaspoon ground cinnamon
3 tablespoons reduced-calorie margarine, melted
Cooking spray
⅓ cup fat-free cream cheese, softened
2 teaspoons "measures-like-sugar" calorie-free sweetener
1 teaspoon vanilla extract
1 cup sliced fresh strawberries
1 tablespoon low-sugar apple jelly, melted
Fresh mint sprigs (optional)

Preheat oven to 350°.

Spread yogurt onto several layers of paper towels; cover with additional paper towels, and let stand 10 minutes.

Combine graham cracker crumbs, cinnamon, and margarine, stirring well. Press crumb mixture evenly into 4 (4-inch) tartlet pans coated with cooking spray. Bake at 350° for 8 minutes; remove from oven, and let cool.

Combine drained yogurt, cream cheese, sweetener, and vanilla, stirring well. Spoon mixture evenly into prepared crusts. Cover and chill at least 3 hours. To serve, arrange strawberries evenly over yogurt mixture; brush with jelly. Garnish with mint sprigs, if desired. **Yield:** 4 servings (serving size: 1 tart).

Per Serving:

Calories 204	**Fiber** 1.0g
Fat 8.5g (sat 0.9g)	**Cholesterol** 5mg
Protein 5.4g	**Sodium** 380mg
Carbohydrate 26.3g	**Exchanges:** 1½ Starch, 2 Fat

Apple-Cinnamon Turnovers

½   cup unsweetened applesauce
1   tablespoon currants
1   teaspoon all-purpose flour
¼   teaspoon ground cinnamon
⅛   teaspoon vanilla extract
4   sheets frozen phyllo pastry, thawed
Butter-flavored cooking spray
5   teaspoons "measures-like-sugar" calorie-free sweetener,
      divided
¼   teaspoon ground cinnamon

Combine first 5 ingredients; stir well. Place 1 sheet of phyllo on wax paper (keep remaining phyllo covered). Coat phyllo with cooking spray; sprinkle with 1 teaspoon sweetener. Top with 1 sheet of phyllo; coat with cooking spray, and sprinkle with 1 teaspoon sweetener. Cut stack of phyllo lengthwise into 4 equal strips, using a sharp knife. Repeat with remaining phyllo and 2 teaspoons sweetener.

Preheat oven to 375°.

Place 1 tablespoon applesauce mixture at base of 1 strip. Fold right bottom corner of phyllo over filling, making a triangle. Fold back and forth into a triangle to end of strip. Place, seam side down, on an ungreased baking sheet. Repeat with remaining phyllo strips and filling (keep covered before baking).

Combine remaining 1 teaspoon sweetener and cinnamon. Coat triangles with cooking spray; sprinkle evenly with sweetener mixture. Bake at 375° for 10 minutes or until golden. Serve warm. **Yield:** 8 turnovers (serving size: 1 turnover).

Per Serving:

Calories 51	**Fiber** 0.3g
Fat 1.3g (sat 0.1g)	**Cholesterol** 0mg
Protein 0.8g	**Sodium** 49mg
Carbohydrate 8.9g	**Exchange:** ½ Starch

White Chocolate Mousse

1   (1-ounce) package white chocolate sugar-free, fat-free instant
        pudding mix
1½ cups fat-free milk
1½ cups frozen reduced-fat whipped topping, thawed
Fresh raspberries (optional)
Fresh mint sprigs (optional)

Prepare pudding mix according to package directions, using 1½ cups milk. Fold whipped topping into pudding. Cover and chill at least 2 hours. Garnish with raspberries and mint, if desired (raspberries not included in analysis). **Yield:** 4 servings (serving size: ½ cup).

Per Serving:

Calories 114	**Fiber** 0.6g
Fat 3.1g (sat 3.1g)	**Cholesterol** 2mg
Protein 3.7g	**Sodium** 232mg
Carbohydrate 15.7g	**Exchanges:** 1 Starch, 1 Fat

If you can't find white chocolate sugar-free pudding, you can use chocolate.

Tiramisù

2 cups ½-inch cubed fat-free pound cake (about 5 ounces)
1 (0.44-ounce) envelope sugar-free mocha-flavored
    cappuccino mix
2 cups 1% low-fat milk, divided
1 (8-ounce) package fat-free cream cheese, softened
1 (1-ounce) package vanilla sugar-free, fat-free instant
    pudding mix
1 (0.43-ounce) envelope sugar-free vanilla-flavored
    cappuccino mix
2 cups fat-free frozen whipped topping, thawed
Grated sugar-free milk chocolate bar (optional)

Place ¼ cup cake cubes into each of 8 glasses. Combine mocha-flavored cappuccino mix with ½ cup milk; drizzle mixture evenly over cake in each glass.

Beat cream cheese with a mixer at medium speed just until smooth. Add remaining 1½ cups milk; beat until smooth. Add pudding mix and vanilla-flavored cappuccino mix; beat at low speed until blended. Fold whipped topping into pudding mixture. Spoon mixture evenly over cake. Garnish with grated sugar-free chocolate, if desired (grated chocolate not included in analysis). Cover and chill at least 3 hours. **Yield:** 8 servings (serving size: 1 cup).

Per Serving:

Calories 157	**Fiber** 0.2g
Fat 1.6g (sat 0.9g)	**Cholesterol** 7mg
Protein 7.1g	**Sodium** 457mg
Carbohydrate 25.5g	**Exchanges:** 1½ Starch, ½ Very Lean Meat

Peanut Butter-Banana Pudding

1   (1-ounce) package vanilla sugar-free, fat-free instant
        pudding mix
2   cups fat-free milk
⅓   cup no-added-sugar creamy peanut butter
1   (8-ounce) carton fat-free sour cream
42 vanilla wafers, divided
6   small bananas, divided
1   (8-ounce) carton frozen fat-free whipped topping, thawed
1   tablespoon lemon juice

Prepare pudding mix according to package directions, using a whisk
and 2 cups fat-free milk. (Do not use a mixer.) Add peanut butter and
sour cream, stirring well with a wire whisk.

Line bottom of a 2½-quart casserole with 14 vanilla wafers. Peel and
slice 4 bananas. Top wafers with one-third each of pudding mixture,
banana slices, and whipped topping. Repeat layers twice using
remaining wafers, pudding mixture, banana, and topping. Cover
and chill at least 2 hours. Peel and slice remaining 2 bananas; toss
with lemon juice. Arrange slices around outer edges of dish. **Yield:**
12 servings (serving size: about 1 cup).

Per Serving:

Calories 236	**Fiber** 1.9g
Fat 7.4g (sat 0.9g)	**Cholesterol** 1mg
Protein 6.1g	**Sodium** 230mg
Carbohydrate 36.0g	**Exchanges:** 2 Starch, ½ Fruit, 1 Fat

Double-Chocolate Pudding Parfaits

1   (1-ounce) package white chocolate sugar-free, fat-free
        instant pudding mix
2   cups fat-free milk
4   sugar-free soft Rocky Road cookies, crumbled
        (such as Archway)

Prepare pudding mix according to package directions, using 2 cups fat-free milk; cover and chill.

Place 2 tablespoons crumbled cookies in each of 4 parfait glasses; top each with ½ cup pudding. Top evenly with remaining crumbled cookies, and serve. **Yield:** 4 servings (serving size: 1 parfait).

Per Serving:

Calories 168	**Fiber** 0.5g
Fat 5.2g (sat 0.2g)	**Cholesterol** 2mg
Protein 5.2g	**Sodium** 459mg
Carbohydrate 26.9g	**Exchanges:** 2 Starch, 1 Fat

Pineapple Fluff

6   ounces angel food cake
2   (1-ounce) packages vanilla sugar-free instant pudding mix
3   cups fat-free milk
1   (8-ounce) package fat-free cream cheese
1   (20-ounce) can crushed pineapple in juice, drained
Shredded coconut, toasted (optional)

Tear angel food cake into 1-inch pieces. Place cake in a 13- x 9-inch baking dish; set aside.

Beat pudding mix, milk, and cream cheese with a mixer at medium speed for 2 minutes or until thick. Stir in crushed pineapple. Spoon pineapple mixture over cake. Cover and chill. Garnish with toasted coconut, if desired (coconut not included in analysis). **Yield:** 8 servings (serving size: 1 cup).

Per Serving:

Calories 155	**Fiber** 0.2g
Fat 0.2g (sat 0.0g)	**Cholesterol** 7mg
Protein 8.6g	**Sodium** 656mg
Carbohydrate 29.0g	**Exchanges:** 1 Starch, ½ Fruit, ½ Skim Milk

Mocha Trifle

1   (2.1-ounce) package chocolate sugar-free, fat-free instant
        pudding mix
3   cups fat-free milk
1   (15-ounce) loaf fat-free chocolate pound cake (such as
        Entennman's)
½   cup strong brewed coffee, divided
1   (8-ounce) carton frozen fat-free whipped topping, thawed
½   (7.25-ounce) package sugar-free chocolate sandwich cookies,
        chopped

Prepare pudding mix according to package directions, using 3 cups
fat-free milk.

Cut cake into cubes; place half of cake cubes in a 3-quart trifle bowl
or glass bowl. Pour ¼ cup coffee over cake; top with half of pudding,
whipped topping, and chopped cookies. Repeat layers. Cover and
chill 4 hours. **Yield:** 16 servings (serving size: ¾ cup).

Per Serving:

Calories 148	**Fiber** 0.8g
Fat 1.4g (sat 0.4g)	**Cholesterol** 1mg
Protein 3.1g	**Sodium** 303mg
Carbohydrate 29.3g	**Exchanges:** 2 Starch

The chocolate pound
cake gives this layered
dessert a double punch
of chocolate, but if you
can't find it, a plain
fat-free or reduced-fat
pound cake will work.

Black Forest Trifle

1   (8-ounce) package chocolate sugar-free, low-fat cake mix
       (such as Sweet 'N Low)
¾   cup water
1   (1-ounce) package chocolate sugar-free, fat-free instant
       pudding mix
2   cups fat-free milk
1   (16-ounce) package frozen no-sugar-added pitted cherries
2   or 3 drops of red food coloring
2   cups fat-free frozen whipped topping, thawed
Sugar-free chocolate curls (optional)

Preheat oven to 375°.

Prepare cake mix according to package directions, using ¾ cup water.
Let cake cool in pan; remove from pan, and cut into cubes.

Prepare pudding mix according to package directions, using 2 cups
fat-free milk; chill at least 30 minutes.

Thaw cherries, reserving ¼ cup juice. Combine cherries, juice, and
food coloring.

Place half of cake cubes in a 3-quart trifle bowl. Spoon half of cherries
over cake; spread 1 cup pudding over cherries, and top with half
of whipped topping. Repeat layers. Garnish with chocolate curls,
if desired (chocolate curls not included in analysis). Cover and chill
at least 8 hours. **Yield:** 12 servings (serving size: about 1 cup).

Per Serving:

Calories 132	**Fiber** 0.9g
Fat 1.7g (sat 0.6g)	**Cholesterol** 1mg
Protein 3.3g	**Sodium** 151mg
Carbohydrate 28.1g	**Exchanges:** 1 Starch, 1 Fruit

Recipe Index

Subject Index

367